P9-AQY-631

The
EVERYTHING
Mother's First Year Book

Dear Reader:

Congratulations on the newest edition to your family! Having a baby is one of the most exciting experiences you will ever have. Your life will change immensely, both in ways that others can see and in ways that only you will know.

Becoming a mother is an in-depth adjustment process. During the first year of your baby's life, dramatic changes will take place. Your baby will transition from a helpless newborn to an active and communicative little person in only a few months. Every moment of a mother's first year is an amazing journey.

While watching your baby grow is tremendously exciting, it is also very difficult. After experiencing nine months of pregnancy, you have to adjust to your new baby's needs and presence, and you must incorporate your new life with the one you had before your bundle of joy arrived. Your body will change wildly, and you'll wonder if you'll ever get it under control again (you will!).

This book will hold your hand as you walk down the path of new motherhood. From dealing with postpartum issues and caring for your baby to getting back into shape and rejoining your husband in the bedroom, this book will give you all the information you need to adjust to your new family.

Best of luck,

Robin Elise Weiss

CHICAGO PUBLIC LIBRARY
SULZER REGIONAL
4455 N. LINCOLN AVE.   60625

OCT - 2006

The EVERYTHING® Series

Editorial

Publishing Director	Gary M. Krebs
Associate Managing Editor	Laura M. Daly
Associate Copy Chief	Brett Palana-Shanahan
Acquisitions Editor	Kate Burgo
Development Editor	Katie McDonough
Associate Production Editor	Casey Ebert

Production

Director of Manufacturing	Susan Beale
Associate Director of Production	Michelle Roy Kelly
Cover Design	Paul Beatrice
	Erick DaCosta
	Matt LeBlanc
Design and Layout	Colleen Cunningham
	Holly Curtis
	Erin Dawson
	Sorae Lee
Series Cover Artist	Barry Littmann

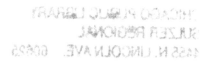

Visit the entire Everything® Series at ✍www.everything.com

THE
EVERYTHING®
MOTHER'S FIRST YEAR BOOK

A survival guide for the first
12 months of being Mom

Robin Elise Weiss,
Certified Childbirth Educator

Adams Media
Avon, Massachusetts

To my sister, Amanda. Thanks for always being there for me.

Copyright ©2005, F+W Publications, Inc. All rights reserved.
This book, or parts thereof, may not be reproduced
in any form without permission from the publisher; exceptions
are made for brief excerpts used in published reviews.

An Everything® Series Book.
Everything® and everything.com® are registered trademarks of F+W Publications, Inc.

Published by Adams Media, an F+W Publications Company
57 Littlefield Street, Avon, MA 02322 U.S.A.
www.adamsmedia.com

ISBN: 1-59337-425-9
Printed in the United States of America.

J I H G F E D C B A

Library of Congress Cataloging-in-Publication Data
Weiss, Robin Elise.
The everything mother's first year book / by Robin Elise Weiss
p. cm
ISBN 1-59337-425-9
1. Infants. 2. Infants--Care. 3. Mother and Infant. 4. Mothers--Psychology.
5. Mothers--Health and hygiene. 6. Mothers--Life skills guides. I. Title: Mother's first year book. II. Title.
HQ774.W42 2005
005.5'7--DC22
2005016168

This publication is designed to provide accurate and authoritative information with regard to the subject matter covered. It is sold with the understanding that the publisher is not engaged in rendering legal, accounting, or other professional advice. If legal advice or other expert assistance is required, the services of a competent professional person should be sought.

—From a *Declaration of Principles* jointly adopted by a Committee of the American Bar Association and a Committee of Publishers and Associations

Many of the designations used by manufacturers and sellers to distinguish their products are claimed as trademarks. Where those designations appear in this book and Adams Media was aware of a trademark claim, the designations have been printed with initial capital letters.

This book is available at quantity discounts for bulk purchases.
For information, call 1-800-872-5627.

R0408241523

Contents

CHICAGO PUBLIC LIBRARY
SULZER REGIONAL
4455 N. LINCOLN AVE. 60625

Acknowledgments

I would like to thank several people for their help with this book: Kate Burgo, for being a patient and kind editor; Barb Doyen, for answering my annoying e-mails and always being my advocate; my family, for allowing me to lock myself in a room with my laptop over and over again; my friends—Kim, Eve, April, Sharon, Marci, and Nicole—for listening; Amy White, Angela Young, and Denay Vargas, for teaching me the value of postpartum support—without you, I may not have made it through some of the roughest but most rewarding times of my life. The work you do for mothers everywhere is a testament to postpartum doulas.

Top Ten Things
Every New Mother Should Know

1. Babies are cute, but they take a lot of work.

2. Postpartum doesn't last forever.

3. Breastfeeding gets easier.

4. Babies do sleep through the night . . . eventually.

5. A few mistakes don't mean you're a bad mother.

6. Everyone needs help.

7. You *will* get your body back.

8. Yes, there is sex after baby.

9. It's okay not to be a supermom.

10. Dirty diapers won't kill you—they just smell like they will.

Introduction

▶ There are a million beautiful moments, exciting events, and fun changes that take place during the first year of motherhood. Probably the most thrilling part is watching your baby grow. Babies learn so many amazing things during the first year. Your baby will go from being unable to hold up her head to being able to crawl, smile, and stand up. Each milestone is a cause for celebration. Caring for your baby will be fun and rewarding, but it will also be a big adjustment. Along with the excitement come challenges, and you will need to work through each one with patience and confidence.

Most families go through at least a few rough times during the first year of their baby's life. This is not to say that you cannot overcome these obstacles, but problems will arise that will be difficult to anticipate and deal with. Anything from a bump on baby's head to baby's runny nose could easily unsettle a new mother. There will be decisions to make, such as who can be trusted to babysit, and when you will go back to work, if at all. Additionally, you will be adapting to your new lifestyle, new body, and new outlook. Your relationship with your spouse will change as well. These aspects just take some getting used to.

One issue you've likely heard a lot about is the postpartum period. The term *postpartum* often brings negative words to mind, such as *depression* and *sleep deprivation*. But the truth is that the postpartum period is much more than misery. It is a time for you to get to know your body as you recover from pregnancy and childbirth, to become familiar with and enjoy your expanding family, and to explore your many roles in life.

Most people would describe the postpartum period as being six weeks long. However, it actually takes the entire first year after the birth of a baby for the family to establish a new sense of normalcy. This period of time can be well spent working on your new family dynamics and dealing with the issues of new parenthood. Still, your time will be consumed with caring for your baby, along with any number of other responsibilities, which could include maintaining a home, working, or fulfilling obligations to other family members and friends. The days may seem shorter, but they will also be much brighter with a new baby in your life.

No matter where you are when you begin the journey of new motherhood, you will be someplace else at the end of this first incredible year. You will learn how to overcome obstacles, how to balance your family life and your social life, and how to grow and change with your child. It's true that your life will never be the same again—but it'll be better! Always remember, there is not a correct path for you to take, but you must simply find your own way. Let this book be your guide as you learn all there is to know about yourself and your new baby. The following pages will take you from your first few days of motherhood right through your baby's first year of life, to the point where you might even be considering another addition to your family! So read on, and enjoy the journey!

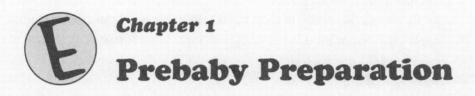

Chapter 1

Prebaby Preparation

Many mothers-to-be begin preparing for their babies the moment they find out they're pregnant. However, most women tend to focus on things like paint colors for the nursery, baby clothing, and toys instead of more pressing issues. Of course, these are the fun aspects of having a baby, and you should take plenty of time to enjoy them. But much of what happens during the birth itself will impact your postpartum period. Early establishment of bigger decisions, like who will deliver your baby and where you will give birth, can help ensure a safe, satisfying delivery and postpartum experience.

People at the Birth

In addition to your husband, there will probably be at least a few other people present for the birth of your baby. One of the first decisions you will make will be with whom you will give birth. Will you choose a midwife or a doctor? You can also choose to have a doula present during the birth, and a doula's services can be helpful to you right through your postpartum period. Read on to learn what these people do and what services they have to offer.

Practitioners

Your first big choice is whether to deliver your baby under the care of a midwife or a doctor. Midwives are trained to assist with normal pregnancy, birth, and other well-woman care (birth control, annual exams, menopause, etc.). Many women with low-risk pregnancies enjoy the care of midwives while giving birth. Midwives may work in a hospital, birth center, or home-birth setting. Midwife training varies widely. Some midwives are nurses with master's degrees, some are certified by organizations like the North American Registry of Midwives (NARM), others have been trained at hospitals or birth centers, and many have a combination of training.

Midwives tend to have a more holistic approach than doctors do. Many are trained to use all of the latest technologies and medications but offer a more personalized approach to birth, realizing that not everyone wants the same type of experience. Those who practice in home-birth and birth-center settings tend to have very low rates of medical interventions.

If you choose not to give birth with a midwife, you might prefer the help of a doctor. There are several different kinds of doctors available to you, including the family practitioner (FP) for low-risk women, the obstetrician/gynecologist (OB/GYN) for nearly every type of pregnancy, and the maternal fetal medicine (MFM) specialist for high-risk women. All of these doctors have attended medical school; what differs is the postgraduate residency course they completed. MFM specialists may not be in every city, but most large cities have these types of practices. If you'd like to use your family practitioner, you must first be sure he delivers babies, as not every family practitioner incorporates birth into his practice.

FACT

If you're not sure what constitutes a safe birth, there is a handy medical text that is easy to read and free online at the Maternity Center Association's Web site. This guide, available at *http://maternitywise.org/ guide*, can help you figure out what kind of medical care you want during your baby's birth.

Each practitioner brings his own expertise to the table, as well as his personal birth philosophy. It is important that you find out if this philosophy is compatible with yours prior to giving birth. Mismatched ideologies can lead to a very stressful experience. The medical professional you choose is your partner in the birth process. You should feel free to discuss all of your questions, concerns, and desires with this person to ensure you have as comfortable and safe a birth as possible.

Start out by asking your practitioner simple questions. This will help you ease into a relationship, so you'll be able to ask the harder questions later. Talk to other women who've given birth with this person, and generally talk to anyone who's been in your situation to hear firsthand experience and get advice. The broader your knowledge of birthing professionals and methods, the better equipped you will be to customize your own experience.

ALERT!

Your informed consent should be given for all medical tests, procedures, or surgeries performed during the birth. Informed consent is not merely your signature on a piece of paper. It means that you fully understand the procedure, as well as its risks, benefits, and alternatives. If your practitioner does not explain these things, there is something wrong.

Doulas

Doula is a Greek word meaning "woman servant." Doulas are trained to help you and your family during the pregnancy, birth, and postpartum period using information, comfort measures, and other local resources. There are both birth and postpartum doulas. A birth doula specializes in helping families during late pregnancy, the birth, and the early postpartum days. A postpartum doula is trained to help the new family during the first few months postpartum. The process involves interviewing doulas and finding the right individual for you. This should be someone that you click with and enjoy being around. Remember, you are inviting this person to participate in a very special time in your life.

A birth doula will meet with you and your husband prenatally and get to know you both. She will help you formulate your birth plan as you figure out what you want out of the experience. She can also be a great resource for information and can facilitate communication with your practitioner. She will not make decisions or speak for you, but she can teach you to ask the right questions and make encounters more comfortable. Your birth doula will tell you how to contact her twenty-four hours a day, and you will make plans for when and where to meet once labor is established. Your doula will stay with you throughout your entire labor and birth, no matter how long that turns out to be.

During your labor, she will help keep you relaxed, show your husband how to take care of your needs (massaging, hand holding, etc.), and generally assist in whatever way she is needed. Many dads love having doulas there for the birth of their children. The doula's presence takes some of the pressure off the father, so he can look after his wife and enjoy the miracle of birth.

FACT

Your doula will not take the place of your doctor, your midwife, or your husband. Her role is to help everyone work together more effectively and provide a continuity of care during shift changes in hospitals and birth centers. Using a doula can help lower your risk of having an unnecessary cesarean by 50 percent. Many other interventions can also be avoided by using a professional doula.

Unlike the birth doula, the postpartum doula doesn't usually stay with you twenty-four hours a day. Instead, you agree on a schedule that works for both the doula and your family. This person will help you with baby-care basics, breastfeeding, light housekeeping, laundry, and meals. Be sure to ask her exactly what services she offers and identify those that she cannot provide. Some postpartum doulas will run small errands or watch older siblings. Some even provide overnight services.

Using a postpartum doula will take the edge off the first few days and weeks of new motherhood. Her presence will allow you to focus on your baby instead of worrying about doing dishes or having dinner on the table. This arrangement is much nicer than the antiquated concept of a baby nurse who took care of the baby while the mother cooked and cleaned!

Important Details

The details of your delivery will contribute to how you feel about your baby, your body, and your life as a new mother. For instance, choosing the location where you will give birth is an important decision. You want to feel completely comfortable and at ease in this place. Additionally, from creating a birth plan to attending childbirth classes, there are numerous things you can do to make your delivery run smoothly. Taking care of these essentials well in advance will save you stress later on.

Location

When visiting potential birth settings, be sure to ask lots of questions and take note of as many details as possible. If you learn a location has routine restrictions on laboring women and high intervention rates, this is probably indicative of the care you'll receive there. Ask about policies and practices that are important to you. Some of these topics may include:

- Intermittent fetal monitoring
- Freedom of movement in labor
- Ability to eat and drink in labor
- Tools available in labor (birth ball, tub, etc.)
- Rooming-in policies

- Visitation policies (particularly for siblings)
- Breastfeeding rate and support

Instead of a hospital or birth center, many women choose to give birth at home. Home birth is an option for low-risk women with qualified practitioners, doctors, or midwives. Today, many families are choosing home birth to have more control over their environment.

FACT

Home birth is a safe practice for well-screened pregnant women with qualified practitioners. Birth outcomes are as good, if not better, in similar populations giving birth in hospitals. Most home births use few if any interventions. Be sure to talk to your midwife or doctor about her training in home birth and what situations she can safely handle at home.

Birth centers offer a homelike environment for delivery, but you have a bit more support than you would at home. Doctors, midwives, or a combination may assist you. The emphasis in birth centers is on the low-risk woman who desires fewer interventions. Typically your stay at a center after birth is not very long, though it depends on your birth, the birth center's policies, and other factors.

The majority of women choose to give birth in hospitals, as they are available for all women. Though many assume hospitals are the birth location best equipped to handle any kind of complication, this depends entirely on your individual situation. Some are not prepared to handle high-risk births or premature babies. Additionally, your desires are less likely to be heard in a large hospital with lots of patients. Be sure to clearly define, with your practitioner as well as with your hospital facility, what you want out of your birth experience. A birth plan can help you with this task.

Birth Plans

A birth plan is exactly what it sounds like: a basic plan, usually in the form of a document, created to help you, your husband, and your practitioner clarify your desires for the birth. A birth plan is not a written contract between you and the doctor or midwife, nor is it a contract between you and the hospital or birth center. And a birth plan does not guarantee you will have the type of birth that you desire.

QUESTION?

Why would I want a birth plan?
A birth plan helps you define your birth philosophy and allows you to convey this information to nurses and other support staff who have not been present during your prenatal visits. It's a sort of cheat sheet to catch up latecomers so they can provide you with a positive, safe experience.

What a birth plan does is allow you and everyone supporting you to have a set of guidelines for how you'd like to approach your labor, birth, and postpartum experience. It particularly applies to your labor and birth and the initial day or two after birth. You should keep your birth plan short and simple. It should never be longer than the front of one page; you can use bulleted points for simplicity. It is also advisable that you break the plan into sections for ease of use. You may choose headings like "Labor," "Birth," "Postpartum/Baby Care," and possibly "Emergencies/Cesarean." This gives your care providers succinct information to reference throughout your birth experience.

ESSENTIAL

Sometimes the hardest part of figuring out what you want from your birth experience is knowing what questions to ask. The Coalition for Improving Maternity Services (CIMS) has a set of ten great questions to get you thinking. Visit *http://motherfriendly.org/resources/10Q* for this and other helpful information.

There is a lot to cover in a birth plan, but it needs to be short and organized. You can reference Appendix B (page 279) for many great resources for birth plans, but here are some basic examples of issues to cover in your plan:

- Fetal monitoring (how much and what type)
- Freedom of movement
- Dealing with pain (movement, massage, relaxation, medications)
- Hydration (IV or not?)
- Interventions (breaking your water, speeding up labor, etc.)
- Episiotomy (prevention techniques, etc.)
- Positioning (standing, kneeling, squatting, etc.)
- Rooming in
- Nonseparation of mother and baby
- Baby care (Do you want this done in your room?)
- Emergencies (Do you want someone with you in the OR?)

Birth plans should be discussed in advance with your practitioners—including the pediatrician—because they will be ultimately responsible for the care your baby receives at birth and during the postpartum period. Birth plans are usually signed by your doctor or midwife, any of their partners, and your pediatrician. Be sure to keep the signed original and give each practitioner a copy. It's also wise to take several copies of your birth plan with you when you give birth.

Childbirth Classes

Childbirth classes educate you and your husband about pregnancy, birth, the postpartum period, breastfeeding, and much more. What is taught in each class will depend on the educator, the theme of the class, and the location. Be sure to ask the instructor what she plans to cover in the series of classes.

Take a class that covers everything, even details you don't think you'll need to know. For example, it is important that everyone understand the basics of cesarean surgery. While you may not think you will need a cesarean, once in labor it sometimes turns out to be the best birth method for women. It is equally important to learn techniques to help get you through labor without medication. That way, if you can't have medication or you prefer not to have it, you'll have the skills to help yourself during labor.

In choosing a childbirth class, it is important to remember that you get what you pay for. Just because a class is cheap, it does not mean you will get what you need out of the class. Be especially leery of free classes. Often these are overcrowded and run by people with their own agendas to push.

In addition to general childbirth classes, there are also specialty classes available. You might want to take an infant safety class or a vaginal birth after cesarean (VBAC) class. There are also classes on multiple births and breastfeeding. Specialty classes allow you to focus on a specific aspect that is important to you. Choose a class that has a great philosophy and an educator you like, and be sure it fits comfortably into your schedule.

There are many ways for childbirth educators to be trained. Most are certified by an organization like Lamaze International, the International Childbirth Education Association (ICEA), or the American Academy of Husband Coached Childbirth (AAHCC, Bradley). Be sure to ask your educator about her certification. Some insurance companies will reimburse your class fees because of the many benefits you get from class, but only if your educator is certified by a recognized organization.

FACT

Lamaze International has established the Lamaze Institute for Normal Birth, which focuses on six care practices that promote normal birth. These practices are based on evidence-based medicine, meaning that each is highly researched and in line with the safest medical guidelines available to date. You can access them online at *http://normalbirth. lamaze.org/institute.*

Packing for the Hospital

There are at least a few things you will need to take with you to the hospital or birthing center when it is time to have your baby. This will vary depending on the facility. Be sure to take a tour of the labor and postpartum rooms before your due date. Ask the staff what they'd recommend you bring and what you can leave home. Do they have a birth ball you can use in labor, or do you need to bring your own? Do they provide music, lotion, or massage tools? Also ask before you bring personal items like hair dryers, as most places will supply you with one. If you'd like to bring a special item like a stuffed animal or a framed photo, feel free to do so.

QUESTION?

Can I bring candles to light during labor?
Candles are not allowed in most hospitals because of the medical equipment and potentially flammable items found there. Some birth centers may have different policies. Be sure to ask. If you can't bring candles, ask about air fresheners and scented lotions if you'd like a certain scent in your room.

Most mothers-to-be worry that they'll forget something when they pack for the hospital. Save yourself the stress! You likely won't forget anything important, and if you do, your husband, a family member, or a friend can easily go back and get it for you. Don't try to stuff everything you own into your suitcase. Don't worry about packing a lot of food, either—a few granola bars and some dried fruit will suffice. Your family can bring you snacks, and some hospitals and birth centers even have kitchen facilities where a family member can make you your favorite meal. That sure beats hospital food! Just be sure to check with your hospital or birth center first.

So, now that you know what not to bring, what items should you pack? Here's a general list of essentials to include in your suitcase:

- Clothes to wear in labor
- Toothbrush and toothpaste

- Massage tools, including lotions or oil
- Birth ball, if not provided
- Baby book, if you're keeping one
- Camera, batteries, and film or memory card
- Phone numbers of friends you'd like to call
- Calling card
- Nursing gown and bra
- Car seat for baby
- Going-home outfit for baby
- Personal items

When packing for labor and birth, pack two suitcases. One should be for labor and include anything that you would need during your labor and the first few hours after birth. The second suitcase can remain in the car until you're in your postpartum room. This should contain extra clothes, going-home outfits, and other items that aren't essential for labor. Remember, someone can bring you anything you forget to pack.

Working Before the Big Day

Many women struggle to decide when to leave work before the baby is born. If you won't be working again for a few years, you might prefer to work right up until your due date. If you plan to return to work soon after you've recovered, you might appreciate more time to relax before the baby comes. Some women are simply worried about being at work when their water breaks. This is a personal decision each woman must make for herself.

When to Leave Work

Because staying at home waiting for your baby isn't productive or fun, you may choose to work right up until the birth. This does not necessarily mean you will go into labor at the office, but that you will work as long as is medically advisable. Some women leave work a day or two before the due date, while others actually head to the hospital straight from the office.

If there is a reason that you should not work during the final weeks of pregnancy, your midwife or doctor will tell you. You may need to leave work if you are experiencing a problem with preterm labor, bleeding, or other complications. You may also be asked to leave work sooner if your job involves physical requirements that are beyond the capacity of a pregnant woman, or if you work with chemicals or other potentially harmful materials or equipment.

If you decide to leave work well before your due date, be sure to schedule visits and outings with friends as long as you are feeling well enough to go out. Stock up on good books and movies, and try a relaxing hobby like knitting or painting to keep you productive and entertained.

There are several benefits to working until the baby comes. For one, working can help keep your mind and body occupied so you aren't consumed with worry about the birth or the baby. If exhaustion is a problem for you, see if you can cut back to part-time or schedule a few work-from-home days each week. Working longer will also mean more income to be spent on necessities for the baby or to put into savings. Just keep in mind that there is no way to know exactly when you will go into labor.

If you plan to work until your due date, you may very well find yourself in labor at work two weeks early. Likewise, if you allow too much time for relaxation before your due date and the baby is late, you might become anxious and frustrated. Be careful that these feelings don't lead you to induce labor. Inducing labor because you're tired of waiting can have serious effects on your labor and postpartum, including increased risk of a cesarean surgery. Labor is easiest when your baby and your body are both ready.

Due Dates

Your doctor will probably give you a due date, or a projected date for the birth. Don't make the mistake of counting on this being the exact date your baby will be born—it's really just a guess. Your baby can safely be born two weeks before or even two weeks after that date. Many women give birth a week after their due date.

FACT

Only about 5 percent of pregnant women give birth on their due date. Most give birth between two weeks before and two weeks after that date. You can still circle this little box on the calendar—just be prepared for your baby's early or late arrival.

If your due date has been changed because of the size of your belly or the size of your baby, the new date may not be very accurate. Ultrasound due dates made after the first trimester are not very accurate either, as babies grow at different rates after that point. A due date is merely an estimate given to help you prepare for the baby.

Maternity Leave

Taking time off from work when you have your baby is partially dictated by your choice. How much time you choose to take off can be influenced by the rules and regulations at your workplace. Other factors would be your health, the health of your baby, your job requirements, the work season, and other details. A combination of these factors will determine how much time you actually take off.

Preliminary Research

Arranging maternity leave with your boss can be a daunting task. The important thing is to have a plan before you go speak with your boss. Talk to your company's Human Resources Department or research your rights according to state or local regulations to educate yourself about the process. You might also consider talking to other new parents at work to see what types of job leave they had when their children were born.

Having an idea of the normal maternity leave process before you approach your boss will boost your confidence. This will also show your boss that you thoroughly understand your position. In showing her you care enough to do the research, your boss will see that you value your job and want to coordinate the best possible arrangement.

Family Medical Leave Act (FMLA)

Federal law on family leave is called the Family Medical Leave Act (FMLA). You must work at a qualifying company, meaning your business has a certain number of employees, to take leave under this act. And your job must qualify, meaning you have worked full-time in your position for a year or more.

If you have questions about the FMLA, address them to your company's Human Resources Department. If the staff can't help you, go straight to the law itself, which is available on the Department of Labor's Web site: www.dol.gov/esa/regs/statutes/whd/fmla.htm.

If you and your place of work meet the requirements, you can take up to twelve weeks of unpaid leave. This time is to be used for the birth of a baby, an adoption, or the caretaking of a sick immediate relative. The good news about the FMLA is that both you and your husband can use it, and in some cases both of you may choose to take some or all of this leave, while having your job status protected. Your husband's work may offer a paternity leave schedule, or he may use part of the FMLA time.

Thorough Planning

It is wise to negotiate your maternity leave by the time you are about seven months pregnant. This prepares you for any surprises in the pregnancy and allows you to relax, knowing that the negotiations are over. As the weeks before your due date start winding down, you should begin mentoring any coworkers who will be taking over your projects while you're out.

One mistake many women make is agreeing to be in touch while on maternity leave. This can create a sticky situation. On the one hand, you don't want to be totally out of touch, but you also don't want them calling you every day. If you agree to keep in contact, be specific about how and when they can contact you. Ask for e-mail updates at the end of each week, but remind them you'll be slow to respond due to your responsibilities at home.

Do not be afraid to show your boss and colleagues that you will be focused on your mothering duties when you're at home. When you decide to call them, be sure to limit the time and energy you spend on the phone. Your leave is designed to help you address the issues of new motherhood. If you feel like everything is under control at home, it will be much easier to regain your focus when you finally return to work.

Budgeting for Baby

You may have heard people say that if you waited to have a baby until you could afford it, you'd never have children at all. While there is truth to this statement, there is also something to be said for being fiscally responsible in planning for your children. A new baby doesn't have to break the bank. The first step to success is knowing what expenses to expect. Then, a little planning can mean the difference between an anxious mom and a confident one.

Pregnancy Expenses

During pregnancy you will want some extra money for a variety of needs. Childbirth classes are one expense, and class fees vary widely depending on the class and its location. The fees for your doula may be covered by your insurance, but if not, you'll have that cost to consider.

In addition to paying the medical professionals for their services, you'll also have to buy a few basics during pregnancy. One of these is maternity clothes. This can get expensive, as your shape and size will change fairly rapidly after the first trimester. However, a good way to save money is to buy secondhand maternity clothes, borrow maternity clothes from friends, or even make them yourself. An occasional pregnancy massage might also be on your list of expenses. Keep these things in mind as you're saving up.

Unfortunately, you can't put your wallet away yet. There are several costs associated with the birth itself. A normal, uncomplicated vaginal birth costs about $5,000, including prenatal care. If you require anesthesia, such as an epidural, that will add another $1,200, and a cesarean costs about $3,000 extra. This total doesn't even include an additional nursery stay for your baby. However, there are a few ways to save money here. If you are low risk, a less expensive option for birth may be to use a midwife or birth center instead of a hospital. These options tend to report higher patient satisfaction rates than hospitals do, in addition to being more cost effective.

QUESTION?

Can you borrow baby furniture and car seats?
Yes. You can use borrowed or previously owned baby equipment to save money. Just be sure to ascertain that the equipment meets the most current safety guidelines, doesn't include lead paint, and hasn't been involved in a previous accident.

Saving Up

If you plan to take a significant duration of unpaid leave from work, it's wise to accrue some savings to be used while you do not have income. Try to figure out your minimum budget. Decide how long you will be out of work and how much you will need to cover that time, then budget in that amount for the months remaining in your pregnancy. Remember to add about 10 percent extra for emergencies or an early birth. It's great if you have a paid leave, but setting aside some money for this time will create a nice cushion in either case.

If you will be leaving work for good, or if you'll be returning to work while your husband stays at home, it's a great idea to use those final months of income to build a nest egg. If you are able to bank vacation or sick days, do this too. Spend your final months in the working world thinking about how you can adapt to life on a single income. Talk to others who've done it, and heed their advice. Preparing for being a stay-at-home parent while you still have the extra income can help pad the pitfalls.

Getting Help and Stocking Up

As the birth approaches, you'll need to do some planning for how things will function once your little one arrives. You'll be focused on your new baby's needs, so who will take care of your other responsibilities? To keep everything running smoothly, you'll need to enlist the help of friends and family and keep your house stocked with the essentials at all times.

Who Will Help?

A postpartum doula is a valuable resource during late pregnancy and the first few weeks after the birth. Your doula might prepare meals for you, do the grocery shopping, or take care of the laundry. You can also ask friends and family for help with these things, though some of these people might be more interested in seeing and holding the baby than helping you with chores. Be sure your helpers are trustworthy and willing to take care of what you need.

As the birth approaches and after the baby is born, friends and family will probably ask you the same question over and over again: "Can I help with anything?" Many people don't like to ask for help, but when you have a new baby at home, you could always use a little assistance. Prepare a list of things you need brought to you or need done around the house and keep it handy at all times. This way, when someone asks what she can do to help, you can offer her a list of suggestions. By giving the person options, she can choose something she's capable of handling, and you won't feel as though you are obligating her to do a particular task.

Essential Items

Other than the usual supply of baby products, it's advisable to have two weeks worth of food and other essentials in the house at all times. Be sure to have plenty of toothpaste, paper towels, toilet paper, soap, and disposable dishes. You will not want to be standing over a sink washing dishes when you're only days away from your due date. Also stock up on nonperishable food items that can be used to make quick meals, such as pasta, rice, and canned soups. Preparing meals ahead of time can also be helpful. Before you get too close to your due date, prepare some large casseroles or pans of lasagna and freeze the leftovers. During the last month of pregnancy, you can simply reheat these for quick meals.

Choosing a Pediatrician

Your pediatrician will be a very important part of your child's life, so put a lot of time and effort into your choice. Interview several pediatricians before selecting one. Whatever you do, don't just choose one from the phone book. You want to know and understand the pediatrician's philosophy. Does he value your opinions and concerns or see himself as the ultimate authority on child rearing? You want someone who has your child's best interests at heart. Finding the right person might take time, but it will save you unnecessary stress in the long run.

To gather a collection of pediatricians to interview, ask close friends who have children which doctors they visit. You shouldn't choose a pediatrician simply because your friend did, but a list of doctors recommended by trusted friends is a far better starting point than the yellow pages.

While the person's philosophy and demeanor are very important, you also need to be practical. The doctor's office should be close to your home or job, accept your insurance, and have office hours compatible with your schedule. It doesn't matter how fantastic the pediatrician is if you can't get to his office. You should also find out if there is a way to reach the pediatrician outside of his office hours in the event of a serious problem.

Chances are you won't find the "perfect" pediatrician, but this doesn't mean you shouldn't try. Don't lower your standards because you're tired of looking. The time and effort you put in now will be worth it in the end. When your first contraction hits, you'll be able to relax knowing you've made the right decision.

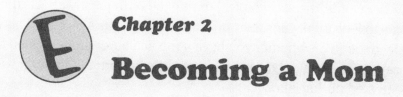

Chapter 2

Becoming a Mom

Congratulations! You are about to be a new mom. Your pregnancy is nearly over and you have very few things left to do. Once you get set up for birth, whether it be at home, a birth center, or a hospital, you will hopefully be able to relax and enjoy the birth experience. You will spend your first few days as a mother relishing your time with your baby and getting accustomed to this new life. Your body and mind will be reeling from the experience, but this is perfectly normal and okay.

Your Birth

It's a fact: having a baby is hard work. But using your birth plan and having people you trust around you will make it much easier. Your birth experience is very important, as it will set the tone for your early days of mothering. In other words, the way you feel during the birth greatly affects the way you come to feel about your baby and your new role as a mother. This does not really depend on whether you have a medicated or unmedicated birth, or a cesarean or a vaginal delivery. Instead, the important thing is how well you are treated during labor.

Vaginal and Cesarean

Having a vaginal birth is the most common experience. Yet within this one experience, there are many factors that will physically and emotionally influence how your first few days as a mother will go.

FACT

The American Academy of Pediatrics (AAP) recommends that breastfeeding begin as soon as possible after birth. If you can't breastfeed immediately, you should do so within an hour of birth.

If you have a vaginal birth without medication, you will probably feel like getting up to move around or go to the bathroom, sometimes within minutes of giving birth. This is perfectly fine, but stick close to someone in case you feel dizzy. If you have an epidural or other pain medication in labor, it will take time to wear off. You may not be able to walk around for several hours. This means you will require a catheter or bedpan to go to the bathroom. You will need help when you do get up, due to residual numbness or dizziness.

Whether or not your cesarean birth is planned, you will not be able to move for several hours. If you have had regional anesthesia such as an epidural or spinal, you may feel some numbness after the surgery. If you have had general anesthesia, you will not feel numb, but you will still be unable to walk around for some time.

Meeting Your Baby

When she is born, your baby may cry, whimper, or be quiet, but none of these is a bad sign. The important thing is that the baby is breathing. Once this is ascertained, your baby should be handed to you right away. The best way to keep the baby warm is by holding her to your bare skin and covering her up with warm blankets. Even before the umbilical cord is clamped or cut, you can hold your baby as high on your chest as the cord will allow.

Cesarean-born babies are just as capable of snuggling skin to skin as vaginally delivered babies. If you don't feel up to it during the remainder of the surgery, your husband can nestle the baby inside his shirt for warmth. You can also ask the nurse to help you breastfeed while the surgery is completed.

Your baby will probably feel a bit wet and potentially be tinged with blood. This is your blood—not the baby's blood. You or your husband can take a clean towel and dry the baby while your newborn gazes up at you (new babies can see best from a distance of about 8 to 12 inches) and listens to the sound of your heartbeat from the outside. Your baby will probably be wrinkled and may appear reddish or swollen. Don't worry if her head looks a bit misshapen. New babies' heads are designed to change shape as they fit through your pelvis. A normal, round head shape will develop as the skull hardens.

During these first few minutes and through the first hour, your baby will likely be in a quiet, very alert state. You will both be taking in so much during this time. In addition to relief that the labor is over, you will likely feel an instant, overwhelming love for your baby.

Does my baby have to be weighed or bathed immediately?
Generally, these tasks can wait a couple of hours until you and your baby are ready to have them done. If you know you want to spend at least one uninterrupted hour with your baby before he is weighed and measured, be sure to mention this desire in your birth plan.

If your baby needs to be seen for emergency reasons or is taken to the neonatal intensive care unit (NICU) after birth, do not fear. This does not necessarily indicate tragedy, and you can still be with your baby in the NICU once you are both stable. While these first few moments are wonderful and precious, you will still have a sense of connection with your baby if these moments must come a bit later. Your and the baby's health are the most important issues.

First Visitors

Everyone will be very anxious to meet your new baby. However, knowing there is an audience waiting outside your door can add to the stress of your labor and delivery. Consider telling everyone to wait at home, promising to call at a certain point in labor or just after your little one has arrived.

In the Birth Room

Having people visit you in labor can be a nice distraction early on, but you'll probably find you don't want visitors once labor is well under way. Know before you go into labor who you have invited and who you haven't. Don't be afraid to let your doula act as your bodyguard if you want to keep visitors at bay for a while.

To keep things comfortable and uncomplicated, go ahead and set a few ground rules. For instance, you can declare that anyone in the labor and birth room must be actively helping with the labor. If you don't allow casual observers in the room, then there won't be anyone staring at you while you pant through contractions. Being a part of the labor and helping out is one thing, but gawking in the corner and taking up space is completely another.

Many hospitals and some birth centers have policies on who can be in the labor room with you. There may be a limit on the number of people, or the rules may define exactly who can be present. The good news is that your doula doesn't usually count in the number you're given.

After the Birth

Immediately after the birth you may wish to spend some time alone with your husband and new baby. Don't worry about offending those who are waiting to see the new arrival. They've already been waiting for a while, so they can wait a few more minutes. In fact, they probably won't even know the baby has been born until you tell them.

Several factors will dictate when you are ready to see visitors. If the delivery room gets a bit messy during the birth (it usually does), you may prefer not to have visitors come in until it has been cleaned up a little. You might also choose to shower first. And you'll probably want to breastfeed the baby before anyone else comes into the room. In a home birth, you might choose to join the guests who are waiting in another room for a few minutes before retreating again with the baby.

One thing you don't want around your new baby is germs. A handy item to keep with you when visitors come to hold the baby is a bottle of gel or foam hand sanitizer. These products are usually small enough that you can keep one or two in your purse or diaper bag at all times.

Above all, remember that *you* are the mother. This means you're the boss. Feel free to insist that your guests wash their hands before holding your baby. On the other hand, also keep in mind that it's impossible for you to keep your baby safe from everything. You can take some basic precautions, but there's no need to keep your baby in a bubble. Babies and small children are remarkably resilient, as you'll soon learn.

Getting What You Need at the Hospital

Chances are, getting what you need in terms of care at home or in a birth center will be fairly straightforward. At home you'll know where everything is and can easily ask someone to get an item for you. A birth center is a bit more difficult, but chances are you won't be there very long. However, you might have to negotiate a little to get what you need at a hospital.

QUESTION?

Can you bring your own food to the hospital or birth center?
Yes, you usually can. Birth centers often have a kitchen for food preparation, complete with a refrigerator. Hospital food is getting better, but snacks aren't a bad idea. New moms are often hungry around the clock for the first couple of days. Check with your practitioner for food limits, particularly if you had a cesarean or other surgery.

Hopefully your birth plan served you well in labor and birth, but there should also be a section of your birth plan that spells out your desires for the postpartum period. This can include details about visitors, getting help with breastfeeding, newborn care, and other areas of importance to you. Because hospitals are busy places with a lot of patients and not so many staff, you'll need to rely on this plan as your form of communication at certain points.

If this isn't successful or if your needs change, do not hesitate to tell your nurse or nurse's aide. The problem in a hospital is that you are on a list with others who also have needs. Therefore, having your own group of friends and family there to help you is a good idea. If your husband and guests can get you what you need most of the time, this will ease some of the burden on the nursing staff. This will also make things run more quickly and smoothly for you.

Assessment and Care of Your Body

You're probably worried about how your body will look after you give birth. What will your bottom look like, and will it ever be the same again? Will you have a scar from a repair or other surgery? Will your husband notice? These are all normal questions that every woman asks, and in most cases, things turn out just fine.

When packing for the hospital or birth center, choose the outfit you will go home in wisely. The jeans you wore at your skinniest aren't going to work, but you don't need a pair of stretch pants from your ninth month of pregnancy either. Just pack a comfortable early pregnancy outfit. You're not pregnant anymore, but your body hasn't returned to its pre-pregnancy state yet either.

One of the first things you might think is how skinny you must be! You look down at your now deflated belly and think, "Wow! I'm thin!" Unfortunately, once you stand up and that loose skin falls southward, you'll have a soft pouch instead of a flat stomach. Don't worry, though—it just takes some time for the skin to tighten back up. Do your best to avoid scales, tight jeans, and pants with buttons in the meantime.

Medication After Birth

Giving birth is taxing on your body, no matter how you do it. You will feel different types of pain in the postpartum process. You will experience soreness from tensing your muscles during labor, aches and swelling at any surgery sites, and general symptoms of fatigue. Additionally, a vaginal birth and a cesarean have different effects on the body. You may choose to take medication to relieve some of these aches and pains, but be sure to consult with your doctor before choosing any remedies, even over-the-counter and herbal products. Some medications will be present in your milk, which can be a serious concern if you're breastfeeding.

If you have a vaginal birth, your muscles will be sore from flexing and moving around while in labor. If stirrups are used, particularly for forceps or a vacuum delivery, then your legs may be sore around the hip area from hyperextension. Usually, a dose of ibuprofen will soothe the majority of muscle aches. For the first few days, you can take this by the clock—you won't want to wait for your pain to come back before taking another dose.

If your pain is severe, which is more likely if you have a forceps or vacuum birth or an episiotomy, there are other methods of pain relief available. Some are narcotics. These tend to make you feel a bit groggy but are very effective in relieving pain. They can also be used in combination with other, over-the-counter medicines such as ibuprofen.

QUESTION?

What is an episiotomy?
An episiotomy is a surgical incision made in the perineum while a woman is giving birth. This helps facilitate the delivery. The incision is closed with stitches or sutures after the baby is born.

Your pain and soreness will be a bit different if you have a cesarean. If you have an epidural or spinal anesthesia, you can be given a medication called Duramorph during or after the administration of your anesthesia. This medication is administered in the same area as the epidural or spinal medications. It can provide pain relief for sixteen to twenty-four hours, without a numbing sensation. The most common side effect from this medication is itching. Be sure to ask your anesthetist about this—some people are allergic to this drug.

After the cesarean surgery is over and the numbness or general anesthesia wears off, ibuprofen can also be helpful to you. You will still feel the same uterine sensations as you would with a vaginal birth—these sensations indicate the healing of the uterus. The ibuprofen will ease the pain from the contractions that shrink the uterus, called afterpains. You may also use narcotics for this purpose. Narcotics for pain relief can be given orally, by injection, or in your IV line, and they tend to make you groggy. Be sure to ask what your doctor or midwife has ordered that you have after your surgery.

Specific Pain Locations

Though your whole body will likely be sore after giving birth, certain areas of your body will be especially tender. Primarily, your vagina will be sore, with or without tearing or stitches. If you do have stitches from a tear or episiotomy, you are more likely to have pain in this area. You may also have hemorrhoids from the pushing process.

FACT

Sitz baths are available to help promote healing and deal with the pain associated with childbirth. They can be done in the hospital or at home. These baths help keep your perineum clean, while soothing the area. Ask your doctor or midwife about this option.

If you have an epidural during childbirth, you may later have a sore spot in your back where the needle entered. A urinary catheter is frequently used in the epidural process, so you may have soreness or a numb feeling in your urethra as well, making it difficult to urinate.

Cold packs can help reduce swelling wherever you have it and particularly in your vaginal area. You can also use spray-on topical anesthetics to numb any painful areas. Ask your doctor or midwife which of these products is available and safe for your use.

Stitches or sutures used after a tear or episiotomy are generally dissolvable. This means that you will not need to have them removed. If you find small black flecks or threads on your toilet paper, don't panic! It's just the suture material dissolving.

Your Emotions

Having a baby puts your emotions on a roller coaster ride. You will transition from a smile to tears in the blink of an eye. Unfortunately, the only thing you can do is work through it. The good news is that for the first day or two after your baby is born, you will be fairly emotionally stable.

Immediately after your baby is born, you will likely be exhausted but euphoric. You might not be able to take your eyes off your baby, even if there are doctors stitching you up and cleaning you off. You may cry out of joy over having your baby in your arms, out of relief that the labor is over, or for no particular reason at all.

ALERT!

If you have a negative birth experience for whatever reason, it is okay to acknowledge this. It is also important that you express this to someone you trust who can validate your feelings. Just because you aren't pleased with your birth experience doesn't mean you don't love your baby. If you ignore these feelings, you can find yourself deep in postpartum depression.

Alternatively, you may feel not much of anything after your baby is born. Exhaustion may take over due to lack of sleep during late pregnancy. Physical symptoms may overshadow the joy of having a new baby—at least for a little while. However, postpartum depression is not common in the first few days. You'll probably just feel weary until your body has a chance to heal.

Newborn Tests and Procedures

Soon after the birth, the doctor or midwife will want to do a few tests and procedures to make sure that your baby is in good health. You may not like being separated from your little one so soon, but you might feel better about these procedures if you have an idea of what they entail and what they will determine. Once you have this knowledge, if you still feel strongly about delaying or avoiding the tests, discuss this with your pediatrician and be sure to address it in your birth plan.

APGAR Scoring

The APGAR scoring system, named for its creator, Virginia Apgar, is a mnemonic device that covers five different ways of grading a baby at birth. This system is used to determine the baby's basic health status. APGAR stands for:

- *Activity*: muscle tone
- *Pulse*: heartbeats per minute
- *Grimace*: reflex irritability
- *Appearance*: skin color
- *Respiration*: absence or presence of breath

Your baby is given a score of 0, 1, or 2 for each category, with 10 being a perfect score. A score of 7 to 10 is considered normal, 4 to 7 might call for resuscitative action, and 3 or below requires immediate resuscitation. Your baby will be graded one minute after birth and again at five minutes. If your baby is having a rough time getting started, you will also have a third score after ten minutes. This scoring usually goes unnoticed by parents. While you are consumed with the emotion of new motherhood, a nurse or midwife will be keeping a sharp eye on your baby for labored breathing or other signs of stress.

Weighing, Measuring, and Blood Work

You'll probably be very excited to know how much your baby weighs and measures. These numbers stick in most mothers' heads forever. Just keep in mind that these measurements do not indicate the health or ultimate body type your child will have. A seven-pound baby can be just as healthy as a nine-pound baby, and one that measures twenty-two inches will not necessarily grow to be taller than a baby born at nineteen inches.

Try to get a picture of your baby on the scale with her birth weight showing. This will be a great photo to send to friends and family in a birth announcement. After a home birth, you might get to weigh the baby yourself; but be sure to hand your midwife the camera first.

Weighing and measuring is usually done in the first couple of hours of life, but it doesn't need to happen right away. After you have spent some time nursing and cuddling with your baby, you can declare that she's ready to be measured.

You may also be asked to permit a routine blood screening for metabolic disorders such as phenylketonuria, thyroid issues, sickle cell, and other problems. This is usually done with a heel stick. Feel free to hold or nurse your baby during the procedure to comfort him and ease any pain. Be sure your baby is at least forty-eight hours old when blood screening is done. If performed prior to this time, the results may be invalid and the screening must be repeated.

Eyes and Ears

Your state law may mandate eye medication following the birth. Check with your local government to find out what the laws are in your community. The eye ointment is administered to prevent blindness in your baby in case you have an untreated sexually transmitted infection (STI). Even if eye medication is mandated, you can still choose when it's done and what medication is used. For example, erythromycin is much gentler than the silver nitrate alternative. Many moms also wait for an hour or two before using the medication because it can cause blurry vision. This may be a bit annoying for your newborn but not harmful.

Where the ears are concerned, many states now require that hearing screenings be done on newborns. These screenings work best when your baby is asleep. So, during the night, a nurse may tap on your door and ask for the baby. Feel free to send the baby with your husband or bring him yourself for this brief test. Bringing the baby ensures that he will return to your room with you as soon as the test is complete.

Common Problems

Chances are your baby will be born happy, healthy, and without complications. However, there are a few rather common complications to be aware of. It is important to know how these are handled so you can be more involved if one should occur with your baby.

Breathing Difficulties

Some babies will have breathing difficulties at birth. If your baby is born early or via cesarean section, she will be more likely to have these problems. Usually, the doctor or midwife can facilitate breathing by rubbing the baby's skin, possibly giving her oxygen. This can be done in any birth setting.

All practitioners are also trained to provide CPR on your newborn, if needed. Long-term ventilation and other breathing treatments may be available only at a Level II or III hospital setting. These measures are the least likely to be needed.

Meconium Staining

Once your water breaks, it may become apparent that your baby has passed his first bowel movement while still inside your body. This is called meconium staining. Meconium is seen in cases where the baby is overdue, stressed, or both. If your practitioner sees meconium, she is likely to listen to the baby more frequently during labor to ensure he is not stressed.

As your baby is born, he will be suctioned before he can breathe or scream. This is done to prevent him from inhaling the meconium. Because meconium is thick and tarlike, it can make it difficult for a newborn to expand his lungs. So, removing it prior to screaming or breathing is important.

In the case of meconium staining, you may have to wait a few minutes before your baby is handed to you. Someone may perform deeper suctioning once the baby is completely free of the birth canal, also to prevent inhalation of meconium. Some babies will still inhale the meconium despite all efforts to prevent this. If your baby does this, he may need further tests, including X rays. In some cases, a baby will also need to stay in the NICU. Your doctor will explain more about this, in the unlikely event that it becomes necessary.

Jaundice

Jaundice is the collection of bilirubin in the blood. This can be discovered through a blood test, but more likely it will be discovered because a baby has turned a shade of yellow. This usually doesn't happen until the first few days after birth.

The best way to get rid of the bilirubin is to encourage as much breast-feeding as possible. Breastmilk, particularly the colostrum it contains during the first few days, acts as a natural laxative, helping your baby to pass the bilirubin. Exposure to natural light through a window can also help.

Extreme cases of jaundice are rare. They are usually treated by breast-feeding and light therapy. Light therapy is usually done by using light blankets. A couple of days are all that is needed to clear up the condition.

The Trip Home

Finally, you've survived through pregnancy, labor, and delivery, and your baby has arrived! Now it's time to take your new bundle of joy home. Bringing your new baby home for the first time is a thrilling and daunting experience. When you last left your home, there were only two of you; now you have a family of three.

FACT

A car seat is one way you can protect your baby during the ride home and other car trips. The problem is that despite good intentions, many parents do not use their car seats safely. Be sure to install and use the car seat every time you travel with your baby in the car. Visit *www.nhtsa. dot.gov/people/injury/childps* for further information on car seats.

In addition to a car seat, remember to bring a blanket or other device to help shield your baby from the rain or sun. You may want to ride in the backseat with your baby during the first car trip or two to watch and comfort her. You may find that you see the world differently once your baby is riding in your car. Suddenly it may seem like every car is pointed directly at yours and every pothole is a deep abyss waiting to swallow her up. These initial fears are normal and will fade in time.

The key to surviving the first days of new motherhood is to be prepared, flexible, and confident. Also, don't be afraid to go after whatever you need. If you need help, ask for it. Be sure to get your questions answered as soon as they come up. And most importantly, enjoy yourself!

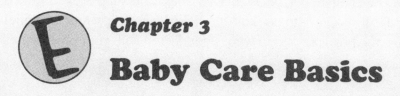

Chapter 3

Baby Care Basics

Transitioning to parenthood can be over-whelming. Suddenly, you have a tiny, helpless baby to feed, clean, clothe, and care for. It's a daunting task! However, if you helped take care of younger siblings while growing up, or did some babysitting to earn extra money when you were a teenager, these experiences will give you a good starting point for raising your own child. If you didn't have either of these experiences, don't panic. They are not prerequisites for being a new mom. Your baby and your instincts will guide you in your new role.

Feeding

If there's one thing you'll be doing more than anything else during the first months of motherhood, it's feeding the baby. New babies don't really eat a lot—they just eat very often. Learning to feed your baby may come naturally or it may be challenging, but with a little help and support, you will come to master it. All you have to do is ask for help. Be sure to see the lactation consultant at the hospital, or one who is connected with your practitioner.

FACT

Newborns have very tiny stomachs. To help you visualize how much milk they need, keep this in mind: A newborn's stomach is the size of a marble. After ten days, it grows to the size of a shooter marble. Even at three months it's only the size of a golf ball. Any myths you hear about new babies consuming gallons of milk in one feeding are wild exaggerations.

Breastfeeding

Breastfeeding is the natural choice for feeding your baby. Your body knows what to do, as does your baby. Even so, you need to learn about breastfeeding. Prenatal classes will teach you basic techniques, as well as explain how breastfeeding benefits both you and your baby. Not only will you learn to read your baby's hunger cues, but you will also learn different nursing positions and how to tell if your baby is getting enough milk.

Your baby is born with the ability to breastfeed. However, sometimes the birth process or the immediate postpartum period produces circumstances that make it harder for your baby to nurse happily and healthily. If you are having difficulties, be sure to talk to other moms who have successfully nursed. You can also get help from a local lactation consultant or through La Leche League International, an organization providing information and encouragement to breastfeeding mothers. The sooner you get help, the easier nursing will become.

Breastfeeding help is available from the Office of Women's Health. Visit their Web site for information, health tips, and questions and answers from other moms, with some in several languages: *www.4woman.gov/breastfeeding*.

Breastfeeding is a lot easier than bottle-feeding pumped breastmilk or artificial baby milk. Coming from the breast, milk is always available and at the right temperature. Support, information, and patience are all you need to create a successful breastfeeding relationship with your baby.

Feeding Artificial Baby Milk (ABM)

Feeding your baby anything but breastmilk is always second best, according to the Food and Drug Administration, the World Health Organization, and the AAP. Not only is breastmilk better for the baby, but there are also risks involved with using artificial baby milk (ABM). Some of these risks include:

- Increased risk of obesity
- Increased risk of allergies and respiratory disease
- More ear infections
- Increased risk of leukemia
- Slower or no return to maternal prepregnancy weight
- Increased risk of SIDS death
- Increased risk of breast cancer for mother

If you make the decision to feed your baby ABM, you will also need to take a class on how to properly feed your baby ABM using a bottle. The bottle and the ABM you choose will be largely dependent on the ABM your pediatrician or hospital provides, as it can be stressful for the baby if you switch to a different milk. However, you may need to switch if the original choice doesn't meet your baby's needs or gives him gas. Be sure to follow the instructions on the ABM can. If you don't follow these instructions, you could cause your baby to become malnourished or even ill. Each manufacturer will be different, so read the labels carefully.

ALERT!

One of the things you miss when feeding ABM instead of breastfeeding is skin-to-skin contact with your baby. This helps establish a bond with your baby, and it comforts her to feel the warmth of your body while she eats. Luckily, you can create a similar sensation by removing your shirt while feeding with a bottle whenever possible.

You will need to choose a premade, condensed, or powdered ABM. There is not really a difference for your baby, but there may be variations in cost and how long each will stay fresh in your home. You will need to heat the ABM using boiling water or a bottle warmer. Do not use a microwave.

While your baby eats, watch for indications that she's getting full. Just because there's still milk in the bottle doesn't mean you should force your baby to finish; this won't make her sleep longer and it may make her ill. Take your time when feeding your baby. Make eye contact with her, talk to her, and switch sides at least once during each feeding, to encourage brain development.

Bathing

While infants don't get dirty the way young children do, they do require occasional baths to keep their skin healthy. Daily baths are not needed until your baby starts crawling on the floor. A bath two or three times a week, in addition to thorough cleansing after feedings and changes, is sufficient before your baby is mobile. There are many ways to accomplish bathing a new baby.

Bathing with Your Baby

In the early days of motherhood while you're still getting used to your new life, try taking a bath with your baby. This will comfort your baby through the new experience of being bathed, as well as prevent you from making the water too hot.

Be sure to lay out everything for the bath before you actually get in the tub or begin washing your baby. Searching for a towel while trying to manage your slippery infant can be extremely hazardous and messy. In fact, storing baby bath necessities near the place where you bathe your baby is a great idea.

Bathing with your little one is also a great way to calm a baby who especially dislikes or fears baths. You can nurse the baby while in the tub to further distract him and passively get him used to the feel of the water; however, be aware that many newborns will have a bowel movement almost immediately after nursing. Bathing with your baby also gives you a chance to clean up, as opportunities for you to bathe will be few and far between during the first busy weeks of motherhood.

Bathing in a Tub

There are several tubs for new babies on the market—some much more elaborate than others. Many are fine for use in the bathtub or the sink. The problem with using them in the bathtub is that you'll probably have to kneel and lean over to reach your baby. This puts you in an awkward, uncomfortable position, which could be potentially hazardous to your baby. Bathing in the bathtub is best saved for when the baby is older and has enough muscle control to sit up by himself.

Always test the temperature of the water before putting your baby in the tub. You can use the inside of your wrist, your elbow, or a bath thermometer to make sure the water is just right. Water that is too hot can quickly burn a baby's skin, and babies chill easily in water that's too cool.

Bathing in a Sink

Bathing your newborn in the sink is easy because you can stand up and do it. No leaning over the tub makes this endeavor much simpler and safer. And the easier it is for you to bathe your baby, the more likely you are to do it (and enjoy it) on a regular basis.

There are a few tubs on the market that fit right over the sink. These are very useful when your baby is tiny, but by the time your baby is learning to sit up, she will really enjoy bath time with a running faucet (with supervision). Lay a towel down on the counter to be used as a drying area after the bath. Keep another clean towel nearby so you can dry her off while she sits on the towel-covered counter.

Changing Diapers

As a new parent, you will spend a good portion of your day changing diapers. The average newborn goes through about eight to ten diapers every day. That's approximately seventy diapers in your first week alone. Gaining knowledge about diapering before you're faced with this nearly constant task can be very helpful.

Until the umbilical cord stump falls off (usually a couple of weeks after birth), regard changing times as chances to follow any cord care instructions from your pediatrician. Changing times are also good opportunities to handle penis care. The AAP offers great advice on caring for the uncircumcised penis and the circumcision wound on their Web site: *www.aap.org*.

Cloth Diapers

Many moms say that they use cloth diapers for a variety of reasons; most frequently cited are fewer rashes for the baby and environmental concerns. Whatever your reasons for choosing cloth diapers, be sure to research the pricing and find a good deal for quality equipment.

Cloth diapers have changed significantly since your mother or grandmother used them. Nowadays, there is no need for diaper pins or plastic pants. Modern diapers and diaper covers are mostly made of waterproof, breathable material and have Velcro closures. There are also diaper services that provide you with the diapers, clean them, and return them to you. However, you can still purchase the cloth diapers yourself and do it on your own the old-fashioned way. Whatever way you choose to do it, consider joining a local or online group where advice, information, and support for home diapering is shared.

Diaper Services

One way to make cloth diapering a little more manageable is to use a diaper service. For slightly more money and depending on your location, you can have clean diapers delivered right to your door.

Many women fall under the false impression that using cloth diapers is less sanitary than using disposable ones. This is not necessarily the case. As long as the diapers are thoroughly cleaned and disinfected between uses, they will be perfectly safe—and often more comfortable—for your baby.

Usually a diaper service will give you seventy diapers and a pail. You simply put the dirty diapers in the pail and once a week on a specified day they will take the dirty diapers and give you clean ones. This option is more expensive than buying and cleaning the diapers yourself, but it saves you the hassle of washing upward of seventy diapers every week.

Disposable Diapers

Diapers are a must for every baby. So, if you're not too thrilled about the cloth-diaper option, you can turn to the disposable-diaper alternative. Just as cloth diapers have developed over the years, disposable diapers have also become more comfortable for babies and manageable for parents.

What do you do if your baby wets right through the diapers?
If this happens with disposable diapers, try using a different brand of diaper. For cloth diapers, you can add a protective lining to the inside of the diaper. The problem could also be that the diapers you're using are too big or too small for your baby.

Disposable diapers are made of paper and are used only once before being discarded. Don't let the word *paper* here worry you—these diapers are totally waterproof. In fact, disposable diaper materials have changed to help keep your baby dry and clean feeling, even while wearing the dirtiest diaper.

Infant Potty Training

No, this is not a typo—infant potty training (IPT) is a real method used by some parents instead of diapers. Elimination communication is not a new idea, but it is making a comeback. To "potty train" your infant, you must learn to watch for cues from your baby that he needs to go to the bathroom. These cues are just as noticeable as those indicating hunger, tiredness, and any other strong sensation your baby might feel. When you realize that your little one has to go, you simply hold a bucket or other receptacle under the baby (or hold him over the toilet) while he relieves himself. Supporters of this method tout its many benefits; for instance, you save money and protect the environment by not buying or throwing away diapers. Additionally, it is suggested that teaching babies to eliminate in diapers and then potty training a couple of years later only confuses children. If you're interested in learning more about IPT, there are several books and Web sites that offer details, products, and advice.

Holding

You will spend lots of time holding your baby—to comfort her, to move her from one place to another, and just to enjoy being close to her. This is one of the ways you and your husband bond with your baby. Go ahead and let friends and family hold your baby as well. It's important that she come to know all the people in her life from an early age.

Skin-to-Skin Contact

Your baby will likely be given to you to hold close to your body as soon as she is born. This is because skin-to-skin contact with you has important benefits, including warming her and helping her to regulate her breathing. However, this contact is not only important on the day of birth; its value holds true throughout infancy. So, take some time each day to hold your baby close to your bare skin during those first few months. Your baby will enjoy the warmth of your body and the sound of your heartbeat, and you'll love the soft sensation of contact with your baby.

Dads should also take time to enjoy skin-to-skin contact with their babies. A mother already has a deep connection with her child from giving birth, and skin-to-skin contact can help a father establish a similarly strong relationship with the baby. In a parent's arms, a baby feels completely safe and comfortable.

Different Holds

Holding a baby comes quite naturally to most new mothers. It's likely that you will inherently know which body parts need the most support. However, there is more than one way to hold your baby. Some holds are one-handed, allowing you to use your free hand for something else. Some holds give the baby a view of the world around him, and others give him a direct view of your face.

Though you will surely discover other useful options through your experience as a parent, here are a few basic holds you can use with your baby:

Cradle Hold: This position is commonly used for nursing. Your baby's head goes in the crook of your arm, and you extend your forearm along the baby's back, supporting her bottom with the palm of your hand.

Shoulder Carry: This hold is great for calming a fussy baby. Just rest your baby's head on your shoulder, hold the baby's lower back and bottom with that arm, and stabilize the baby's head with your other hand.

Football Hold: With your dominant hand faceup and at your side, place the back of your baby's head in your palm and support her body with your forearm, holding her close to the side of your body. This is a great position for nursing after a cesarean because the baby is not hovering around your scar.

Hip Carry: This position is for older babies who can hold up their own heads. Rest your baby's bottom on your hip bone so she is facing outward and wrap that arm around the baby's body. This keeps your other arm totally free for another task.

ALERT!

Plagiocephaly is a condition in which a baby develops a flat spot on the back or side of her head from too much pressure there. This usually happens if a baby spends every night and too many hours of the day lying in any one position. To help prevent this, carry your baby using a variety of different holds and promote tummy time during play periods. If your baby does develop a flat spot, take her to the pediatrician right away.

Crying

Many new parents become very distressed if their babies cry often or for long periods of time. But it's important to remember that babies cry—it's just a fact of life. Without verbal abilities, your infant doesn't have too many options when it comes to getting your attention. Crying doesn't necessarily mean that your baby is hurt, and it doesn't mean you've done something wrong. Your baby will cry for many reasons. The cause could be physical (he's hungry, tired, in pain, or wet/dirty) or emotional (he's frustrated, scared, lonely, overstimulated, or bored).

When your baby cries, try not to get frustrated. Instead, be a problem solver. Assess the situation by asking yourself questions. Could your baby be hungry? Does he need to be changed? Might he be tired? In some cases your baby will be asking you for a change of environment. For instance, if he is in a swing, moving him to a calmer place—like a blanket on the floor—might help him relax. If you are in a noisy room, try moving him to a quieter area.

Unfortunately, your baby will sometimes cry for seemingly no reason at all. You might try every trick in the book, but to no avail. This can be extremely frustrating for both you and your baby. When this happens, hand your baby off to someone else, if possible. This will allow you to calm down and might even distract the baby from his carrying on. If there is no one else around, put your little one someplace safe, like in his car seat on the floor, and briefly leave the room to regain your composure. Shaking your baby out of frustration can have fatal repercussions.

FACT

Contrary to popular belief, crying is not your baby's only way to communicate with you. In fact, it is usually his last signal that something is bothering him. Your baby will give other cues (facial expressions, heavy breathing, etc.), and you should learn to recognize these. This way, you'll be better able to respond to your baby before crying becomes necessary.

Sleeping

Choosing bedtimes and sleeping arrangements can be a challenge for new parents. The more sleep you lose, the harder it will be to think rationally about this topic. Your decision will depend on your lifestyle, your beliefs, and your baby. Keep in mind that your baby's bedtime will change as she gets older. In the beginning, it may be easier to have the baby keep hours similar to yours. This allows you to get more sleep when you are naturally tired and sleep well.

The Basics

Newborn babies sleep about twelve to eighteen hours a day during the first month of life. Generally, periods of wakefulness become longer as they get older. The problem with this is that most babies will not sleep for long stretches of time—especially at first—preventing you from getting sufficient sleep. But take heart: as time goes on, your baby will sleep longer and longer, and so will you.

Partially determining how well your baby sleeps will be the environment in which she sleeps. If you suspect your baby is not getting enough sleep, consider her environment. Do you leave the lights on? Does your baby share a room with a sibling who snores loudly? Is your baby's temperature comfortable? These and other details play a major role in how well your baby sleeps at night.

Sleeping through the night is really only possible when your baby is neurologically ready. It cannot be forced by feeding your baby cereal, letting your baby cry, or any other rumored "cure." Always be skeptical when presented with surefire methods to make your baby sleep through the night.

Co-sleeping

Co-sleeping, or having your baby sleep in bed with you, is the natural way to parent at night. In many cultures, parents have their children sleep in or very close to their bed. This enables them to respond quickly to the child's needs.

Co-sleeping, also called sleep sharing or the family bed, is a safe practice when executed using common sense. It is beneficial for you as well as your baby and will not cause your baby to become dependent on you to sleep. Your baby will eventually leave your bed, when you are both ready.

Sharing sleep with your baby is a natural extension of baby care, particularly during the first months of life. Sleeping with your baby will make breastfeeding at night very simple, as there is no need to get out of bed, turn on lights, and sit up to feed your baby. This will probably help both of you get more sleep as well.

Many babies sleep better when comforted by the presence of their parents. It has also been shown in some studies that babies who sleep with their parents are less likely to have problems with sudden infant death syndrome (SIDS). Researchers speculate this is because the baby falls into your sleep patterns.

FACT

Do not sleep with your baby if you are taking pain medications or if you have been drinking. This is dangerous, as certain medications and alcohol can cause you to act without regard for your baby. If you need to take medication, your baby should sleep in a crib, where she will be safe.

The rules for co-sleeping are simple: Don't sleep on a water bed. Don't be crowded in bed—use a queen- or king-sized bed if possible. Don't go to bed intoxicated or on pain medication. And end co-sleeping when you feel your child is naturally ready to sleep alone.

Crib Sleeping

You may decide that a crib is the best place for your baby to sleep. Be sure to choose a crib that meets the most current safety standards, to prevent injury to your baby. This includes ensuring that the crib has slats that are close enough together, the crib does not contain toxic paint or other materials, and the mattress is of safe firmness.

Consider holding or rocking your baby into a light stage of sleep before trying to lay her down in the crib. If your baby wakes up as soon as you move her, you may need to wait until she is in a deeper sleep stage. Remember that even if the baby is not sleeping in your bed, or maybe not even in your room, you still need to be physically responsive to her at any time of night. Make sure she is relatively close by so you can hear any sounds of distress.

ALERT!

Don't be seduced by cute crib toys and decorations. Bumpers might match your baby's nursery, but they could potentially harm your baby. It is best for her to sleep with nothing but a small, lightweight blanket. This means no toys, bumpers, pillows, or other items should be in the crib with her.

Leaving the House

Most new parents worry about taking a new baby out of the house. They don't want to expose their child to unknown dangers, especially while driving in the car. To get accustomed to leaving the house with the baby, start with short trips first. As you build your confidence, longer trips will come naturally. Don't be afraid to take your baby with you. He can actually learn a lot from being in different environments.

In addition to the act of taking the baby into the outside world, the amount of supplies you need to take with you can be very daunting. Before becoming a parent, most people need only their keys and wallet when leaving the house. Things are a little more complicated once you have a baby. You'll come to feel like you're carrying everything but the kitchen sink in your diaper bag, and it'll seem like you're emptying out the grocery store every time you go shopping. This just takes some getting used to.

In addition to carrying a stocked diaper bag everywhere you go with your baby, it's also a good idea to keep an emergency kit in your car. This could include an extra outfit, two diapers, and a small baggie of wipes. Just don't confuse this with your diaper bag and remove it from the car.

You will need to tote around quite a few things in your diaper bag. These may include several changes of clothes, a blanket, a few toys, several diapers, wipes, medications, and much more. If you regularly carry a diaper bag, be sure to restock it as soon as you come home. This will ensure you're always ready to go. You should also put your diaper bag near the door, making it easy to grab on your way out.

If you are traveling by car, you will need a car seat. You may also wish to pack a sling to carry your baby around in, or another soft carrier. When your baby is older, you can use a sling, which can fit in your diaper bag, or a stroller. All of these items can fit easily in your car.

Routines

A new baby is an all-around challenge. This addition to your family will knock your former lifestyle, schedule, and habits completely out of whack. Fortunately, your new life with a baby will eventually fall into patterns, and you will be better able to make advance plans and follow a cycle.

Though you're used to operating by the time on the clock, your baby operates on a natural, instinctive schedule. His tiny tummy can't go as long without eating, and your baby requires more frequent sleep, for shorter periods of time. It will take time to join this way of life with your own, but it will happen.

QUESTION?

If your baby seems like he could feed forever, does this mean he's not getting enough to eat?
This baby is exhibiting what is called cluster feeding behavior. This means that at a certain point in the day, your baby will eat about every hour or two. Don't panic—this is normal and healthy. The good news is that after cluster feeding, your baby will likely have his longest period of sleep for the day.

You should not be rigid about when your baby does something and for how long. Follow the cues your baby sends you to show when he is satisfied and when he needs something. As your baby begins to disengage and appear sleepy, try putting him to bed for a nap. If your baby is alert and interacting with you, sing and play to entertain him. Your baby will let you know what he needs from you. Your only challenge is learning to read his signs and signals.

Don't let the thought of caring for your new baby overwhelm you. Remember that everyone makes mistakes, and these mistakes are rarely disastrous. Try out different techniques until you find what works best for you. And no matter how busy you get or how hectic life becomes, always take time to enjoy the experience of being a parent.

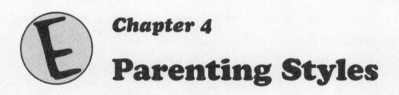

Chapter 4

Parenting Styles

Y ou've probably received endless "advice" from well-meaning friends and family on how to raise your baby. Despite what anyone tells you, your parenting style must be developed over time—by you. However, you can still pick up tricks from existing parenting styles, including those that seem like fads. You can also take advice from friends and family—but with a grain of salt; a few of their methods might work for you, but others might not. Simply keep an open mind and consider your baby's unique characteristics when making these decisions.

Just One Right Way?

There is not simply one correct way to raise a child. Every child and every family has unique needs. It's helpful to have a general idea of how you'd like to parent, but your methods will adjust and change to accommodate your child's individual qualities and requirements. Be leery of any person or parenting program that claims a one-size-fits-all method is the answer to all your problems—it's not true. With some patience and persistence, the right path for your family will present itself in time.

One set of research says that there are four styles of parenting: indulgent, authoritative, authoritarian, and uninvolved. Some research also suggests that it is your overall parenting style rather than individual practices that make you a successful or unsuccessful parent.

Attachment Parenting

The words attachment parenting might conjure up images of a child being dependent on his parents forever. Actually, this is the opposite of the outcome this method produces. Attachment parenting is a technique in which parents read the baby's cues to figure out what he needs. By learning to recognize the needs of your baby and meeting those needs, he will develop into a confident child with a healthy attitude, who is not afraid to venture out into the world. Here are some characteristics of attachment parenting:

- Baby's needs are met immediately.
- Physical punishment is not used.
- Parents read signs from baby to learn how to best handle situations.
- Babies are seen as unique individuals.

The baby builds self-confidence because his parents always promptly meet his needs. To facilitate this relationship, the baby must always be in close proximity to one or both parents. For this reason, many parents who follow the attachment parenting model co-sleep with their children, at least for some part of their lives. Attachment parenting subscribers usually breast-feed their babies as well.

Baby wearing is another component of attachment parenting. Dr. William Sears says that babies who are worn in slings are better able to relax, sleep, eat, and play. He feels that baby wearing is a natural extension of pregnancy.

QUESTION?

How old must a baby be to carry him in a sling?
Slings can be used with newborns all the way up to hefty toddlers. Using your sling is just a matter of practice and imagination. There is good information on baby wearing available online at *www.askdrsears.com/html/5/t051100.asp.*

Fussy babies especially love being worn, as the positioning close to the parents' bodies helps keep them calm. Even if other parts of attachment parenting don't work for you, you might consider wearing your baby if he ever gets fussy. This is also a great way to discreetly nurse your baby.

Pediatrician-Directed Parenting

Some parents who like to have guidance as they develop their parenting methods prefer to follow the advice of the pediatrician. Hopefully, the guidelines your pediatrician follows come from the American Academy of Pediatrics (AAP).

FACT

The AAP is the governing body of pediatricians in the United States. They have an extensive Web site with tons of parenting information for anyone to read. Visit *http://aap.org/parents.html.*

Pediatrician-directed parenting might be a great way to start if you are unsure of how to proceed with your new baby. The problem with this method is that you are effectively letting someone else raise your child. Try this only as a starting point, and then as you gain confidence in your ability to raise your baby, start making your own decisions. As you grow confident that you can meet the needs of your baby, you will be able to transition into your own style of parenting. At this point, your pediatrician will become a resource rather than a leader.

Scheduled Parenting

Parenting by the clock, or scheduled parenting, means that your child consistently does everything at a certain time of day. Supporters of this method believe that if you find a predictable schedule for your baby, then he will grow confident and thrive. These infants are usually crib sleepers, with scheduled times for eating, playing, and sleeping.

ALERT!

According to the World Health Organization, scheduled breastfeeding can lead to a variety of neonatal problems. Be sure that your baby is eating well and gaining enough weight if you breastfeed on a schedule. Sometimes a baby who doesn't cry could be having a problem instead of just being a "good" baby.

Unfortunately, real life doesn't work like this for most parents. The fear of falling off the schedule can lead to some serious issues for some parents and babies. One of the biggest problems of scheduled parenting can be feeding issues, particularly early on in your baby's life. Newborn babies have very small stomachs. They are not designed to hold large amounts of food. Therefore, they need to eat small, frequent meals. Scheduled feedings can lead to weight gain issues, including problems with malnutrition and dehydration.

As with any other decision concerning your baby, you need to figure out what works for your family. Don't worry if you can't manage the scheduled-parenting method—it's not for everyone. But if you find that some of the method's tips are helpful, go ahead and incorporate them into your parenting style.

Discipline

The definition of discipline that you learned as a child may be a bit different than the one you'd like to use with your baby. In the past, many parents used physical punishment to discipline their children. Fortunately, most modern parents realize that this can be a very harmful experience for your child. A far better choice is the use of positive discipline in your home. One of the first steps in using positive discipline is to recognize the distinction between a bad child and a bad action. A child who is told he is bad will develop very low self-esteem. You must instead show your child that his actions may be bad, but he is not.

FACT

Shaken baby syndrome (SBS) is a form of child abuse. This is a collection of symptoms seen when a baby is shaken. If your baby is crying and you can't control your frustration, put your child in a safe place and step away. Go in another room and call a trusted friend to come help you. For more information about SBS, call 888-273-0071.

Positive discipline is generally defined as nonviolent. Respect is shown for both the child and the parent. Typically, there is no hitting or yelling. Punishment is enacted in a variety of forms, from time-outs to removal of privileges. Punishment may also include natural consequences. For example, for little children, this means that if they break a new toy, they do not get a new one. There are many ways to incorporate positive discipline into your parenting technique.

Your baby is not plotting against you, though some days you may come to feel this way. Babies cry for a variety of reasons, but spite is not one of them. Young children sometimes test the boundaries by touching off-limits items or ignoring parental instructions, but these are just ways that children exert their independence. You can curb these behaviors, but you usually can't eliminate them completely through discipline.

That said, you should begin developing your own philosophy about discipline while your baby is still very young. Watch other parents interacting with their children to get an idea of different options. As your child grows, slowly integrate your preferred discipline method into your child's life.

When Parents Differ

The first step to dealing with differences between your and your husband's parenting theories is recognizing these differences. You must realize that each person has a different view of things, and that each person's opinions have merit. Try to educate each other about the style you've developed, why you've developed it, and how you think it works. Remember to be open to suggestions from the other side. Your best chance for success lies in finding a common ground.

Start a conversation with your spouse about the topic. Some questions to begin with might include:

- What did you like best about your parents' parenting methods?
- What would you do differently from your parents?
- Describe your philosophy toward meeting your baby's needs.
- Are there things you definitely want to do as a parent?
- Do you see yourself as a partner in raising your child? Or would you prefer a more laid-back role?
- Should only one parent be the disciplinarian?
- Do you believe in spanking children, and if so, for what offenses? When is your child old enough for spanking?
- What are your beliefs about punishing children?
- What is the best style of communication with your child?
- Do you think yelling is necessary?

As you explain your ideas to one another, create examples and even act them out to demonstrate your rationale. Ask that your husband do the same. If you claim to have gotten your information from a certain source, go ahead and show the book, Web site, or other resource. Thoroughly explaining each of your opinions will make it easier to compromise. Remember, parenting is a team effort. The earlier you compromise to establish a parenting style, the better. This will save you and your child stress later on.

Be aware of tactics you use in discussing parenting issues with your spouse. Avoidance, arguing, and ignoring are not conducive to meeting your final goal. Serious compromise and dialogue are necessary from both sides to make change happen.

Once your baby is born, parenting really begins in earnest. No longer are these questions of philosophical debate. Where will your baby sleep? Will you respond immediately to her needs? Conflict here can be very uncomfortable. Be prepared to have differences, but be sure the major kinks are worked out before your baby is born. Conversely, you can also agree to put some decisions on hold. Don't waste your time and energy arguing about the age at which your baby will be allowed to date when she's still in the womb. Agree to wait and see what kind of person your baby develops into. These questions might have much clearer answers in fifteen years.

Advice from Others

As soon as your belly starts to blossom, words of advice will probably start flowing in from all directions. During pregnancy, excess advice may be easy to shrug off, as your baby has not yet arrived. But once the baby is born, you may be a little more likely to worry. If someone suggests holding your baby too much will spoil him, you may begin to second-guess your choice to use the attachment parenting method.

Just remember to listen only to advice that seems to be practical. Think about how it might apply to your life. Does it make sense? How would you feel if you applied it? Does it go against any of your major beliefs about parenting? If an idea seems to meet all your requirements, consider trying it out. Remember, you can always scrap the idea if it doesn't work for you.

Grandparents

Unfortunately, the stereotypical new grandparents you see on sitcoms might actually turn out to be a reality for you. Your and your husband's parents might actually hover over you with advice, citing thousands of their own experiences when you two were little. Though they probably mean well, this unending "guidance" from your parents can drive you crazy. But unlike strangers with bad advice, you can't just ignore them and walk away.

Keep a couple of things in mind when dealing with unwanted advice from the baby's grandparents:

- They probably mean well.
- They probably don't know about the new technologies, products, and knowledge available to parents today. Don't be afraid to try to educate them—they may actually enjoy it.
- Listen to their advice; use what you can and discard the rest.
- Divide and conquer: if it is your spouse's parents who are driving you nuts, ask him to step in. Be willing to do the same if your parents act up.
- Remind them that ultimately, you are the baby's parents and your word is law.
- Most importantly, do not feel guilty for discarding advice that doesn't work for you.

Of course, not every set of grandparents will overwhelm you in this way. You may be lucky enough to have parents who offer to babysit and visit with the baby with no strings attached. If this is the case, enjoy it! And don't take this to mean that your parents can't offer advice if you need it. Feel free to ask, even if they aren't offering it up on a daily basis.

Friends

Your friends may also fall into the well-meaning category, but that doesn't make hearing their incessant advice any easier. Sometimes, however, friends are well connected, up-to-date parents themselves and have great advice to offer. In this case, listen to their advice, but heed it only if it fits your own parenting ideals.

Beware of childless friends with theories. You might find that the parenting theories you hold before you have kids will fly out the window when your little ones actually arrive. This is probably the same for many of your friends who don't have children. Still, these people just want to help, so be gentle if and when you must refuse their guidance.

If your friends have kids, they probably have some ideas that are similar to yours, and that might be what drew you together in the first place. Separate out the helpful advice using some of the same principles you use with grandparents. Try to laugh off or ignore what doesn't work for you. Be kind but remind friends to give you your space in parenting.

Parenting differences can seriously affect your friendships. If you and your friends have very different styles, it will be apparent and may cause tension. Try not to let parenting differences ruin your friendship. Agree to disagree and go on from there. This usually works well for all involved.

Strangers

One day, you might be standing in line at the grocery store holding a huge package of diapers. The lady behind you might tap on your shoulder and tell you that the brand of diapers you've chosen always leaks. Is this helpful? The answer probably depends on how much sleep you got the night before.

Advice from strangers can be very helpful or downright awful. How you chose to deal with it will depend on many factors, including the nature of the advice and your mood when you receive it. Try to be kind to nosy strangers offering tips or tricks, even if you don't find them helpful. They might be exhausted new mothers just like you.

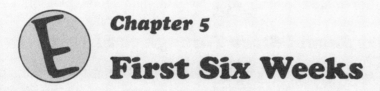

Chapter 5

First Six Weeks

A wise woman once said that if a new mother can survive the first six weeks of motherhood, she can make it through anything. Once you make it to the magic six-week mark, you'll probably agree. With some knowledge and patience, you can get through those first few challenges and proceed with confidence and enthusiasm. Just be wary of myths, allow yourself to make mistakes, and take care of yourself in addition to your baby.

Common Myths of New Motherhood

As if you needed another challenge on top of learning to be a mom and getting to know your baby, there are a bunch of myths about new babies in circulation. By ridding yourself of some erroneous bits of information, you can streamline your life and make your days and nights more pleasant.

Myth: Babies Should Sleep Through the Night

Lack of sleep is an oft-cited reason to dislike the first months of new motherhood. Sleeping like you did prior to pregnancy is not going to happen for a while. However, there are a couple of key things to remember about nighttime sleep when you're a new mom.

ALERT!

If your baby sleeps most of the day away and rarely cries or fusses, you need to take her for a visit with the pediatrician. What you might regard as great baby behavior can be a sign that your baby is ill. Periods of wakefulness or distress in babies are common and completely healthy.

For one thing, no one actually sleeps deeply through the night. If you look at what sleep researchers have known for years, the truth is that everyone passes through different cycles of sleep each night. These are periods of both light and deep sleep. Many adults have minor waking episodes at night. When your baby wakes you up with crying, it might not be much different from those experiences.

Second, in many cases, it is dangerous for babies to sleep through the night. This is because a baby has a tiny belly that cannot hold enough food to get her through the night. By waking to feed, even in small amounts, babies get what they need to survive and thrive. In the beginning, most babies wake up two or three times each night. By three months of age, this has gradually decreased for most families, though it is not uncommon to have a baby who is still waking up once a night even at nearly nine months of age.

QUESTION?

Does it help to give a baby cereal before bed?
Though you may have heard about this "miracle cure" for restless babies, cereal before bed will not help them sleep through the night. If you give your baby cereal prior to the time recommended by your pediatrician, you could introduce the potential for food allergies. Pediatricians generally recommend starting solids around six months of age.

Additionally, waking to feed your baby a few times a night gives you the opportunity to meet some of her other needs. This might include changing a dirty diaper or moving your little one into a better sleeping position. Some mothers are also anxious about sleep periods that last too long, so night waking can ease these worries.

Myth: You Will Get Skinny Right Away

You will probably be sad to know that you'll most likely wear maternity clothes home from the hospital. Though you lose a lot of weight when your baby is born, you may also suffer from some swelling, particularly if you have intravenous therapy in labor or postpartum. You will have stretched your abdominal skin, which will take a while to return to its original shape. Remember, it took you nine months to put on the weight, so you can't expect to lose it overnight. However, you will see the most dramatic changes during the first six weeks after birth.

The good news is that breastfeeding can burn up to 1,500 calories a day. It also taps stores of maternal fat that were established in your body specifically for breastfeeding during pregnancy. This makes breastfeeding the natural way to shed unwanted pregnancy pounds.

Myth: The First Six Weeks After Birth Are Unbearable

Surely you have heard this one. Everyone says those first six weeks of little sleep, endless feedings, a sore body, and other physical issues will nearly kill you. Truthfully, many women actually find the first six weeks interesting and pleasant. Many of the sweetest moments you will share with your baby come during late-night feedings and other supposedly "terrible" moments. Don't expect the first six weeks postpartum to be miserable; you may end up pleasantly surprised to find these few weeks go more smoothly than you thought.

Myth: After the First Few Days You Should Feel Like Your Old Self Again

Giving birth is hard work. You will likely feel drained from pregnancy and birth for weeks to come. You'll probably also be a bit overwhelmed by the task of shaping your parenting theories, not to mention tired from a few sleepless nights. While the physical issues are normal and simply take time to heal, your new role as a mother will take the place of certain other activities you enjoyed as your "old self."

It will take at least six weeks for the majority of the physical healing process to occur. During this period of time, your uterus will shrink back down to its prepregnancy size. You will lose the majority of your weight, though it will take additional work to strengthen and tone your muscles. Your hormones will start to level out, and your body will heal any wounds incurred during the birth process.

Leaking Everywhere!

Many women are unprepared for some of the body changes that come with giving birth, particularly leaking. Your breasts, eyes, sweat glands, vagina, and bottom will be leaking fluids you never saw before. This is your body's way of ridding itself of fluids retained during pregnancy, labor, and birth.

Vaginal Discharge

Regardless of how you give birth, vaginally or via cesarean surgery, you will experience vaginal discharge after you give birth. For the first few days, this discharge will be in the form of bleeding, which may seem heavy at times, particularly when standing up after lying down. It will also include clots. This postpartum bleeding comes from your uterus. At the place where the placenta attached to your uterus, you will have a large open wound. The blood indicates the healing of this wound.

You must not wear tampons or place anything else inside your vagina while you are bleeding. Wearing pads is the only way to deal with postpartum bleeding. If at any point during your bleeding you revert back to a heavier or a brighter red flow, you need to slow down. Take this as a signal that you need to lessen your activity to heal, and mention the change to your doctor, just to be on the safe side.

As your uterus heals, the bleeding will slow. A second phase of bleeding will be more like your regular period and may last for a week or two. The final stage of bleeding is more of a brown or beige discharge. It may come and go over a couple of weeks. There should never be a foul odor to this or any discharge. It should smell about the same as your period. If you run a fever, have a tender abdomen, or notice a foul smell, be sure to call your doctor right away.

Leaking Breasts

Right after your baby is born, your breasts produce a premilk substance called colostrum. Colostrum is rich in antibodies and helps your baby pass his first stool, called meconium. Colostrum comes in very minute quantities, because your baby needs only a tiny bit. In the first few days after birth, your breasts will begin to produce what is called mature milk.

At first your body will seem to produce enough milk for the whole neighborhood. This is because your body is trying to satisfy even the heartiest appetite. This quantity can support more than one baby if you give birth to multiples. Because of the extra quantity, you may notice that milk leaks from one breast when your baby is nursing on the other side, or from both breasts when your baby cries. (Leaking when your baby cries is a conditioned response to your baby's needs, which lessens drastically as your baby gets older.) Sometimes you will leak if your breasts are overfull, showing you that your baby needs to eat.

The easiest way to deal with leaking breasts is to wear breast pads. It's important to ensure that the breast pads you select are not backed with plastic. You need breathable material to help prevent nipple soreness and potential yeast infection. These pads simply fit inside your bra. You can buy disposable pads for one-time use. There are also thick cotton washable pads available for repeated use.

QUESTION?

What do you do if you leak when you're not wearing breast pads?
You might notice a tingle in your breasts before your milk begins to flow. If this happens when you are not wearing pads, simply cross your arms over your breasts and apply a bit of pressure. This should solve the problem. Also, wear patterned shirts if leaking is a problem, as stains will be less obvious.

As your body and baby get in sync as far as your milk supply goes, your leaking will decrease dramatically. This will lessen your need for breast pads, though you may still have an occasional leak. It usually takes a couple of weeks for leaking to slow drastically. After the first few weeks, you may not leak at all. This is not a sign that your milk has dried up; it simply means that your body has adapted.

Excessive Perspiration

Shortly after giving birth, your body will decide it must rid itself of all the extra fluids it gained during pregnancy. If you received IV fluids during labor and birth or even during the postpartum period, you may have even more fluid to lose. One way your body will expel fluids is through perspiration.

You may notice throughout the day that you are warmer than everyone else in your home. You might also wake up drenched in sweat in the middle of the night. The increase in sweating usually lasts only a week or two, and the only way to deal with it is to stay comfortable. Try showering at least once a day. You can also change your clothes as frequently as you need to stay dry and comfortable.

Lack of Sleep

The image of a new mother as a disheveled, exhausted woman with a tiny baby on her shoulder may be more accurate than you hope. Some days, you will certainly feel this way, but it won't be your everyday experience. However, one thing most new moms do complain about is lack of sleep. The more sleep you lose, the harder it becomes to catch up and get back on track.

Sleep When the Baby Sleeps

Sleeping when the baby sleeps sounds like a good plan. Unfortunately, it's not as easy as it sounds. This method often fails because, just as you lay your baby down for a nap, you might notice a toy strewn carelessly on the floor and put it back in its place. Or maybe you'll walk by the overflowing laundry basket and decide to throw in a quick load of wash while you've got the chance.

In modern society, people are conditioned to be productive during the daylight hours. This being the case, you'll probably try to get a few things done around the house while your baby sleeps rather than consider your own exhaustion and take a quick nap. Don't make this mistake! Whenever possible, lie down and try to take a nap when your baby does. Even if you can't actually sleep, take the opportunity to flip through a magazine in a reclining position. Rest promotes healing and will do your body good.

The Art of Napping

The next hurdle is learning to sleep like a baby. The art of napping is difficult to perfect. Not only are people used to staying awake from early in the morning to late at night, but most people also question the value of a quick thirty- or forty-five-minute nap. The truth is, even a short burst of rest and relaxation can do wonders for your tired, healing body.

ALERT!

Be very careful when you're sleepy. Driving in the car with your baby when you're tired puts both of you at risk. Don't be afraid to ask for help from a friend or family member when you need a break to catch up on your sleep. Even a short nap can refresh you enough to keep you out of harm's way.

If you are having trouble getting to sleep in your bed, try drifting off in different settings, like on the couch in front of the TV. You can maximize the amount of sleep you get by minimizing the struggle to fall asleep. The problem is that people don't have on and off switches. It will take some practice to be able to fall asleep when you have a brief chance.

Leaving Your House

After being in the house for the first few days after birth, you may get a touch of cabin fever. This is perfectly normal. To refresh yourself, consider a quick walk around the neighborhood or a trip to the store to buy a new outfit for the baby while your husband watches her. Just be cautious if you decide to go out, particularly if you had surgery. If your body is still recovering, try a car ride instead.

ALERT!

If you give birth via cesarean or have to have an extensive repair on your perineum, you may not be able to drive for several weeks. Be sure to ask your doctor or midwife when you will be able to get behind the wheel again.

If you want to take your baby with you, choose a low-key destination. Don't choose a busy mall or grocery store, as the crowds may add stress to your little outing. Instead, select a place that will allow you to meander and stop when needed. Also make sure there is a place to change or nurse your baby if the need should arise. The key to a successful first trip out is to be sure that you and the baby are up for it. Neither of you should be too tired or too hungry to deal with whatever situation might befall you. Asking a friend to join you for this quick outing might also be a good idea.

Cleanliness

Your job as a parent is to protect your baby. Part of this job is keeping your baby's environment clean and safe. As with everything, there are two extremes separated by a middle ground when it comes to the issue of cleanliness. Some women fall at either end of the spectrum, but your goal is to settle somewhere in the middle.

Two Extremes

Some moms are so nervous about their new baby that they become obsessed with cleanliness and germ control. You know the type. They practically make you put on a space suit before letting you touch their baby. This is obviously extreme behavior. Healthy children come from various types of homes, and very few of them are squeaky clean every minute of the day.

On the other end is the mom who picks up a dropped pacifier that fell nipple-side down on the floor and puts it right back into her baby's mouth. While your floor should be clean enough for your baby to crawl on, you probably still wouldn't want her licking it. The mom who is too laid back about cleanliness might find her child constantly riddled with cold symptoms. This is not the environment you want to provide for your baby either.

Middle Ground

Obviously, neither of these extremes are what you want or need as a mother. It is important to realize that your baby will be exposed to germs no matter what you do. Some of these germs will be harmful, while other germs will serve to boost your baby's immune system.

Be reasonable. If someone is sick, ask that they respectfully refrain from holding your baby. You may choose to have people wash their hands prior to holding a tiny newborn, but that may not be as feasible (or necessary) for an older baby.

Wash your breast pump parts, feeding utensils or soothers, and teething toys frequently. Some things you may choose to sterilize more frequently than others. Consider purchasing microwave sterilizers to make the task easier. Beyond that, keep your house as clean as you can without going crazy. Generally keep floors and furniture free of dust, wash dishes and clothes regularly, and clean up any spills or leaked fluids right away.

Fashion Sense for New Moms

Luckily, today's new moms don't have to wear frumpy clothes. Gone are the days of baggy pants and potato sacks for your in-between wardrobe. There are many fashionable clothing lines available for new moms to wear with pride and style, and they won't all break the bank. Being comfortable and looking good are important components to building self-esteem after giving birth.

Wardrobe Basics

There are very few hard-and-fast rules about what to wear postpartum. One of these is don't wear your maternity clothes after you've given birth. They're very comfortable, but they won't help boost your body image. On the other hand, avoid the temptation to go out and purchase a new wardrobe two weeks after your baby is born. This is not your permanent shape. Buying a couple of transitional items is fine. However, you'll also need some clothing that provides easy access for certain motherly tasks.

Underwear

During the first few weeks after having a baby, you will need to wear underwear that is capable of holding a pad. The purpose of this is to catch vaginal discharge, which will persist only temporarily. If you have a cesarean incision, you will probably want to avoid bikini-cut underwear. These can irritate the scar and make it sore, or even make it bleed. If big, comfy underwear don't meet your style requirements, try the thigh hi-cut, which is a bit more attractive.

Though you won't know exactly what size will fit until after your baby is born, buy a few postpartum clothing items before you give birth. This way, you won't have to go shopping during those first few days—you'll already have some basics. Once you regain your strength, you can go shopping for some better fitting, more stylish items.

A good bra is also a must for any postpartum mom. Having someone fit you for a bra after your baby is a week or two old is a good idea. Milk production can enlarge your breasts significantly, so your old bras probably won't cut it. If you're breastfeeding, you'll also need a bra with openings for nursing. Some bras have snapped flaps, while others allow you to slip your breast through a movable fabric panel. Figure out which style best suits your needs.

Everyday and Dressy Clothes

Since you won't want to sit around the house all day with your new baby, you'll need outfits to wear when you leave the house and even a few for those rare dressy occasions. For everyday use, choose a couple of shirts that make nursing easy—ones with buttons or large neck holes. These should also be patterned to hide any leakage from your breasts or spit up from your baby. You can also layer shirts and sweaters to give you the functionality you need and the style you want.

FACT

Shorts, skirts, and pants are the easiest options for everyday wear, rather than dresses or one-piece outfits. It's a good idea to have a nursing dress on hand as well. These items make it easy to breastfeed, go to the bathroom, dress, and undress.

In the first few weeks, you won't really need or want to dress up. More comfortable, flexible clothing is conducive to your purposes as a brand-new mom. However, if you have the need for a special outfit, consider a basic black dress with a fancy scarf to liven it up. This will work for many occasions, from the office holiday party to a wedding.

Six-Week Checkup

After nine long months filled with visits to your practitioner's office, you will have one final visit. This will consist mainly of a physical exam. Though they'll tell you to make your appointment for six weeks after you give birth, you may need to be seen sooner if you have problems or if you had surgery. Be sure to call and ask the practitioner's office if you need to be seen, rather than waiting for the six-week visit.

There are some practitioners who will also use the six-week checkup to go over your birth with you and discuss what happened, how you liked it, and how you would do it differently in the future. If your practitioner doesn't do this, consider scheduling a meeting to have this discussion. This will help you sort out your feelings about your experience.

The Physical

The whole point of the six-week visit is to ensure that you're in good physical health. At this point in the postpartum period, you should have done the majority of your physical healing from the pregnancy and birth. This visit will also include some preventative health measures. The following are a few procedures and issues that may be performed or discussed at this time:

Pap smear: This will give your practitioner a chance to look at your perineum. She can talk to you about how this area is healing, if you required any stitches from an episiotomy. Your practitioner should discuss the resumption of sexual activity as well.

Breast exam: During this exam, the practitioner will be looking for irregularities or masses that have appeared since your last exam. You can also ask any breastfeeding questions you may have and inquire about doing breast self-exams while nursing.

Follow-up procedures: If you require any follow-up lab work or procedures such as hernia repair, now is the time to discuss them with your practitioner. You may also need to have some immunizations; the one new mothers commonly need is the rubella vaccine.

Birth control: Bring any questions you have about birth control with you. Consider writing them down so you don't forget.

Saying Good-Bye

One of the hardest parts of the six-week visit is realizing that it is the last one. Be sure to bring your baby so that everyone you got to know in the office can meet the fruits of your combined labor. It's okay to feel a bit weepy. After all, these people have played a huge part in your life over the last year.

The first six weeks are the most difficult time of your first year. At the same time, they are wonderful weeks of change and exploration. Despite sleep deprivation and awkward body changes, you'll emerge with fond memories of your baby's first life experiences.

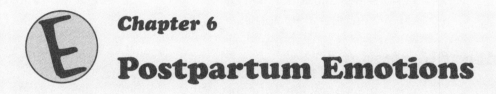

Chapter 6

Postpartum Emotions

I f there's one postpartum experience that pretty much all women share, it's extreme emotions. Some women say it's like a roller coaster: one minute you're smiling and glowing over your new baby, and the next you're crying your eyes out for seemingly no reason. You've probably already had some experience with these mood swings through having your monthly period. However, the emotional highs and lows you'll reach during the postpartum period will be more extreme than ever before.

Hormone Fluctuations

During the first few days postpartum, your body will go through some amazing changes. Unfortunately, these aren't all as wonderful as the birth of your baby. The biggest change occurs with your hormones. When the placenta detaches, a series of hormonal events is triggered, causing a wide variety of physical and emotional responses.

About Hormones

During pregnancy, the amounts of two hormones, progesterone and estrogen, in your body greatly increase. Your body uses these hormones to sustain the pregnancy. After you have given birth, your body no longer needs these hormones in such high pregnancy levels. They rapidly drop back to prepregnancy levels.

It is this drop that is often blamed for the mood swings and other not-so-fun feelings during the postpartum period. Some scientists explain that this is the same type of reaction that many women experience just before their periods, often called premenstrual syndrome (PMS). There is nothing you can do to avoid this hormone drop. It's a necessary part of your body's return to normalcy.

Dealing with Fluctuations

It is said that patience is a virtue, and this holds true for the postpartum period. There isn't much you can do about hormone fluctuations except hang on for the ride. However, there are a few handy tips that can help you deal with the mood swings and physical exhaustion.

Primarily, it is very important that you eat well. No matter how busy you get, never skip meals. Eat a variety of healthy, natural foods and be sure you are getting the recommended daily supply of vitamins and minerals. This will help your body heal and make you feel better.

Another tip is to sleep whenever you can. You may not get a full night's sleep very often, but even several bursts of a few hours each day can work for you. Getting sufficient sleep helps your body heal and keeps you in a rational frame of mind.

Have you ever heard the term babymoon? This concept means that you and your family ignore the outside world for a while after the birth of your baby. You turn inward and take care of only yourselves. The purpose is to help you strengthen your body as well as your bond with your baby.

For most new mothers, the hardest part is the first few days. If you can manage to laugh at some of the ridiculous things you think and feel during those first few days, the rest will be a breeze. Tell your husband all about what to expect postpartum before the baby comes. If he anticipates and understands your hormone fluctuations, it will be easier for him to deal with them.

Postpartum Elation

One postpartum emotion that is rarely talked about is postpartum elation. This can include the sheer joy of being a new mother, the thrill of surviving through labor and delivery, and the pride you feel when you look at your new baby. When you feel postpartum elation, you won't be able to stop talking about how happy you are. No, it's not all pain and misery!

Sharing Your Joy

When experiencing postpartum elation, you'll want to tell everyone how great you feel. Telling your birth story and the story of your first days postpartum is an important part of the whole experience. You'll be thrilled and want to share and generally be gushing to anyone who will listen. This is perfectly healthy! Tell your friends and your family all about your experiences and feelings.

Small details in your memories will fade fairly quickly, so be sure to write down your birth story as soon as you get a chance. You can choose to write it in your journal or your baby's book. Your husband should also write his version, as the two of you probably had very different experiences. Writing your birth story will help you express that joy and elation you feel.

FACT

Your birth doula is a good person to talk to about the birth of your baby since she was there and experienced it with you. She is also trained to help you talk about the experience without tainting your thoughts about how it went.

The Downside to Elation

Unfortunately, when you go to share your story, you'll find there are those who don't want to hear it. They may let you know they're not interested, or you may be hurt to discover they aren't listening to a word you say. If this happens, simply end your story quickly and change the subject.

Even worse than those who don't pay attention are those who try to downplay your experience. They might tell you your birth was easy compared to the hard work they had to do during labor. Or they will tell you that it was a lucky experience and that's why you're so happy. Just ignore these people. Their bad attitude has nothing to do with you or your birth.

There are also those who want to steal the spotlight and tell their own story. Often these people have a horror story to share. They are working through their negative birth experience by searching for others who had the same problems. They can't even begin to hear the good news of your birth. It simply doesn't compute. Be careful to gush only to trusted individuals who are genuinely happy for you.

Postpartum Depression (PPD)

During the first weeks after birth, many women experience minor depressive episodes lasting anywhere from a few hours to a few weeks. These are usually bouts of the baby blues. Postpartum depression, or PPD, also surfaces within the first weeks after childbirth but is more severe than the baby blues. It lasts longer and feels more intense. Unlike the baby blues, which merely take time to pass, PPD usually requires medical treatment.

When discussing PPD with your practitioner, be sure to tell him if you are breastfeeding. Certain medications are better for breastfeeding mothers than others. If you're not sure about a particular drug's safety with regard to breastfeeding, consult Dr. Thomas Hale's Medications and Mothers' Milk, or go to *http://neonatal.ttuhsc.edu/lact/*.

Who Gets PPD?

PPD can happen to anyone. You can get PPD with your first child or your fifth. The one thing that's certain is, if you have experienced PPD with one child, you are more likely to experience it again with subsequent pregnancies.

Many of the symptoms of PPD can also be caused by a hormonal imbalance in the thyroid. When you talk to your doctor or midwife about the possibility of PPD, ask for a quick blood test to screen your thyroid levels too.

The symptoms of PPD go beyond those of baby blues, both in duration and intensity. Some of the major symptoms include:

- Feelings of depression or sadness beyond what would be considered usual under the circumstances.
- Weight loss or weight gain.
- Insomnia or feelings of extreme tiredness.
- Inability to concentrate or make decisions.
- Being overly worried about your baby or not worried at all.
- Finding no joy in life, particularly with things that used to give you great pleasure.
- Lack of interest in sex or your partner.
- Fear of hurting yourself, your baby, or someone else.

Clearly, many of these symptoms might be difficult to distinguish from regular postpartum symptoms. The difference is that these symptoms continue for longer than a couple of weeks, or they are much more intense. You might not recognize the signs that you are experiencing PPD; your husband, a family member, or a friend may be the one who notices and says something to you. Be sure to report these occasions to your doctor or midwife.

The Cure for PPD

There is help for those suffering from PPD. With counseling and sometimes medications, you can usually see dramatic results. The key to improving your situation is recognizing the problem and reaching out for help and support.

FACT

If anxiety is one of your symptoms, along with nervousness, rapid heart rate, rapid breathing, dizziness, or chest pain, you may be suffering from postpartum anxiety and not postpartum depression. Mention any and all anxiety-like symptoms to your doctor so you can be correctly diagnosed.

It's possible that at your six-week postpartum visit, you won't want to complain about feeling tired or sad. Perhaps you'll think that it is something you are doing wrong. However, to be accurately diagnosed with PPD, you must be honest with your doctor about your symptoms. Don't leave something out because it seems irrelevant; let your practitioner make that decision. The information you provide will help him determine what form of treatment is best for you.

Postpartum Psychosis

Thankfully, postpartum psychosis is very rare, occurring in only 1 to 2 births out of 1,000. Postpartum psychosis is an intensive and severe medical emergency that requires immediate medical attention. The mother is not going to realize she has this condition; only others around her will be able to identify the signs.

Who Gets Postpartum Psychosis?

Postpartum psychosis is more common in women who have a history of bipolar disorder, schizophrenia, or severe depression. There is also an increased risk if you have these diagnoses anywhere in your family. Additionally, if you have previously suffered a psychotic episode postpartum, your chances of having another episode dramatically increase.

FACT

If you have a history of psychosis or of bipolar disorder, schizophrenia, or severe depression, you will need to discuss medications during pregnancy to help protect yourself from postpartum psychosis.

Have your husband learn the signs of postpartum psychosis before you give birth, so he can identify them if this happens to you. Symptoms usually start within the first two or three weeks after birth. Symptoms of postpartum psychosis are:

- Auditory hallucinations: hearing things that aren't there.
- Visual hallucinations: seeing things that aren't there.
- Disordered thinking or behaviors.
- Severe sleep disturbances.
- Delusional behavior or thoughts.

Getting Help

Getting help is the key to getting well. The sooner treatment is started, the better the chances for a speedy recovery from postpartum psychosis. Hospitalization is mandatory for this illness, to protect the mother. Some hospitals have specialized units where the baby can spend some time with the mother under the nurses' watchful eyes. This is considered a beneficial approach to care.

There are also other forms of treatment that can be used during and after hospitalization. Medications are mandatory to facilitate recovery. Individual, group, or couples counseling is also an important part of the process. This helps address all areas of the woman's life.

Birth Trauma

Someone may try to tell you that a negative birth experience won't affect you after it's over. The sad fact is that you can have such a horrible birth experience that it leads to post-traumatic stress disorder (PTSD), or birth trauma. Signs that you may be experiencing birth trauma include depression, difficulty sleeping, nightmares, and anxiety that last longer than a month.

FACT

Certain experiences make you more susceptible to PPD, postpartum psychosis, or birth trauma. For example, if you have an emergency cesarean, you are six times more likely to experience depression after giving birth.

Prevention of Birth Trauma

The best way to deal with birth trauma is to prevent it. One way to do this is to develop a trust-based relationship with your doctor or midwife. Discuss what you'd like to have happen for your birth with this person during your prenatal visits. Perhaps you have very strong ideas about certain subjects such as medications used in labor. It may be that you are concerned about pain in labor. These are all examples of important things that need to be communicated to your doctor or midwife.

Building that trust between you and your practitioner will help you communicate during labor. One main key to satisfaction in birth and avoidance of birth trauma is the feeling that you are in control of the situation. This is possible even in labor. That relationship with your practitioner means that with only rare exceptions, everything is presented fairly to you and you are given an opportunity to make the decision that is best for you and your baby. The lack of this decision-making ability is what causes birth trauma.

Loss of control is a hot topic when it comes to birth trauma. This is partially because loss of control is defined so differently from woman to woman. What you consider a loss of control in birth may contribute to another woman's ideal birth. The key is identifying the deciding factors for you.

ALERT!

If you have previously been sexually abused, the loss-of-control issue may be more dominant. Birth is a time when residual issues of sexual abuse tend to arise. Be sure to discuss this not only with your practitioner, but also with your counselor and husband. They must be prepared to help you through any trauma that results from your birth.

Healing from a Traumatic Birth

If you have suffered a traumatic birth, you will need to heal from the experience. If you do not heal, you will have a tendency to suffer depression, restlessness, fear of birth, and other symptoms. The healing process will take some time, and you must be patient.

Healing can usually be accomplished with a combination of counseling and time. You will want to address the issues of birth trauma before you decide to have another baby. If you don't, the feelings will rise up again during your next pregnancy and make you feel frightened about repeating your experience.

When to Get Help

Recognizing that you have a problem with a postpartum emotional disorder is difficult. The problem lies not only in diagnosing yourself but also in the fact that society rarely recognizes postpartum emotional distress. Many tend to write it off as just one of those postpartum "things." This disregard can be very dangerous.

Education

As you learn what the normal postpartum variations are, you should share the information with those around you. Be sure to talk to your husband, family, and friends about the normal ups and downs of postpartum. If they are all aware of what normal is, they can more easily spot the abnormal symptoms of a postpartum emotional disorder.

If you plan to attend a postpartum class, invite anyone who might be helpful to you in the early postpartum period to come with you. Remember that if you are suffering from PPD or worse, you will be unable to take care of yourself. You will also be unable to say, "I'm in trouble and need help." Those around you will be the ones who make that call for you and seek help.

Many family members worry about having to be the ones to say something is wrong. This can be very dangerous. You absolutely need to have people around you who can help you determine if you need help. Assure your family early on that you'll be grateful for any help they can give you.

What Constitutes a Problem?

You should certainly think of postpartum as a bumpy ride. Mood swings, lack of sleep, and crying episodes. These can be normal. What you and your family are going to look for is what exceeds the norm, either in duration or severity.

Any feeling of unease, be it depression or anxiety, that lasts more than a couple of weeks should be reported to your practitioner. She can determine whether you need further evaluation or treatment through physical and mental examination. Sometimes just hearing that you may have a problem can motivate you to seek help and treatment. Even counseling alone can be beneficial for you.

Where to Find Help

The key to getting well is getting help and support. Getting that support early on can make a huge difference in your recovery. Finding support can be a difficult task if you aren't sure where to look. Talking to professionals in your area can often help you uncover what local resources are available.

Support Groups

You may not be crazy about the idea of support groups, especially if you associate them with alcoholism or other serious problems. However, the close community of a support group could be very comforting to you. These groups do not have to be officially sanctioned PPD support groups to be helpful. The members simply need to be willing to listen to you talk about postpartum life.

FACT

Postpartum Support International has both information and support group listings online. Their Web site can point out local or online support groups to help you deal with postpartum emotional disorders. Visit *www.postpartum.net.*

Oftentimes a new mothers' group will help you sort out your issues. However, there are also more specific support groups tailored to those who've had certain experiences. Depending on the severity of your depression, a professionally led support group may be more useful for your situation. In any case, you may come to think of your support group as just a group of friends.

Professional Help

Professional help is necessary in all cases of extreme postpartum disorders like PPD and postpartum psychosis. You can use group therapy, lay and professional, as an adjunct, but you will need to seek the care of a professional in these cases. It is best to find someone who has experience working with postpartum mothers.

You can ask your doctor or midwife for a recommendation to a counselor, psychologist, or psychiatrist. He should maintain a local listing of helpful providers. If you can't find someone through your practitioner, consider asking your insurance company for help.

If you suffer from PPD, you have a 25 percent chance of having symptoms that last for up to six months. However, when left untreated, many women still report symptoms at one year. If your husband or a trusted friend tells you he thinks you might be suffering from postpartum depression, see your doctor immediately.

Medications

Probably low on your list of ideals is the need for medication to treat postpartum emotional disorders. The good news is that not everyone who suffers from postpartum emotional disorders will require medications. Even if you do need medications, there are many that you can take that are safe for you and your baby.

Antidepressants

Antidepressants are commonly prescribed to adults in the United States. While once unheard of, more and more new mothers are being prescribed medications for symptoms of PPD. These are usually only to help you get over the hump of your depression and are not a long-term therapy.

The hard part for you might be deciding when the time is right for medications. There are a couple of factors to take into consideration. Have you already tried every other nonmedication solution? Have you tried healthy diet, exercise, and extra help (extra sleep)?

FACT

Dads can suffer from PPD as well, though less is known about this depression in fathers. Since the only thing that sets PPD apart from other depressions is the timing of its occurrence, it makes sense that men could suffer too.

Remember, medication is not an instant cure. Many medications can take up to six weeks to get into your system and take effect.

Medications can be given to nearly every new mother. There are very few restrictions on who is able to take medications. If you are nursing your baby, there are certain medications found to be safer than others, so be sure to talk to your doctor about the medications he is prescribing for you. Do not accept the statement that nursing mothers cannot take medications. It is simply false.

Herbal Remedies

If you have an aversion to taking medications, you may want another alternative to help you through your depression and fatigue. Luckily, there are alternatives out there. These aren't usually as strong as prescription medications, but they can take the edge off. One of these alternatives is herbal remedies. Consult your physician about these possibilities.

Herbals have their place in your life. However, in a situation as potentially serious as PPD, you must talk to your physician about what is the best course of action for you. If you have a mild case of PPD, your physician might be willing to monitor you while you take an herbal depression remedy. You simply need to have medical follow-up. This remedy may be all you need to feel like yourself again.

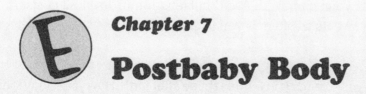

Chapter 7

Postbaby Body

It's happened—the baby is here, and you've finally returned home. After a couple of days of feeling really skinny, you realize that you're only skinny compared to your former nine-month-pregnant self. Now, your belly is saggy where the baby used to live. You have lines and marks all over your body, like a road map of new motherhood. Your hair is falling out. Your skin is dry. What can you do to look and feel normal again?

Avoid Full-Length Mirrors!

Part of being kind to yourself these first few months involves taking the time to uncover the beautiful, glowing woman hidden under the wear and tear of pregnancy and birth. This means taking some reasonable precautions. Don't look at yourself naked. Avoid full-length mirrors at all costs. And feel free to wear sweats as often as you like.

FACT

Not everyone's body is in terrible shape after birth. How your body looks and feels depends largely on how well you took care of yourself during pregnancy. If you didn't gain excessive weight, you probably won't have much to shed. You may also find you weigh less than prior to pregnancy, if you took better care of yourself after becoming pregnant.

Try to focus on where you're going instead of where you have been. Give more attention to the positive aspects of your body. Do you have more curves than you did before your baby was born? Maybe you're enjoying an enhanced bra size? These positives will help you through the tough parts of regaining a healthy and attractive body. The keys to looking good, particularly as a new mom, are creating goals and staying motivated enough to meet those goals through good, healthy habits.

Changing Skin

Now that you've had your baby and your hormones have settled slightly, you've probably noticed some skin changes. The skin changes in postpartum are usually simply reversals of whatever happened during pregnancy. Most women develop stretch marks, acne, and dry skin during pregnancy, which means big changes to your skin postpartum. During the postpartum period, your skin will generally work its way back to normal, with only a few small exceptions.

Stretch Marks

Now that you can actually see your entire belly, you may find a couple of gifts your baby left you. Stretch marks are basically points in your skin where you were not able to stretch any more. The indentations of the skin show where your skin gave way to make room for your growing baby. These marks can be found anywhere on your body. The most common spots would be on your abdomen, thighs, breasts, arms, and above your buttocks. While nothing can prevent these stretch marks, there are ways to deal with them after birth. The good news is that the red, raw look of early postpartum stretch marks is not permanent. In fact, most stretch marks fade rather rapidly and become silvery or white.

There are plenty of touted cures for stretch marks, though none of them are very beneficial. Some new procedures have been developed to help you rid yourself of these marks, but pursuing this fix is not always the best idea, particularly if you are considering having more children. If you do plan to have more children, many of the treatments, which tend to be expensive, may need to be redone and may not be as effective the second time around.

Acne

If you started looking like a teenager with serious skin problems while you were pregnant, you'll be glad to know that the acne usually clears up in the first six weeks postpartum. You may find this acne on your face or other oily parts of your body. This is because the hormone levels are returning to normal levels. It will take a bit of time before your skin is completely normal again. Not all women will suffer from acne during pregnancy or postpartum. Those who do may find it takes a bit longer to clear up, depending on their hormone levels.

ALERT!

Some skin creams used to treat acne and other blemishes are not allowed in pregnancy, like those containing large doses of vitamin A. Talk to your dermatologist about safe alternatives, and consider using something postpartum as well.

Continue to treat whatever blemishes you have with your own resources. Clean skin is usually the way to go. You may also try some over-the-counter products or a visit to the dermatologist to help stabilize your skin.

Dry Skin

Your skin may also feel drier during the postpartum period. This dry skin is also caused by postpartum hormone changes. Treat yourself to a nice bottle of your favorite lotion. As soon as you leave the shower, rub this lotion in, prior to drying off. This can help seal some of the moisture back into your skin.

For an extra treat, ask your husband to use your lotion to give you a nice massage. This will give you a chance to relax and reconnect with your husband, while moisturizing your skin. Do this as often as you can manage. Just don't be surprised if you fall asleep during the massage!

If you notice skin flaking from your body as well as your face, assess your bath regimen. Are you showering at least every other day? Do you take the time to use a washcloth, loofah pad, or other exfoliating product? These can help remove dead skin cells from your body, allowing the healthy skin beneath to shine through.

Issues with Hair

During pregnancy, your body was so busy working on the growth of your healthy baby that it neglected to fulfill one of its regular jobs: releasing hair. This means that you might have enjoyed a glorious, full head of hair in pregnancy. The bad news is that all the hair you uncommonly retained during the last nine months is going to go now.

You're Not Going Bald

While washing your hair in the shower you're probably going to notice clumps of hair coming away in your hand or dotting the floor of the shower. Try not to panic. You are not going bald, even if it looks that way. The hairs that are lost in the immediate postpartum period are the hairs that didn't go during pregnancy. If your hair loss continues at a rapid rate past the first few months postpartum, consider having your thyroid levels checked. In this case, there's a chance your hair loss might not be due to pregnancy at all.

Treat Yourself

During pregnancy, you probably enjoyed having such a full head of hair. Now that your body is changing, you'd definitely benefit from a new look. There's no need to go overboard and do something drastic, but you would probably feel better with an updated hairdo. Consider treating yourself to a visit to a nice salon. Spend time talking to a stylist. Tell her what your life is currently like and ask for hair suggestions. She'll probably be able to give you something low maintenance. After all, as a new mother, you don't have the time or the patience to spend more than five minutes a day on your hair. If you can't decide on a cut you like, just get your hair washed and styled. The pampering will be good for you.

Your First Period

After having a baby, you may wonder when you can expect your next period. You may also wonder what changes your period will experience after your body has given birth. The answers widely vary from mom to mom.

When to Expect Your Period

When to expect your period will have a lot to do with how you feed your baby. Breastfeeding mothers tend to have a longer delay in the return of their periods. This is because the hormones of breastfeeding suppress ovulation, which triggers your cycles to begin. Some mothers wait for six months to a year before their periods return. Some nursing mothers find that their periods do not return until their babies go long stretches without nursing, like lengthy periods of sleep at night.

If you are not breastfeeding your baby, you will find that your periods return much sooner. Most nonbreastfeeding mothers will find that they can expect their periods to return about six weeks after the birth. It is also important to note that you usually ovulate before you bleed, so do not assume that you are not fertile simply because you haven't gotten your period back yet.

Changes to Your Period

You may not notice any changes to your period when it does return. However, some women do experience changes, with flow and/or cramping. There is no hard-and-fast rule about who will experience changes or not. Either situation could happen to you.

Some of the changes may be for the better. You may notice that your flow is lighter. You may also experience less cramping than before. The downside is that you could just as easily wind up with more painful periods or a heavier flow. If you are concerned about your periods, be sure to talk to your doctor or midwife. The good news is that problems with your period are usually short-lived and work themselves out within a couple of cycles.

Bone Movement

You have probably figured out that your body will never be the same after having a baby. However, you may not anticipate certain changes, and your girlfriends may forget to tell you about them. One of these unexpected changes is bone movement.

Hips

During the last moments prior to the birth of your baby, you probably felt strong tension in your hip area. This occurred because your hip bones needed to separate to allow your body to give birth to your baby. For this reason, many women notice that their hips seem more prominent after giving birth. Most people assume bones are a strictly stationary, inflexible part of your body, but this is not so much the case in childbirth.

FACT

After giving birth, your hips may ache quite a bit. This can be a result of different positions you assumed in labor or of having your legs positioned too far apart while pushing. Using a heating pad on the sore area will help. You might also consider getting a massage from a professional who specializes in women who have given birth.

Unfortunately, even if you lose every single ounce of weight you gained in pregnancy, you might never fit into the same clothes. You can even lose extra weight, but to no avail. Don't panic. This doesn't mean your hips are visibly bigger than before. The change is usually fairly imperceptible, except in the tightest of clothes.

Ribs

Yes, you guessed it. What can happen to your hips can happen to your ribs as well. This expansion of your rib cage usually happens toward the end of pregnancy. Rib expansion happens less frequently than hip expansion, but it does happen. The expansion of your ribs is caused by the pressure of your growing uterus in pregnancy. In essence, your ribs move slightly to make room for your baby. You may or may not have experienced sore ribs in pregnancy due to this phenomenon. The good news is that most shirts are forgiving enough that it's rarely noticeable.

Weight Loss

You've had your baby. You're anxious to get back into your old clothes. What do you do next? The combination of a healthy diet and exercise will be your fastest way back to the body you want. There are many different ways for new mothers to work on losing the weight they gained in pregnancy. You may enjoy the group efforts of some diets, such as Weight Watchers, or prefer a stand-alone diet option. No matter what you choose, you can be successful.

Calories

Burning more calories than you take in is the key to losing weight. Your body burns calories all day; even breathing uses up calories. Find small ways to expend calories during your day, in addition to eating well. Beware of fad diets while you are in the postpartum period. Your body is taking on the enormous task of repairing itself. Your body really needs the calories to help repair the damage done by pregnancy, which takes a great toll on your body. During this time, it is very important to eat a balanced diet.

Recent research has shown that the sooner you lose the postpartum weight, the easier it comes off. In fact, after the first six months postpartum, you are very unlikely to lose the weight you gained in pregnancy. So make the most of the energy you have and get started!

Your diet should consist of a variety of fruits and vegetables, fiber, protein, and other nutrients. All of these will help replace nutrients lost in the pregnancy process, as well as rebuild stores of certain vitamins and minerals used in pregnancy, like iron. Eating a wide variety of foods helps ensure that you are getting the nutrients you need.

You should eat when you are hungry. Your body will send you signals to eat. Do not ignore these signals; they're your body's way of telling you it requires energy. Drink plenty of water. This helps you avoid becoming dehydrated. Even slight dehydration can make you feel tired and sickly, an experience you definitely don't need in the postpartum period. (See Chapter 9 for more information on feeding yourself and your baby.)

Breastfeeding Helps

Breastfeeding is one of the best ways to help your body lose weight postpartum. The fat stores that your body accumulated during pregnancy were designed to help you breastfeed. These fat stores won't be tapped into unless you're breastfeeding.

Do you have to eat a special diet when breastfeeding?
No. Your regular diet, whatever that may be, should be fine. Some people say that you should avoid certain foods, like Indian or Mexican food. But Indian and Mexican women certainly don't, so why should you?

Breastfeeding your baby will burn between 500 and 1,000 calories a day. It would take a good workout to expend that many calories. Feel free to consider breastfeeding your secret weapon of weight loss, but don't assume it will do all the work for you.

Treating Yourself Right

It can be so easy to become totally focused on your baby in those first few months after birth. While loving and caring for your baby is never a bad thing, it is also important to take care of yourself. Don't neglect your own needs during this time. You can't help anyone else if you aren't feeling good yourself.

Some of the biggest complaints from new moms relate to physical stress: the strain of lost sleep, the physical changes to the body, the inability to focus or concentrate. Taking care of yourself can help relieve these issues. Of course, this doesn't mean you should abandon your family each day and spend six hours in a spa (though it's a tempting thought). Instead, consider doing small things for yourself to regain balance and control.

For instance, while the baby naps, avoid the laundry and grab a good book to read instead. Consider writing a letter to a friend you've lost touch with. Don't do the dishes. Instead, paint your nails and rub some lotion on your sore legs and shoulders. If your husband can stay home with the baby, go out and get a haircut. Read and send a few e-mails to stay connected with distant friends and family. In short, do what you need to do to stay healthy and in a good mood.

When to Call the Plastic Surgeon

Plastic surgery may seem like the easy answer to all of your postpartum body-image issues. Even a night in the hospital might not sound too bad at this point. However, most postpartum moms are not great candidates for plastic surgery, at least not right away. If you choose to have surgery, you will have a preliminary meeting with the surgeon to discuss the issues you have and their potential solutions. The surgeon will also take photographs and document your health history.

ALERT!

Before you have plastic surgery, be sure that you are done having babies. Getting pregnant after having plastic surgery will reverse its effects. There is no sense going through all the trouble and expense just to have a procedure redone at a later date.

The Right Weight

One of the biggest issues will be your weight. The majority of good plastic surgeons will not even consider working with you until you're at or near your ideal body weight. The reason is that your surgery won't really help or last if you aren't close to this weight when you have the procedure. Liposuction and other plastic surgery methods are not meant to help you lose weight. These surgeries are designed to help reshape and contour your body. Being overweight when you have surgery adds risks to your surgery, including the potential of poor wound healing.

Common Reasons for Plastic Surgery Postpartum

The most common reasons for plastic surgery after a baby are actually not cosmetic in nature. There are some medical reasons to have a surgical repair or plastic surgery after your baby is born. Here are some examples of surgery common in the postpartum period:

- To repair a hernia after your pregnancy.
- To repair separated rectus abdominis muscles (a condition referred to as diastasis) after carrying a large baby or multiples.
- To reconstruct veins, usually in the leg, after suffering from severe varicosities in pregnancy.
- To remove excess abdominal tissue that hangs around the waistline.

Choosing Your Surgeon

Choosing the doctor who will perform your surgery is a huge step. You may need to interview several practitioners before deciding on a particular one. Ask lots of questions during these meetings.

Stretch marks may be indicative of the way your body will heal after surgery. If you have deep or multiple stretch marks, you may have more scarring from surgery due to your skin's lack of elasticity. Be sure to question your surgeon about the elasticity of your skin and what you can reasonably expect from surgery.

Be sure to ask surgeons you interview if they have had experience working with postpartum moms. Ask to see before and after photos of women who had body issues similar to yours. Also ask for a realistic estimation of what you can expect. Talk to your plastic surgeon about alternative treatments. Are there nonsurgical things you can do to help your condition?

In the end, be sure the decision to have elective plastic surgery is the right one for you. Many moms are very happy with the results. However, if your problems are more emotional than physical, all the surgery in the world won't help you.

Loving Your Mom Body

When all the weight is gone, all the stretch marks have faded, and all the flab has re-formed into firm skin, your new mom body will be evident. Short of drastic measures like plastic surgery, this is the new you. This can be a scary prospect. Do what you can to make loving your mom body an easier transition.

Clothes

The clothing you wear can have a lot to do with how you feel about your new body. Do your clothes accentuate your new body? Are they appropriate for how you feel in your life? Are you wearing the same clothes you've worn for years? Consider getting a couple of new outfits that make you look and feel confident and attractive. If you've fallen into a cycle of alternating different-colored stretch pants, try wearing some nice skirts or dresses for a change. This can make you feel more feminine and refreshed.

Makeover

Consider a new mom makeover for yourself. Get a new hairstyle and a new bottle of perfume. Even if you're not a big fan of makeup, just a bit of lip gloss and some eye shadow can make you feel glamorous. You don't even have to spend a fortune on this. Many cities have department stores or independent consultants who will provide you with a free makeover just for learning about their products. Do this with a friend for a fun afternoon activity.

In addition to making over your body, make a change in your overall outlook. Look at your body and your baby with fresh eyes and put any pain from pregnancy and labor behind you. Embrace the new you and move forward with your life. Learning from first pregnancies can help you make changes in future pregnancies. So don't worry; chances are, it will be easier the next time around.

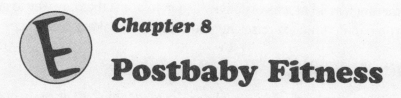

Chapter 8

Postbaby Fitness

Probably one of your biggest personal worries is the changing shape of your postpartum body. You've gone from no belly to a big, round, hard belly, and now you have a jelly belly. You may have also noticed other changes to your body. Luckily, you have a lot of control over how your body looks after you have a baby. It just takes a bit of effort on your part.

Finding Time to Work Out

Time always seems to be lacking when you have a new baby. It's hard to find time to read a magazine article, let alone get a workout in at the gym. However, you can find creative ways to make it work, if you put your mind to it. Remember, solid blocks of activity at a gym aren't the only way to get in shape. You can do little exercises here and there to make a difference.

Tips to Make It Work

Don't view working out as a chore. Instead, think of it as a luxury: time spent by yourself working on your own needs and goals. It gives you a chance to get back into that skirt you love, or to reach your ideal mile time. Also, the healthier you are, the more energy you'll have to handle the demands of your new baby. Of course, it won't always be easy. Here are a few tips to guide you through the rough spots.

- **Stick to a schedule.** Keep a workout appointment with yourself, much as you would keep a dental or hair appointment. Once you develop a workout schedule, this task will come as easily as any of your other regular duties.
- **Incorporate your baby.** Take your baby out in the stroller, and speed-walk or jog while pushing the stroller. Or try a fun stroller aerobics class with your baby.
- **Quick and easy exercise.** Take the stairs instead of the elevator whenever you can. Park at the back of the parking lot and walk the rest of the way to the store rather than wait for the perfect spot to open up. Do different exercises during TV commercials.

QUESTION?

Can you use a pedometer to get in shape?
Pedometers offer a great way to challenge yourself when walking for exercise. Try wearing one on a normal day to gauge how many steps you take. Then try to increase the number of steps you take each day. This is a great way to get in shape and have fun.

Child-Care Options

Child care is another issue when it comes to being available to work out. When your husband isn't available, and you don't have a regular babysitter, it can be nearly impossible to gather enough alone time for a workout. However, there are a few options out there that can improve your situation. Consider the following:

- **Help from family members**—If your husband isn't available to watch the baby, ask the baby's grandmother to come over and keep an eye on her while you do an aerobics video or go for a run. Other family members will likely be willing to help in this way as well.
- **Mom co-op**—Groups of mothers can get together to offer free babysitting to other members of the co-op. You simply have to take your turn watching their kids too. This is a great way to make friends and get exercise.
- **Gym with child-care facility**—Many gyms have child-care facilities built right into them. The only catches are that there may be age restrictions for children, and the child-care services may cost extra.

Workout Common Sense

Part of the problem with working out after your baby is born is that you probably won't be as protective of your body as you were during pregnancy. Yet, just because the baby has been born does not mean that you can get away with overworking your body at the gym. Remember, you are still recovering from giving birth and must take precautions when getting back into shape.

Body Changes and Fitness

After a few weeks of recovery, you may feel pumped and ready to get back in the game. You might be excited to pick up where you left off in your running workouts a year ago. It's true that you are able to work out after having a baby. However, you may not be able to exercise as long and as hard as you'd like, due to some body changes.

Relaxin is a pregnancy hormone that helps your body adapt to being pregnant. It allows your joints to be more flexible for ease in giving birth. But once you've had your baby, there is little use for relaxin. The problem is that it takes a while for your relaxin levels to drop. For this reason, you need to take it very easy on your joints; you are more prone to injury during this time.

Be careful that you do not overextend your arms and legs as you work out. If you begin to feel pain during stretching or other activities, stop. This means that you are stretching too far. But don't worry; you should be back to your normal capacity by the three-month mark.

Common Postbirth Pitfalls

One exercise pitfall that many moms face is not being able to resume their prior physical activity level. You can't simply jump back into the level of exercise you were doing before you got pregnant. Even if you continued to work out throughout your entire pregnancy, you still lost some of your fitness level and muscle mass.

FACT

If you severely cut back your workout intensity or did not work out at all during pregnancy, you may find that it takes you more time to physically recover and get back up to speed. It may also take you more hours in the gym to regain your previous fitness level and muscle tone.

Be sure to ease back into your workouts. Start slowly and gradually increase. Do not attempt to increase the intensity or duration of your physical activities by more than 10 percent per week. At this safe rate, you'll be back up to your prepregnancy fitness levels in a few months.

Another common exercise problem for new moms is that they do not eat enough. Because your body will be healing and repairing itself, you will simply need more calories to support increased physical activity. You may be trying to burn calories when working out, but it's very possible to go too far. If you are not adequately nourished, you could suffer from fatigue, dehydration, injury, and other problems.

New Mom Trouble Spots

Even after you've lost most of the remaining weight from pregnancy, you will probably still have a few weak areas that need attention. For many women, these areas include the abdominal muscles, the hips, and general flexibility in muscles and joints. The hardest part is making the decision to work on these areas. You may find you actually like the exercises designed to improve the trouble spots.

Abdominal Muscles

Your belly is the most obvious area of change in pregnancy. The further along you are, the more your abdomen protrudes. Since this area becomes stretched out during pregnancy, it obviously takes some time and effort to get it back in shape.

ALERT!

Be sure that you check for a separation of the rectus abdominis muscles before working on your abdomen. You may have a separation that requires some work to heal before you can get busy with crunches. You are more likely to have a separation if you had multiples, carried a very large baby, or gained a large amount of weight during your pregnancy.

Abdominal work can begin within a couple of weeks of birth, assuming that you don't have any separation of the muscles. Start slowly with a few abdominal exercises a day. Slowly increase the amount of repetitions. Once you're comfortable, you can increase the frequency. Luckily, abdominal muscles are very forgiving and can withstand a significant amount of activity. In time, you will find that your flabby stomach skin has firmed up again, creating a slimmer, sleeker you.

Hips

Your body stores some extra fat to aid you in pregnancy and in breast-feeding, right on your hips. These maternal fat stores deplete somewhat when you breastfeed, but it takes more than breastfeeding to completely slim them down. Exercising the hip area should be slow and specific. Remember that early on in the postpartum period, you still have a lot of the hormone relaxin in your system. This can make it easy to hurt your hips.

As you firm your hips and trim your rear, you will notice your old shape coming back. You may even be pleasantly surprised to find a nice fullness in this area that you never had before. There's nothing wrong with a pair of curvy, healthy hips.

Flexibility

During pregnancy and the early postpartum period, you probably won't be stretching very often. However, your flexibility is very important, and you need to get it back as soon as you can. There are some very simple exercises you can do in a few spare minutes to regain flexibility in problem areas like your neck, chest, and hips. Certain exercises can also enhance your posture and balance. Do these while sitting in front of the computer, watching TV, or folding laundry.

Neck

Sit or stand with your spine straight. Hold your shoulders up and back. Slowly drop your chin to your chest and hold for five to ten seconds. Bring your head back to a neutral position. Now slowly drop your left ear to your left shoulder and hold for five to ten seconds. Do not bounce. Repeat this on the right side. Complete the whole series of stretches three to five times. This exercise will reduce tension in the neck that results from breastfeeding.

Chest

Stand with your feet shoulder-width apart. Tuck in your pelvis and flex your abdominal muscles. Stretch out your arms at shoulder level. Slowly bend forward, bringing your arms around to the front. As you return upright, pull your arms back, just enough to feel a stretch. Imagine that you are pushing your shoulder blades together. This stretch will help alleviate tension from carrying your baby.

Hips

Sitting upright with good posture on an exercise ball, place your hands on your hips. Picture a figure eight in your mind and begin to trace this with your hips. Your feet should be firmly on the ground for stability. This is great for stretching out hips sore from delivery.

Posture

While standing, place your back flat against the wall. Walk your feet forward until they are six to eight inches in front of you. Press your rear, your shoulder blades, and the back of your head to the wall. Raise your arms at a 90-degree angle and press them against the wall. Slowly raise your arms above your head, while keeping them to the wall.

Balance

Get down on your hands and knees, tighten your abdominal muscles, and breathe naturally. As you exhale, extend your right leg and left arm, extending each limb as far as you can without pain. Hold this pose for three to five breaths and repeat up to ten times on each side.

Where to Work Out

Where you work out is important. Your success in getting in shape depends largely on the space you choose. Factors such as proximity, ease of use, and cost can make or break your plan to get fit. Whether you choose to work out in a gym or a spa, or even in your own home, the important thing is that you create a plan and stick to it.

Gyms and Spas

Working out at a gym or spa is a fairly popular option. Being surrounded by other people striving to stay healthy can serve as a great source of motivation. You may also find benefits at a local gym or spa, such as specific classes you want to take, workout equipment you may not have at home, and child-care facilities.

Be sure to factor in the location of a gym or spa before getting a membership. If you choose a facility too far from home or work, you probably won't use it as much as you hope. Not only would this detract from your fitness goals, but you wouldn't get your money's worth either.

Cost may be a big factor in whether or not you choose to use a spa or gym. Many of these facilities charge a monthly membership fee, as well as a significant start-up fee. Use of child-care facilities in the gym or spa might also cost extra. Depending on where you live, use of a gym or spa could cost you anywhere from $20 to $150 per month. The cost may be worth it to you to have the company of others and use of equipment while working out, but if you can't afford this option, you'll have to consider other possibilities.

Working Out at Home

Sometimes the best place to work out is right in the privacy of your own home and neighborhood. This option doesn't require a membership fee, but you will have to pay the up-front cost of any equipment you might need. However, you can probably find secondhand equipment for sale in the local paper. The home option allows you to work out on your own schedule, for as long or brief a duration as you like.

You can also personalize your own private gym area at home. If you like to work out with only an exercise bike and hand weights, you can have those items in a free corner of your bedroom, living room, or basement. You can set up a TV and VCR or stereo in your workout area, too. Motivational posters or quotes can be pinned up on the walls for further customization. All this can be done more cheaply than attending a gym or spa, and you might find you like the privacy better, at least until you've lost some of your excess pregnancy weight.

Overcoming Obstacles

One of the biggest problems many people have when it comes to keeping in shape is lack of consistency. Some studies say that it is better not to exercise at all than to have big lapses between workouts. This is because inconsistent exercise can make you more prone to injury. However, if you can fight through the days when you feel little motivation, you'll ultimately reach a comfortable, consistent exercise schedule.

ALERT!

Consider looking into a gym membership at a local university. Many have great facilities but a lack of student members. To attract more members, they often sell inexpensive memberships to people in the community.

You may have the determination, the drive, and the physical ability to work out, but other challenges can still stand in your way. If you're lacking time, money, and/or easy child care, your motivation to get in shape may not be enough. In this case, you might need to make sacrifices or special arrangements to make it work. Consider the following:

- **Time:** If you can't find the time to work out, trick yourself into doing it. Allocate a certain number of hours each week to working out and schedule these time blocks on your calendar. Treat these blocks like doctor's appointments and consider them nonnegotiable. Do whatever it takes to keep these appointments with yourself.
- **Money:** You may believe that it takes lots of extra money to work out. The truth is that in most cases, you can work out for only a few dollars a month, or even for free. Use what you already have in the house. Don't buy hand weights; use filled water bottles instead. Don't buy a treadmill; go run outside in the sunshine. If you do need a few items, put a few dollars into a jar each week until you have enough to buy what you need.
- **Child care:** If you can't afford a gym with child-care facilities, there are other options to try. Put up a sign in your local grocery store, advertising your desire to pair up with another mom and provide child care

while you exercise. With this arrangement, you can work out while she watches your child, and she can work out while you watch hers.

Fitness Fashion

While you might like some new, attractive workout clothes to help inspire and motivate you, your appearance while working out is not very important. Purchasing workout clothes to fit your new mom body is a good idea, but you should choose them based on comfort, not fashion. Also, don't buy too many items at once, as your body size and shape are sure to change as you move toward your fitness goals.

Clothing

The clothing you wear while working out will influence your success. Though the easiest and most affordable option is to throw on an old T-shirt and a pair of shorts, well-designed athletic wear can make a big difference. Certain materials keep you comfortable by wicking moisture away from your body. Also, some fabrics allow your skin to breathe while you work out. Not only will you feel better wearing quality clothing, but these items can actually allow you to work out more safely and effectively.

FACT

Be sure that you choose a good, supportive sports bra to work out in. You need to wear a well-fitting bra that prevents bouncing. If you aren't well supported during workouts, your chest can become sore and achy. Sports bras aren't cheap, but they're worth the expense.

In addition to choosing clothes made of the right materials, you need to make sure they fit well. Clothes that are too tight can restrict your breathing and trap body heat. Clothes that are too big and baggy could cause you to trip and fall, and the extra fabric might make you overheat. Ask a knowledgeable employee at a sports store for suggestions on what items to buy in what sizes.

Shoes

The shoes you wear should correspond with the type of exercise you do. For example, if you do running workouts, you want to ensure that you wear proper running shoes. You need plenty of cushion and support to handle the stress on your feet, ankles, and knees. There are also specific shoes made for walking, tennis, hiking, and aerobics. If you do a variety of sports, consider investing in a pair of cross trainers.

You don't have to spend a fortune on athletic shoes. There are very expensive styles out there, but you can certainly find a good pair for under $50. Just keep an eye out for sales and promotional deals in local sports stores. Staff at the stores may also be able to tell you if a sale will be coming up in the near future.

Breastfeeding Considerations

Just because you are breastfeeding doesn't mean that you can't work out. There is nothing about breastfeeding that would preclude you from working out. In fact, the combination of working out and breastfeeding may be your fastest ticket back to your previous fitness levels.

While the quantity and quality of your milk isn't affected by exercise, it is considered best to breastfeed prior to exercising, so that your breasts are not as full. There are also higher levels of IgA, an infection-fighting agent, in your milk prior to exercise, but they return to pre-exercise levels within sixty minutes of rest.

Breastfeeding Fitness Myths

You may have heard a couple of rumors about breastfeeding and working out. These often circulate around groups of friends with children, and many are untrue. It is important to know the truth to ensure you're healthy and well taken care of. Here are some common myths about breastfeeding and fitness:

- **Myth:** Working out while breastfeeding will dry up your milk. Fact: Working out does not decrease milk production at all.
- **Myth:** Working out will cause your milk to sour. Fact: Working out can increase the lactic acid in your milk, but this is never harmful and rarely noticeable to your baby.
- **Myth:** Your baby will wean too soon if you work out because the milk will taste bad. Fact: Some babies will refuse to nurse immediately after you exercise due to increased levels of lactic acid in the milk or the salty taste of sweat on the nipples. However, this is always short-lived, lasting less than sixty minutes or until you shower.

Precautions

There are only a few reasons to pay attention to your body when exercising as a breastfeeding mother. However, these issues do deserve mention. Discuss any further worries you have with your doctor before beginning a workout regimen. Keep the following issues in mind:

- **Weight loss:** If you lose weight too rapidly, you may find that your baby is not gaining weight quickly enough. This is very rare. But if you are losing more than four pounds a month (after the first two months), you may want to lighten up on workouts for a while.
- **Joints:** Just like in pregnancy, you have hormones during lactation that can make your body more prone to injury. Your joints can be particularly susceptible. So don't overdo it, and remember to stretch lightly before and after workouts.
- **Fad diets:** Beware of diets that involve anything excessive or restrictive. You should not be starving yourself or straining your body. Also, talk to your pediatrician before consuming any product, even if it's supposedly all natural or herbal.

Remember that fitness is an important part of regaining your self-confidence after birth. A solid exercise routine and a healthy diet should help you shed pregnancy pounds, regain muscle mass and tone, and provide you with enough energy to care for your family. Do whatever it takes to get inspired and stick to your plan.

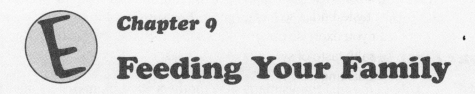

Chapter 9

Feeding Your Family

Nutrition is a very important issue for new mothers and their babies. The last thing you want to do after giving birth is worry about what to eat, but you need certain nutrients to heal after birth, and your baby needs the proper nutrition to grow into a healthy child. There are also different methods of feeding your baby to consider. Will you breastfeed or bottle-feed? When will you start feeding solid foods to your baby? This chapter will give you all the information you need to make these decisions.

Your Nutrition

The food choices you make are always important, but these are especially crucial to a new mother's health. During the postpartum period, your body is in the process of healing from pregnancy and birth. Continuing the great habits you formed while pregnant will contribute to keeping you healthy and strong during the first few months after birth.

Your First Meal

One of the first things many new mothers want immediately after birth is food. The hard work of labor and delivery will likely leave you ravenous. Unfortunately, most labor and birth units don't have very appetizing options available. You may be offered only gelatin, pudding, or broth at first. If you're lucky, you'll get a sandwich. It's better to send a family member out for food that will actually satisfy your hunger. However, if you have a cesarean, you may not be able to eat at first and might be put on a clear-liquid diet for twelve to twenty-four hours.

FACT

Birth centers often have a kitchen located within the facility. Families are encouraged to use the kitchen to cook for themselves and for the new mom. Ask if your birth center offers this great option. If so, tell your family members about it in advance so they can plan to bring groceries when you go into labor.

Once you're out of the delivery room and in the regular postpartum unit, meals will be served regularly. Despite the many jokes about hospital food, many hospitals go to great lengths to serve nutritious, delicious meals. Many times you will be given a couple of choices from a menu for the duration of your stay. If you have any special dietary needs or concerns, you will want to talk to your doctor or midwife as well as your nutritionist at the hospital prior to birth. Examples of special cases include lactose intolerance, keeping kosher, vegetarianism or veganism, and food allergies.

It's also a good idea to discuss your postpartum diet with the nutritionist. If there is no nutritionist available to you at the hospital or birth center, consider speaking with the nutritionist from your practitioner's office. A basic understanding of good postpartum nutrition will be very helpful as you take care of yourself and your growing family.

A Healthy Plan

Armed with your new guidelines from the nutritionist or your own basic knowledge of nutrition, you should be ready to take care of your body. During the first few weeks, you will probably want to increase the amount of protein you would normally consume. This will help to heal your body after birth. Eating enough fruits and vegetables and taking in the right amount of carbohydrates are also important.

Protein

Protein is found in almost every food, though some foods are particularly rich in protein, such as beans, peanut butter, cheese, and meat. However, not all protein-rich foods are healthy for you. You need to create balance by choosing protein-rich foods that are low in fat. For example, if you want to eat cheese, try to choose cheese made with skim milk, or eat only small portions at a time. When you eat meat, choose lean meats with a low fat content.

By removing the skin from meats you eat, you can eliminate a lot of the excess fat without losing flavor. Remove the skin after cooking but before eating to retain the moisture in the meat. Other low-fat choices such as skim milk and light yogurt can also help you keep up a healthy diet.

Fruits and Vegetables

Probably the biggest challenge for most American families is eating the recommended five to nine servings of fruits and vegetables a day. Most people are more likely to reach for a bag of chips than an apple for a quick snack. However, most of the vitamins and minerals you need will come from your fruit and vegetable selections.

One serving size of fruit or vegetables is actually not that daunting. One medium piece of fruit, ¼ cup of dried fruit, 1 cup of leafy vegetables, ½ cup of cooked/canned/fresh vegetables (including beans and peas), or ¾ cup of juice constitutes one serving. That doesn't sound so bad, does it?

FACT

Vitamin supplements are okay, but they simply don't work as well as the real thing. Many vitamins supplements don't contain minerals and vitamins in a bioavailable form, meaning your body doesn't fully benefit from them. Taking a pill is quick and easy, but it might leave you with a false sense of security.

Try some quick tricks for adding these wonderful foods into your diet. Slice a banana into your morning cereal. Snack on a handful of dried fruit during the day. Chop up some baby spinach and add it into almost any dish for a hidden serving of green leafy vegetables. Remember, this doesn't have to be a chore. Fruits and vegetables have natural flavor, and they feel a lot better on the way down than a bag of greasy chips.

Carbohydrates

Carbohydrates are the primary source of fuel for your body. Some recent fad diets have given carbs a bad rap, but the truth is, your body needs carbohydrates. Pasta, bread, and rice are all carbohydrates that make great bases for meals. You can supplement these main items with almost anything, from sauces and vegetables to meat and cheese.

Just as with any other food, some forms of carbs are better than others. Unrefined carbohydrates or ones from natural sources are better for you than overly processed and refined choices. For example, wheat bread is better than white bread. Both offer carbohydrates, but the white bread has been processed so extensively that it actually has very little nutritional value remaining. This doesn't mean you should never eat white bread. Just be sure to get your carbs from a wide variety of sources, including whole grains.

Fast Food for New Families

No, fast food doesn't refer to drive-through restaurants when you're a new mom. Your body needs healthy food to recover from birth, but this doesn't mean it has to be difficult. There are many ways to make cooking at home simple and fun. The keys to success are planning ahead, preparing ingredients beforehand, and using simple cooking techniques. There are many products and cookbooks out there to help you with this task.

Planning Ahead

The easiest way to ensure your family is fed well is to plan ahead. One specific thing you can do is choose four or five meals to make every week. You don't always have to eat the same thing on the same day, but keeping your options simple and defined will help you stay in control.

With only four or five meals planned, you still have room for spontaneity but won't become overwhelmed. If lasagna is one of your core meals, make a vegetarian version one night for some easy variation. Or start out your meal with a salad instead of the usual soup. Have fun and keep it interesting.

If you have several meals planned in advance, you will also have a fairly regular grocery list. This will make shopping trips a snap. In time, you might not even need a list. Once you have this down, it will be easy to throw something new into the cart for a little variety.

Cooking Ahead

There are a couple of different ways to cook ahead, and either can work wonderfully for a family. You can either double the recipe each time you cook and freeze half for another day, or select a single cooking day each month and prepare large enough quantities to last for the next few weeks.

Both of these options make it easier for a family to eat nutritious, home-cooked meals every day.

Doubling recipes is probably the more realistic choice when you have a tiny newborn. It doesn't really require any extra time—just a bit of math. If you decide to try the more ambitious monthly cooking method, be sure you can handle the details. It will involve one huge grocery shopping trip and a full day of cooking each time around. You'll also need a lot of freezer space to store all the food. If you can work out the logistics, this method can make the majority of your meals extremely simple and quick.

Cooking Simply

The two things you must balance as a new mother are nutrition and time. If you were used to cooking gourmet meals in the past, your new situation will be quite a shock to your system. You simply won't have the time to prepare such elaborate meals. However, this doesn't mean you have to sacrifice flavor. Many simple meals can be quite delicious, even if they didn't take forever to make. Don't fall into the trap of equating good food with lots of work. Instead, use a few simple tricks to make great food with ease:

- **Casseroles:** Dishes like lasagna and potpie fit into this category. These are basically simple one-dish meals that are easy to serve, eat, and store. If you get tired of having the same casseroles over and over, don't be afraid to vary ingredients and try new recipes.
- **Slow cookers:** Simply throw a bunch of ingredients into a slow cooker early in the morning, turn it on, and leave it for the day. By dinnertime, you'll have a hot, nutritious meal all set to go. You can make almost anything in a slow cooker, from meat dishes and stews to breads and desserts. For recipes, check out The Everything® Slow Cooker Cookbook.
- **Rice cookers:** For perfect rice, there isn't much to do except pour the ingredients in your rice cooker and turn it on. You can make white or brown rice in most rice cookers. Some also have a feature that will cook oatmeal overnight so you have a warm breakfast waiting in the morning.

Breastfeeding

Feeding your baby is obviously a huge part of the first year. Breastmilk is a species-specific milk, meaning it is made by a human specifically for a human baby. Breastmilk is the best food you can give your baby. Though your breastmilk is pretty much all ready for your baby as is (and your baby is ready for your breastmilk), there are certain things you can do to make breastfeeding go even more smoothly.

Tips for Breastfeeding

The best advice you can get as a breastfeeding mother is to relax. Your baby will let you know how much milk she needs and when she's ready for it. Also, your breasts are designed to follow your baby's lead. After the first few days of life, look for five to six wet diapers a day and two to three bowel movements. The bowel movements may lessen as your baby ages. These are the signs of a baby who is getting enough to eat.

Furthermore, don't be tempted to watch the clock. There is no determined time limit on how long your baby should eat at each feeding. Your baby will pull away from the breast when she is ready to do so. Likewise, there is no set minimum amount of time that should pass between feedings. Your baby will give you hunger cues when she's ready to eat, and it's best not to ignore them or make her wait.

ALERT!

Crying is a late sign of hunger. If you wait until your baby is crying, you've missed other feeding cues, like REM sleep and hands in the mouth. It is always best to feed your baby when she is showing early signs of hunger, as opposed to crying out for food.

You don't necessarily have to feed from both breasts at each feeding. Some babies will fill themselves at one breast. You should offer the second breast and see how your baby reacts. If she doesn't want to nurse right then, begin the next feeding with the fullest breast when she is ready.

Where to Breastfeed

One of the many benefits of breastfeeding is the convenience of always having breastmilk available no matter where you are. This means that you can feed your baby anywhere, though some places are less common than others. Ask any mom who has breastfed to tell you the funniest or oddest place she's ever breastfed. You might be surprised by what you hear.

QUESTION?

Do nursing clothes help you nurse discreetly?
Yes they do, because they are designed with discretion in mind. However, you don't have to buy specially designed nursing clothes to nurse discreetly. You can either make your own or use button-down shirts from your existing wardrobe.

Yet, just because you *can* nurse anywhere doesn't mean you *want* to. You need to feed your baby where you feel comfortable and safe. Part of doing this is learning to nurse discreetly. Nursing discreetly takes practice, so don't panic if you don't master the skill right away. Keep trying it out in different places until it comes naturally.

Breast Pumps and Pumping

There will be times when you need to be away from your baby and yet you want to give your baby the benefits of breastmilk. In these cases, you'll need to extract and collect your milk, either through the use of a breast pump or by hand expression. Hand expression is fairly simple—you just use your hand to express the milk into a bottle. However, there are a few intricacies to take into account when it comes to pumps, including different sizes and styles. You need to ask yourself how often you will use a pump and how much milk you will extract each time to make the right choice.

Big Pumps

The more often you intend to use your breast pump and the more milk you need to extract, the more likely you are to need an electric pump. These can be hospital grade, meaning the motor is designed to help you pump lots of milk at one time, fairly quickly. Electric pumps also allow you to double pump, meaning you can pump both breasts at once.

FACT

Most breast pumps are for single users only; this means you shouldn't share with your friends. The hospital-grade pumps can support multiple users, but all parts that touch your breasts and/or your milk must be sterilized before the pump can be used by someone else.

There are also single-user electric pumps available for purchase. These are a good option for women returning to work or those who need to express a lot of milk at once. Most of these pumps enable you to double pump as well.

Small Pumps

Smaller breast pumps are usually hand or battery operated. They are fairly portable, and most do not provide you with the ability to double pump. These smaller pumps are designed for occasional use. They are perfect for a single replacement feeding every couple of days, but it would be difficult to use these on a daily basis for very long. These pumps use less power and are not designed to extract lots of milk quickly.

Pumping Tips

It may take you a while to get the hang of pumping. Remember, your baby is the expert at extracting milk from your breasts—pumps will be only second best. Consider practice pumping by nursing your baby on one breast while simultaneously pumping the other. This lets your baby help regulate the hormones of letdown and increase your milk supply at the same time.

Pumping your breasts should not hurt. If it hurts, stop and ask for help from your lactation consultant or the company that made the pump. You can damage your nipples by incorrectly using a breast pump. Follow to the letter any instructions that come with the pump.

If you're pumping while you're away from your baby, try to think of your baby. Some mothers bring pictures of their babies with them to look at while they pump. Others just try to close their eyes and relax while thinking of their baby's smile. Thoughts of your baby will help stimulate milk production.

In addition to the pump itself, there are other products you can buy to make pumping easier. For one, you can find hands-free pumping bras for sale at many locations. These bras allow you to hook up the pump and keep your hands free for other tasks. If you're returning to work, you might want to invest in a breast pump microwave sterilizer. You simply rinse out the parts and put them in this round device with some water on the bottom. It takes only five minutes in the microwave to sterilize your pump. Also check your workplace for a place to store your milk after you've pumped. If there isn't a fridge, invest in a small insulated bag and blue cold packs to cool it. This will keep your milk cold until you get home.

Bottle-Feeding

Bottle-feeding is not as straightforward as you might imagine. It's not as simple as popping a bottle in your baby's mouth. There are many different types of bottles and nipples, as well as some safety information you should know before feeding your baby with a bottle. With a little time and research, you can have a safe and satisfying bottle-feeding experience.

Tips for Bottle-Feeding

One thing to remember about bottle-feeding is that you must hold your baby while you feed him. You should hold your baby close and talk to him while feeding, as well as switch sides and arms during feedings.

ALERT!

Never prop a bottle for your baby, as it could cause choking and even death. If your baby cannot hold his own bottle, then someone else must hold the bottle for the baby. Milk flow does not stop even if the baby quits sucking on the bottle. A young baby cannot remove the bottle to protect his airway.

Holding the baby close and talking to him makes the experience feel safe and comfortable. Don't consider feeding something you have to do to keep your baby alive; it's also a time to bond with your baby. Make sure everyone who feeds your baby a bottle understands how you feel about feedings and does what's necessary to keep the experience calm and comforting.

Choosing Bottles

There are many types of bottles. Some are plastic; some are glass. Some are disposable and some are reusable. The types of bottles that work best for you will depend on several factors. How often do you intend to use a bottle? Who will be feeding your baby with a bottle? Will you be feeding stored breastmilk in the bottle? How will you wash the bottles?

FACT

Nipple flow is important. You should ensure that your baby has the slowest flow appropriate for your baby's age. Using a faster-flow nipple can actually cause your baby to choke and spit up, not to mention waste food. Check nipple packages for age appropriateness before buying.

Disposable bottles can cost more in the long run and are worse for the environment than reusable alternatives. However, disposables are great for traveling, as you won't have to carry used bottles with you until they can be washed. Regular reusable bottles require washing and sterilizing. They also take up a lot of room. However, they are more cost-effective and kinder to the environment than disposable varieties are.

Cleaning and Storage of Bottles

Except for disposable bottles, all bottles must be washed out. You will need some special tools to help you accomplish this task. A bottle brush is a must, as is a nipple brush. These tools thoroughly remove bits of food that remain after rinsing.

ALERT!

You should never put cereal or any other solid food in your baby's bottle. This can cause choking in your infant. Solids can also clog the bottles, rendering them useless. When your baby is ready to ingest solids, he should be fed using safe, child-size utensils and dishware.

If you hand-wash your bottles, you may wish to invest in a wooden drying rack to allow the bottles to air-dry. To sterilize your bottles, you can boil them in water, sterilize them using a special sterilizing pot made for this purpose, or use a microwave sterilizer. Putting bottles in the dishwasher (after an initial rinse) is a great option, as it will both wash and sterilize your bottles. You may also wish to buy a dishwasher-safe cage for your nipples and nipple rings, which prevents them from flying around loose during wash cycles.

Weaning

Weaning from the breast and weaning from the bottle are two different things. They can occur at different times and may be met with different attitudes. Whether you wean your baby suddenly or gradually is a matter of choice, but don't be surprised if your baby seems opposed to the idea.

Weaning from the Bottle

By the age of one year, most babies should not be using a bottle; a cup will be sufficient for drinking. Your child may fight you on this, but it needs to happen. Choose to quit using bottles all at once or remove them gradually. For the cold turkey option, you might pick a certain day to say bye-bye to the bottle. Perform some sort of ceremony to present weaning from the bottle in a positive light. Tell your baby what a big boy he is now that he drinks from a cup. There may still be tears shed over losing the bottle, but your baby will adapt to the change in time.

Bottles should never go to bed with your baby. Not only can this cause baby-bottle tooth decay, but it can also cause choking if the baby falls asleep with the bottle in his mouth. To stay on the safe side, keep all bottles away from your baby's crib and feed him only when he's in your sight.

If you choose to gradually wean your baby off the bottle, you may decide to start by removing the bottle from one meal a day. This may be easier in the daytime, as most toddlers prefer the bottle early in the morning and at bedtime. Remember, the action of sucking is comforting to babies. To wean gradually, just continue to remove the bottle from meals one at a time until the baby is no longer using the bottle at all.

Weaning from the Breast

Weaning from the breast can be led by the baby or by the mother. Around one year of age, if the mother wishes to wean, she will start cutting out one feeding a week. Generally, a one-year-old nurses only two or three times a day in short bursts, so feedings will decrease relatively rapidly at this rate.

The American Academy of Pediatrics (AAP) recommends that your baby breastfeed for at least one year. After that, the choice is left up to the mother and child, though the AAP also notes that there are physical benefits to breastfeeding beyond one year.

Another approach to mother-led weaning is to discontinue offering the breast to the baby. If you normally wake up and immediately nurse your baby, try a new ritual instead. If the baby forgets he usually nurses during this time, don't remind him. However, if he shows he wants to nurse, go ahead and breastfeed. When he's ready, he'll stop asking for the breast.

Weaning from the breast is usually easier than weaning from a bottle because it can be replaced with the cuddling and loving associated with nursing. Most children will eventually wean themselves. The key here is that as long as mother and baby are happy with their nursing relationship, there is no reason to end it right on the baby's first birthday. Many happy nursing pairs nurse well into the second or third year.

Starting Solids

One of the most exciting milestones in your baby's first year will come when you can begin to give her solid food. The first thing to do is determine when to start feeding solids to your baby. Be sure you don't start too early, as this can cause choking and instigate food allergies. The AAP recommends that you don't start solids until at least six months of age. However, there's not a definite start date; your baby will show signs of readiness, such as interest in food, ability to grab small food pieces between thumb and forefinger, and ability to take food into the mouth without tongue thrusting. These signs usually appear in combination around the sixth month, but don't be fooled by a random early sign.

ALERT!

Never give cow's milk, honey, or eggs to a baby under one year of age. These foods have the potential to harm your baby by way of allergies and disease. Talk to your pediatrician before including any of these items in your baby's food.

Once you have decided to start feeding solids to your baby, you'll need to choose which solids to feed. The general consensus is that a low-allergen item like rice cereal is a good starter food. You simply reconstitute the dried cereal with breastmilk, ABM, or water. Your pediatrician may recommend that you try a couple of other cereals, too, before moving on. After cereals, babies generally move on to vegetables.

You should stick with one food for at least five days before introducing something new. This allows you to observe your child for signs of allergies, from general crankiness to rashes. Use a calendar to keep track of when you start which foods, and jot down any noteworthy reactions your baby has.

After vegetables, you can move on to fruits, and eventually meats, if you wish. Remember to keep each new food separate from others so you can watch for allergies. Once you have gone through the spectrum of foods, with no sign of allergic reaction, you can feed your baby whatever you wish. Of course, just be sure textures are not too sharp or hard and serving size pieces are small enough to chew thoroughly and swallow.

Feeding Baby from the Table

Now that you've figured out what your baby tolerates and enjoys in terms of food, you can get a bit more creative. Make baby food from scratch and have your baby eat at the table with you and your husband. Making baby food is fun and cost-effective, and feeding the baby from the table makes things easier for you. All you need is something to grind food with. A regular food processor will do the trick, but there are also special baby-food grinders on the market.

When you make dinner for the family, simply throw some of the dinner into the baby-food grinder and serve it to your baby. This simply makes it easier for the baby to swallow and digest the food. There is no need to avoid spices or certain ingredients, as long as your baby has not shown signs of food allergies. If your baby really likes a dish, consider saving the leftovers. You can store ground food in small plastic containers for ease of later use, or grind it after reheating for the next meal.

FACT

Your child's tastes will certainly change as he grows older. Even if he refuses to eat ground-up spaghetti as a baby, he might still come to love spaghetti as a toddler or young child. Also, many children tend to be picky about the foods they eat, which can be aggravating for parents. Take heart—the pickiness usually fades with age.

Eventually you won't need to grind foods for your baby; you will simply be able to feed him from the family's dish of food. As your baby develops teeth and chewing motions (with or without teeth), he will come to enjoy the texture of foods. Unfortunately, this may bring some playing with food and refusal to use silverware. Don't panic—it's actually a very good sensory experience for your baby.

Chapter 10

Developmental Milestones

One of the best experiences you'll have as a mother is watching your new baby grow. You've probably heard that babies grow quickly; but you won't realize how quickly until you see for yourself. As your baby grows, she will also gain new skills. Many babies reach certain milestones around the same age, while some jump ahead or fall behind the norm. The most important thing to remember is that all babies are different. Crawling, walking, or talking sooner does not necessarily indicate greater intelligence, athleticism, or health than doing so later on.

Newborns

Newborn babies are much more complex than they're given credit for. Though their future skills have not yet become evident, much of the groundwork has already been laid for these abilities. For example, your baby has a fully developed body. What she lacks is coordination and control. This is the reason why she might occasionally slap herself in the face with a flailing arm, or knock into your shoulder as she swings her head around.

ALERT!

If your baby was born prematurely, you will want to analyze development in terms of her corrected age instead of her actual age. The corrected age is the age your baby would be if she were born on her due date. Talk to your pediatrician about what to reasonably expect as your baby develops.

Your new baby actually has a lot of really neat reflexes, some of which will disappear as she gets older. Ask your pediatrician to show you which reflexes are generally tested in a newborn physical exam. You can amaze your family and friends by showing them your baby's stepping reflex, which looks like your baby is trying to walk. Learn all you can about newborn reflex development so you can monitor your baby's progress.

One thing you can do to encourage physical development in your newborn is give her lots of skin-to-skin contact. Consider letting her lie in only a diaper on your or your husband's chest. Hearing the familiar sound of a heartbeat and feeling the warmth of your body will relax her, and maybe even put her to sleep. To keep your newborn warm, simply place a blanket over the top of you both. This is important, as newborn babies do not yet have good temperature regulation abilities.

First Month

The first month is an adjustment for everyone. Your baby is getting used to extrauterine life. You and your husband are just starting to figure out your new roles as parents. By the end of the first month, life will begin to settle into a manageable routine. There are several developments you can expect to see in your baby during the first month.

Physical Development

At this point, your baby still does not have much control over his body. You still need to support him as you hold him, particularly his head. His neck muscles are weak, so even when resting on your shoulder, his head can flop around, which can cause damage. Be sure to always hold your baby's head secure. Tummy time will help him learn to develop his neck muscles.

Your baby will periodically see your pediatrician for well-child visits throughout the first year. At these visits, you will be asked a few questions about your baby's actions. Be sure to ask for a copy of the pediatrician's assessment and inquire about what to expect in the coming months.

Though your baby cannot yet reach for objects, you may notice him staring intently at certain things. The best range for vision is still about eight to ten inches away. Don't listen to anyone who tells you new babies are blind and deaf. Your baby knows your voice and responds to the sound of it.

Mental Development

Your baby will particularly enjoy looking at faces in this first month. Smiling at your baby may inspire a partial smile in response, though a full smile is not to be expected right away. High-contrast patterns will also amuse a one-month-old.

In terms of voice development, your baby will begin some spontaneous cooing in the first month. You may find you can carry on little conversations with your baby as you speak to him and he coos in response. At this age, your baby will also cry if over- or understimulated.

Months 2 and 3

By the second and third months, the postpartum period as most people think of it is coming to an end. Life has found a rhythm and is calming down. However, this doesn't mean that your baby stops changing. Change is constant in a new baby's life.

Physical Development

Your baby's movements will begin to take on a purpose. Her muscles will begin to relax and her hands uncurl. First, your baby will begin to extend her arms and legs. Then, she will more deliberately extend and retract her limbs. Your baby will also begin to gain control of her head and neck. Your baby may be able to lift her head at about a 45-degree angle.

FACT

Your baby will begin to discover her hands in the second or third month. You may catch her staring at them for lengthy periods of time. When bouncing her arms around, she may very well knock herself in the head. Fortunately, injuries rarely occur this way.

Your baby may even be able to hold a small object like a rattle for a brief while. This duration will increase in length as time goes on. By the end of the third month, your baby may be rolling one or both ways. So never leave your baby on the couch or any other raised surface. Even if you haven't noticed this new skill, take the precaution around this age to be on the safe side.

Mental Development

Your baby still loves to look at you, and now you are rewarded with intentional coos and giggles. You may notice that your baby's babbling is also taking on a more verbal quality. Listen for some long vowel sounds coming from your baby.

Your baby's personality will also begin to show in the second and third months of life. Your baby will be able to convey basic emotions with facial expression. She will also begin learning cause and effect and making use of that knowledge. For instance, she will learn that if she cries, you will respond. This may become tiring for you, but your baby gets her sense of security from your quick and consistent response.

Crying is not always a bad thing. In fact, crying is an important form of communication. By this point, you will probably have learned that your baby has different cries for different situations: she may cry out when she's hungry, whine and whimper when she's sleepy, and shout to get your attention.

Months 4 and 5

This is a very exciting age for your baby. He will notice everything in his environment and respond to each thing with great enthusiasm. This is one of the last periods of time where your baby is still largely dependent on you to get around. But watch out, because mobility is close at hand!

Physical Development

Your baby has much better head and neck control now. Your baby's head really needs support only when he is tired or asleep. Your baby should be able to hold his or her head up to about a 90-degree angle.

FACT

Remember that there will be natural variations in growth and development from infant to infant. Just because your neighbor's baby of the same age is already sitting up and your baby isn't, doesn't mean that your child is behind. He's just on a different schedule.

Your baby will also begin to move objects from hand to hand. This passing game can last for lengthy periods of time and helps develop hand coordination. Also, with a bit of help your baby can stand up. He will likely roll a lot as well. Eventually, toward the end of this time, your baby may begin to wiggle forward (or backward) on the floor. This is the beginning stage of crawling.

Mental Development

Your baby is now aware that everything has a name. You may even hear some forms of words coming out of his mouth. When Daddy comes into the room, you may hear your baby say, "Da da." Don't be sad if it's Dad's name that he calls first. This is normal.

QUESTION?

What is infant sign language?
The theory behind infant sign language is that the brain is ready before the voice. Signing gives your baby a way to communicate before he can speak. You can teach your baby simple terms, like more, eat, drink, change, please, and thank you.

Babies of this age love colors and contact and are captivated by speech. Your baby will laugh hard when tickled or when he finds something funny. Your baby has also developed the ability to communicate his dislikes, usually by pushing away something or making a signal like he's wiping his nose. On the other hand, your baby will also make motions to indicate that he wants to be picked up or played with.

Months 6 and 7

Watch out world . . . here she comes! During these months your baby will be exploring his mobility options, and reaching for and grabbing things more easily than before. Just make sure you have the house babyproofed before you let him wander at will.

Physical Development

Sitting is a skill your baby has been working on and will likely successfully complete during these months. He'll also be able to support himself on his hands and knees. Your baby will be able to reach up and actually get what he is going after as well, which may worry you. Increased fine-motor skills and the pincher grasp (baby uses his thumb and forefinger to pick up small items) will follow.

The best way to childproof your home is to get down on your hands and knees and crawl through your house. Take note of what items are in sight and within reach. Remove any items to which you don't want your baby to have access.

Plastic baby utensils and dishware are great for babies of this age. Choose spillproof cups for your little one to use. These items help your baby develop self-feeding skills, which will be perfected in the coming months.

Mental Development

Your baby is now much more vocal than before. You may even hear some two-syllable sounds coming from your once quiet child. You might even catch your baby having a conversation with a toy or his reflection. This babbling helps your baby express himself.

Is it normal for a baby to get fussy just before he learns a new skill?
Yes, this is perfectly normal. Dr. T. Berry Brazelton calls these bouts of fussiness that precede new developmental accomplishments Touchpoints. Rest assured; this happens to a lot of babies.

Your baby is still a great imitator at this age. He loves mimicking your facial expressions. Don't be surprised if your baby gets anxious when spoken to or held by strangers or people he doesn't know well. A preference for his parents is common among babies at this age. Your baby may also begin to respond to his name at this time.

Months 8 and 9

At this point in your baby's life, she will look more like a toddler than a baby. She will still crave bonding time with you, but she will also be exerting a bit more independence. You will notice your little one really flirting with mobility now. Get ready because crawling is just around the corner.

Physical Development

You'll see definite signs that crawling is on the way. Once your baby is on hands and knees, you may see her rocking back and forth, as if in anticipation of motion. This is a precrawling posture. Eventually your baby will find a way to propel herself forward.

From rolling both ways to sitting supported and then unsupported, the next step is obvious. It's time to move upward. Around this time, your baby will start pulling herself up with the use of stable objects like furniture. Typically, your baby will be so excited by the accomplishment that she will immediately thump back down again.

Mental Development

Your baby has learned a lot since birth. Now he may understand that toys or objects may be hidden under a blanket or behind your back. You may also enjoy playing nesting games using stackable cups or dolls with your child. These are really intellectually stimulating and help develop spatial relations.

Language ability is also growing by leaps and bounds. This month you may actually begin to hear a first few words, though some babies are fairly quiet at this age. As long as you hear some babbling, your baby is fine. Remember, there is a wide range of normal in all areas of development.

Months 10 Through 12

It's official! At this age your baby is a toddler. You'll learn why the name toddler is given to a child of this age as you watch your wobbly little one move about. Things will start to get a little more complicated as your toddler gains access to off-limits items and pulls himself up onto furniture.

Physical Development

Crawling is mastered by this point. A few babies begin walking at this age, but this is rare. Most babies exhibit a behavior known as cruising, in which they pull themselves up to a standing position using furniture and other steady objects for support and then take small steps as they continue holding on.

From crawling to walking, your baby will learn to stabilize himself and move around. This doesn't mean that falls won't happen, so keep an eye on him as he wobbles around. As your baby masters walking, the falls become less frequent and less traumatic.

Mental Development

At this time, your baby is a social butterfly. She will be smiling and giggling up a storm. Simple games are lots of fun at this age. A big favorite for your baby will probably be peekaboo—a game she could play for hours. This is also a great game for toddlers to play with babies.

By now your baby's language skills are also more developed. Not only is your baby trying to communicate with words, which you may or may not understand, but your baby is able to understand words. If you point at an object and say the name, your baby is likely to mimic.

FACT

Babies often make up names for objects or people that you don't understand. It may be a poorly developed word they are trying to say or nothing you recognize. Don't fear—your baby will learn to speak her native language fluently and correctly when she's ready.

One of the words your baby will quickly learn and love to overuse is *no*. Whenever you issue a command, her response will probably be "No." Even if you were to ask, "Would you like a cookie?" "No" is what you'd hear. Don't worry—this defiance lasts only a little while, until she becomes equally infatuated with the word *yes*.

Taking Precautions

It's very normal for new mothers to worry that their babies are not developing at a healthy rate. It's also normal to compare your baby to other babies, including siblings and cousins. While all children grow and develop at different rates, certain lapses or deficiencies do indicate that your baby needs to be watched or evaluated more closely by your pediatrician or another health-care provider.

Is This a Problem?

Many times you might think your baby has a problem, but you are unsure. This can really wreck havoc on your life. To be on the safe side, you should seek help as soon as you suspect that there is a problem in your child's development. You might be overly cautious, but it's better to be safe than sorry.

ALERT!

If your gut tells you something isn't right, get it checked out. If your pediatrician says you're overreacting, continue to bring your baby in until you get a referral, or consider getting a second opinion. You know your baby best, and your suspicion may very well be correct.

If you think your child might have a problem, do some research. Read books on early child development and compare the information to your child's situation. Discuss your suspicions with friends who have children. If they've noticed similar characteristics in their own children that turned out to be nothing, your child will probably be fine as well.

Where to Seek Help

Where to seek help for your child will depend on what you or your pediatrician thinks is wrong. There are some issues that can be managed within your pediatrician's scope of practice. These may be minor issues common among children of your child's age, such as an innocent heart murmur.

Most major cities have a specialty hospital for children. Here you will find all types of medical specialists who have expertise in anything from disease to developmental issues. Specially trained health-care providers such as physical therapists, occupational therapists, and speech therapists might be able to help with your child's developmental issues. If there isn't a local children's hospital, ask your pediatrician if he knows of any local programs for babies with developmental problems. Many states have specialized agencies just for this purpose. If you have a baby who is at a higher risk of developmental delays because of a preterm birth or other issue, you may be given this information before your baby leaves the hospital.

Be sure to ask your pediatrician if your baby needs a referral to a specialist rather than being seen in his office. Many times, a pediatrician may try to handle something, thinking that is how the parents want it handled. Ask if there are specialists in this field in your locale to be sure your child gets the best possible care.

There are also many national and international organizations for children who have developmental delays or difficulties. These can easily be found online or by asking your practitioner for local resources. Some groups have educational literature and personal stories from other parents who have been where you are. They may also have support groups to help you deal with the day-to-day aspects of having a child who needs some extra attention.

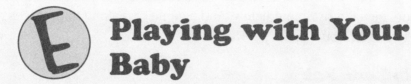

Chapter 11

Playing with Your Baby

One of the biggest joys of parenthood is playing with your baby. The smiles and giggles your little one gives will delight you to no end. Becoming a parent reminds you of all the fun kids can have and how much they actually learn through play. The essential skills your baby will learn in the first year are foundations of lifelong learning. While these foundations are vital, they are also lots of fun. As your child's first playmate and teacher, do all you can to enrich her early life.

First Toys: Voices and Faces

Toys aren't always colorful plastic shapes you buy at the store. Almost anything can seem like a toy to your newborn. Before she can even hold a conventional toy in her hand, she'll become infatuated with two toys you didn't know you had: your voice and face. Your baby will learn and love the sound of your voice almost immediately. And a game of making funny faces could occupy her for hours.

Talking to Your Baby

One of the best ways to teach your baby is to talk to her. Through hearing your voice, she will learn a lot about language and other rhythmic patterns in speech far before she can use these skills herself. She will also pick up tone and emotion in your voice.

You may have spent time talking to your baby before birth. Maybe your husband even had a few one-sided conversations with her through your belly. Immediately after your baby was born, you might have talked to her a little as well. Perhaps you told her how happy you were to finally meet her. Talking to your baby in the hours and days that follow these initial conversations is a natural continuation of your relationship with her.

The question is, what do you have to talk about with a newborn? If she can't respond, how can you make effective conversation? For many new parents, talking to their babies does not come easily at first. To ease into it, just try giving her a rundown of her daily activities: "It's bath time! Let's get you undressed. First we take off your shirt. Now it's time for your diaper. Feel the warm water? Do you like the water?"

Over time, the conversations will become more natural and your baby will seem more and more interested in the words you say. Your baby will learn to understand not only patterns of speech, but schedules as well. Soon she'll associate all your babbling about getting undressed with bath time.

Singing to Your Baby

When it comes to your baby, there are no singing lessons needed. Your baby doesn't care if you hit the notes or get the words right; she simply wants to hear the musical quality of your voice. Babies love to be sung to sleep with a soft lullaby or hear a playful tune while they bounce on your knee. Don't get embarrassed about singing to your baby. You'll soon find it's even easier than singing in the shower.

Making Faces

Your face is such a cool toy! Not only will your child love to watch and mimic it, but it doesn't cost a penny and it can't break. At first, your little one might just stare at you as you make silly faces, but as time goes on, she'll start reaching for your face and even imitating the funny faces you make at her.

Studies have shown that babies as young as a few hours old will imitate faces and stick out their tongues. The sooner you can engage your little one's attention in this way, the better. Making funny faces can be your first form of parent-child communication. How much fun is that?

In addition to making silly faces, try overexaggerating different emotions to teach your baby about feelings. Show her what a huge grin looks like and then say "happy." Show her looks of anger, surprise, and sadness, too. Your baby will get a huge kick out of watching your one-man show and may even try to mimic you right away.

Dust off the Nursery Rhymes

Nursery rhymes are timeless favorites for babies and toddlers. These silly rhymes never seem to go out of style, as they have continued to delight children for decades. Whether you stick to the classic Mother Goose variety, explore the more modern works, or invent your own style, goofy rhymes and funny tales will delight your little one over and over again.

Why Are These So Popular?

One of the strangest things about nursery rhymes is that they aren't always so sweet. Think about it: Humpty Dumpty falls off a wall and no one can fix him. Jack is a poor boy who runs through the streets jumping over candlesticks. A spider frightens Miss Muffet away from her breakfast. You might ask yourself, what kind of nonsense is this?

The truth is, most kids don't even recognize the weird nature of the tales. They simply enjoy the sounds of rhyming words and love the interaction with you. In fact, if you're reciting a rhyme for your baby and you forget the words, he probably won't even notice. You make up words to fill the gaps or hum along until you get to the next verse you know. All your baby needs is the musical sound of your familiar voice.

Find Your Own Style

If the classic nursery rhymes don't really fit your style, choose an alternative to read to your baby. More modern authors like Dr. Seuss and Shel Silverstein have written countless books bursting with goofy rhymes and stories. Again, your baby just wants to hear your voice and watch your face as you recite the rhymes.

If you don't like the old stuff and the newer rhymes aren't up to par, go the extra mile and write your own rhymes, stories, and songs. This is a great option, as you can personalize your rhymes to include your baby's name. Your baby will recognize his name and will love to hear you repeat it over and over again in a musical voice. As your baby gets older, you can add more names. Name Mommy and Daddy, pets, friends, and any other familiar folks whose names your baby will recognize. You can even put on a little play featuring characters named after close friends and family. Your baby will love this, and you might even have some fun with it too.

Books for Baby

You may think your baby won't develop any reading skills until she enters school, but this is actually not the case. Studies suggest that reading to your baby while she's still in the womb and reading to your infant after she's born are great ways to interact with and teach your baby. But with thousands and thousands of books to choose from, where does a mother start?

Choosing Books

Choosing a book for your baby needn't be a difficult task. If you would like suggestions, visit a bookstore or library and ask the staff for recommendations. Select a couple of books with big, bright pictures and very few words to start. These are usually durable laminated board books, which are convenient for use with a baby since they wipe clean. However, your baby will inevitably spill drinks and drool on his books, so don't be surprised if they don't stay pristine for long.

From simple words and pictures, you can move on to simple story lines. Singsong or rhyming words and lyrics work really well. Keep in mind that your baby may not sit still through the entire story or may even become attracted to one particular page. That is normal. He will gain more concentration skills as he develops.

How to Read to Your Baby

With a very young baby, simply sit him on your lap. Open the book and rest it on your knees at a comfortable viewing height and distance for your baby. As your baby ages, let him help you turn the pages. He will enjoy the feel of the pages, as well as any special textures that are included in the book. Putting his hands on the book will also give him a sense of ownership.

Be sure to find time to read adult books you're interested in as well. Chances are that if your baby sees you reading both with him and on your own, he will come to think of reading as a lifelong pleasure. The more books he sees and touches, the more comfortable he'll be when they become a big part of his life in school.

In the latter half of your baby's first year, he will start reading to you. The words he says may be mostly unintelligible, and the stories he tells may not make any sense at all, but this is a very healthy form of self-expression. Plus, he will take great pride in "reading" to you. He will want to hold the books and turn the pages the way you do when you read to him.

When to Read

Reading to your baby before bed is a great way to transition him from the hustle and bustle of the day to the calm hours of the night. You may find this helps you establish a bedtime routine, in which your baby gives you less grief about going to bed.

Of course, reading should not be an activity your baby associates only with bedtime. You should also read to him during the day and pretty much anytime he seems interested. If he picks up a book and hands it to you, he is probably telling you he'd like to be read to. When this happens, drop everything and sit him on your lap for a story. The goal is to make your little one so comfortable with books and reading that they continue to be a natural part of his later childhood and adult life.

Music for the Mind

Music, specifically classical music, is thought to be a great source of stimulation for babies. Studies are showing that infants exposed to classical music develop into smarter children than those who do not hear the classics early on in life. Of course, this doesn't mean that other music genres won't be beneficial to your baby. Any type of music will be helpful to your baby as it will develop her sense of auditory recognition.

Incorporating Music into Your Life

There is no specific music regimen guaranteed to boost your baby's intelligence. While classical music is touted as the key to success, you can choose a collection of different genres to stimulate your baby. Play classical music during calm times, like before naps, and play more lively tunes with beats during playtimes.

In addition to playing music at home for your baby, also turn it on when you and your baby are in the car. Feel free to sing along with the songs you know. Soon your baby may start imitating the sounds you make and sing some funny little tunes of her own. Encouraging this freedom with music will build her self-confidence and maybe even help develop your little one into a future singer or musician.

Babies love to wiggle and move to the sounds of music. Though she won't be able to dance on her own at this age, she will love spinning around and moving to the beats of different songs from the safety of your arms. So, tune the radio to your favorite station, pick up your baby, and dance until your heart's content.

Do It for Free

You do not need to feel pressured to spend a fortune on music. You can buy secondhand CDs, borrow music from friends and family, or just turn on the radio. Don't let advertisements convince you that you need a specific music kit or product for your baby. The old-fashioned methods work just as well.

That said, there are a few musical activities you might consider trying out with your baby. Some schools, libraries, or other organizations might offer sing-along programs that you can attend with your baby. These programs allow you to meet other members of the community, sing and play simple instruments with your baby, and generally have a lot of fun.

Choosing Toys

Nowadays, there are overwhelming possibilities when it comes to buying toys for your baby. From different materials to different technologies, boys and girls today have far more options than the simple truck or doll of years past. However, this doesn't mean you have to give your child one of everything. In fact, simple is often better when it comes to your child's playthings.

Babies under one year of age really don't care much about characters. They aren't into marketing, and they don't know about the latest movie or fad. Any colorful toy with various textures is fine for this age, so don't get tricked into emptying your wallet for the last Tickle Me Elmo on eBay.

Keep It Simple

There are very few rules to keep in mind when buying toys for your baby. The main one is that the toys need to be safe. Look out for removable parts that can be swallowed, long strings or cords that can be choking hazards, and other potentially dangerous aspects. The truth is, the simpler the toy, the better it is for a baby. Your little one is more likely to show interest in the box a toy comes in than in the toy itself.

A basic, soft ball is a classic toy for your baby. Even very small babies love to watch a ball roll around. It's great for babies to become acquainted with this common shape early on. An unbreakable mirror is also a great toy. Remember, babies love to look at faces, and they become especially infatuated with their own reflections. Your baby may also start to hold the mirror up to you as he learns what a reflection is. And of course, simple toys that make noise, like bells and rattles, are big favorites. Balls, mirrors, and rattles will all give your baby his first lesson on cause and effect.

QUESTION?

Why are there so many red, black, and white baby toys?
Some studies show that newborns see high contrast best. This information has led to the creation of lots of red, black, and white toys, which are supposedly more interesting to a baby. Use your judgment before spending a lot on these special toys.

It's also nice for baby to have a stuffed animal or doll to play with. However, until your child is out of a crib, he shouldn't take this toy to bed with him. Older babies and toddlers love to play with stuffed toys and dolls and pretend to care for them like pets or children.

Tactile Stimulation

Tactile stimulation, or appealing to the baby's sense of touch, is a great thing for even a small child. You don't have to spend lots of money on fancy toys—you can make your own tactile toys. For instance, put a few different objects with different textures into a paper bag. You can choose cotton balls, cereal pieces, one of your baby's socks, or whatever else you have around. Let your baby reach in and hand you an object. Talk to him about the object that he's pulled out. Your baby will love choosing objects and hearing your voice as you explain them.

Tactile foods are also a great idea. As your baby gets older, change the texture of his foods. Watch how he rolls the food around in his mouth and hands. It's a messy process, but it serves to stimulate your baby's brain. Tapioca pudding is one example of a tactile food your baby will love.

Encourage Pretend Play

Pretend play is so important for your baby. This is one of the best ways for your child to express himself creatively. Your baby will begin pretend play by simple imitation. This begins nearly from birth as your baby begins to imitate facial gestures. From there your baby will begin to learn to move around alone, from rolling to scooting to cruising and finally walking. Each of these physical phases of development will add a new dimension to the pretend play.

Babies love to mimic their parents' daily lives. Popular toys for kids reveal this, as they are often replicas of grown-up items like phones, vacuum cleaners, cars, and the like. Encourage this kind of imitation in your child. It means he looks up to you and is interested in your life.

To encourage pretend play in your baby, give him plenty of free play. Not every moment of playtime needs to be orchestrated. You can simply set a few small and simple toys down with your baby. Big, fancy toys won't do anything for your baby that simple toys won't. In fact, the more simple a toy is, the more likely your baby is to use his imagination when playing with it. Remember, the best power for toys is brainpower, not battery power.

Encourage Creativity

Creativity is the ability of your baby to be expressive in art and music. There are plenty of simple ways to encourage this in your child. The first thing to do is offer your baby creative freedom. Give her a couple of crayons and some blank paper. Coloring books are fun too, but these suggest your child should color within the lines. Blank paper helps children feel free to draw whatever they like.

Musical instruments can make great creative toys as well. Babies can make noise and learn about rhythm. This helps them learn about patterns and mathematics. Eventually, you'll see your little one playing along with the rhythm of a song. Clapping is another variation of this skill development.

From Tummy Time to Cruising

Your baby's physical development can be tracked by her change in movement. Your baby first begins to roll from one side to the other, and then back again. Then your baby learns to sit. Maybe scooting comes next, followed by crawling. The stage between crawling and walking is called cruising. This is where your baby holds on to furniture, people, or whatever she can grab to support herself while she moves around. Each of these milestones is fun and important.

Tummy Time

Tummy time is a way for your child to build muscles in her upper body. As she learns to push up on her arms, she'll gain arm strength. Your baby will also gain strength in her neck muscles, which are used to help your baby lift and turn her head. These are important skills for every baby to learn.

When playing on the floor, you may wish to lay down a clean blanket when your baby is very small. This will cover any small things you may have missed with the vacuum. Warn other people in the house that the baby is on the floor, and keep pets clear of her to avoid injury to your little one.

In addition to fundamental development time, tummy time can be playtime—a chance to look around and explore. For very young babies, simply put a mirror to one side and let her enjoy talking to the "other" baby. As your baby gets older and learns to lift her head, other toys may be fun for her. Eventually, as your baby expands her movement base, you can place toys slightly out of her reach so she can practice reaching for the toy.

Don't be afraid to get right down on the floor with your baby. Lie down next to him and talk to him while he's small, or lie head to head and rest on your chin, watching him while he watches you. It is also okay to simply leave the baby to play on his own, as long as you always have him in your sight.

Cruising

Cruising is a wonderful time of anticipation. It's clear that walking is just around the corner, and you're ready. Perhaps you have cameras poised in every room, waiting to capture those first wild steps and your baby's excited face. However, the cruising milestone is also an important one. Unfortunately, it brings some dangers that you may not be expecting.

FACT

Remember, baby gates are not just for keeping your baby out, but they also work to keep your baby in. This allows you to give your baby complete freedom in a room you have thoroughly safeguarded, without your having to worry that she will get into something dangerous in the next room.

Now is when it is very important to get down on your hands and knees and assess your home for potential dangers. Are there glass objects on the table that your baby could grab? What about power cords that could trip the baby or even be chewed on? Can your baby reach the cords hanging from the window blinds?

Anything that could potentially be dangerous to your baby needs to be removed or separated from your baby. This includes gating off areas that could cause problems, like stairs, rooms with slick floors, or rooms with sharp-cornered furniture. Take these precautions early to save yourself stress later on.

Beware of Rough Play

Rough play is any type of play that puts your baby in danger. This can be something that is simply developmentally inappropriate, like bouncing a baby on your knee when the baby doesn't have neck control. This is perfectly acceptable for an older child, but not for a small newborn. Rough play can also be something you just shouldn't do, like throwing your child in the air.

Learn What's Rough

The best plan of action for rough play is to know your baby and follow your baby's lead. If you are tickling your baby and your baby is obviously out of control, even if it seems like pure laughter, stop. If you try something and your baby physically can't handle it, stop. Sometimes your baby's facial expression will tell you when play gets too rough; you may notice a look of shock, fear, or anxiety.

Be careful to notice the age requirements for toys and games. For example, a bike helmet shouldn't be used on a baby until he can hold his head up with the helmet on. This generally happens between eight months and one year of age. Until this point, your baby should not be carried on your bike, even in a baby bike seat.

Who Plays Roughly?

Dads are often stereotyped as the initiators of rough play; however, this is not always true. In fact, this can be a dangerous stereotype. Truthfully, anyone can play rough, from siblings and cousins to aunts and uncles. As your child's guardian, you need to ensure that anyone who babysits or plays with your child knows how you feel about rough play. Most of the time, these people are not trying to harm your child—they simply don't know any better.

Playing safely with your child is a matter of understanding infant development and knowing your baby's personal limits. Follow your instincts about playing with your baby. Choose only safe, appropriate toys and keep your baby's playing space free of all potential dangers. Always encourage your baby to have freedom in play, but also teach him the right way to do it.

Chapter 12

Baby Gear

One ironic part of having a tiny newborn baby is all of the equipment that goes along with him. There is an incredible selection of products to buy, all of which claim to make your life with a new baby easier. From car seats and cribs to slings and swings, the choices can be overwhelming. How will you know which ones are right for your family? Also, how do you know if you're getting good deals? This chapter will help you sort out what you need and how to get it.

Car Seats

A car seat is a necessity for a new baby. The problem is that there are so many styles of car seats that it's hard to determine which is the best for you. The key to choosing a car seat will always be safety. Once you've found a safe, reliable car seat, good looks and fancy features are just perks.

Infant Car Seats

Infant car seats are designed to face backward in your car. The reason that infant car seats face backward is that it is easier for your baby to deal with the force of a crash with their weak neck muscles in this position. Infant car seats should be used until your baby weights at least twenty pounds. In general, your baby is always safest in the rear seats of your car.

ALERT!

Every year, the AAP publishes a car-seat guide for parents. It is available free online at: *www.aap.org*. You can also find other useful information on this site to guide you in your first year of parenting.

These types of car seats fit directly into the seat of your car and are strapped in with your regular seat belt. Another option is the use of a base. The base is strapped to the seat of your car with the seat belt, and you simply snap and unsnap the car seat from the base. This eliminates the need to mess with the seat belt every time. The good news is that the car seat can be used without the base, or you can buy extra bases if you have multiple cars. It is also handy to use the car seat as a carrier.

Toddler Car Seats

Toddler car seats are seats that face forward in your car and are used for babies who weigh more than twenty pounds. They are not usually used until your child is also one year of age and over twenty pounds. Most toddler car seats are designed to carry children until they are sixty to eighty pounds, though state laws vary on how old and how large your child has to be before he can leave a car seat. There are also older child options for those too small or young to leave a car seat but too mature to sit in a baby seat.

When you buy a new car, be sure it comes equipped with the new LATCH system for safely securing car seats. This is the most up-to-date and simple car seat system available in vehicles. Car seats can work in older cars, but the LATCH system makes things a lot easier.

A toddler car seat attaches to the car via the seat belt in your car. It can be moved from car to car, but it is less convenient than the infant car seats. It does not double as a carrier. Speak to other parents about their toddler car seat choices before purchasing your own.

Convertible Car Seats

The convertible car seat is supposed to be the best of both worlds. It can fit the smallest newborn in a rear-facing position and also converts to a forward-facing toddler seat. This also means you need only purchase one car seat as opposed to two car seats for your little one.

However, there are complaints about the convertible car seats. The main complaint is that it can't be used as a carrier. Others dislike the fact that it's quite large for a tiny baby. If you know someone who has a convertible car seat, ask to borrow it and try it out before making your own purchase.

Bassinets, Cradles, Co-sleepers, and Cribs

The crib is the classic place for a baby to sleep; in fact, you most likely slept in a crib as a baby. However, there are many options for places for your baby to sleep. Some are long-term options, while some are appropriate for only certain age ranges. From bassinets and cradles to co-sleepers and cribs, the items you select should fit your lifestyle.

Bassinets and Cradles

Bassinets and cradles are typically used for the first few months of your baby's life. Many families choose to use them to keep the baby closer to them while they sleep. These are smaller than the usual crib and don't allow the baby much room to move.

ALERT!

Be sure to check out any antique or heirloom bassinets or cradles prior to use for your baby. There are certain safety features that your baby's new bed should have. Check out the Consumer Product Safety Commission (CPSC) Web site for more information: *www.cpsc.gov.*

These short-term options are very useful for the first couple of months. Since you will have your baby close to you during the night, these items can make night feeding much easier on your family. Unfortunately, you need to discontinue the use of these products when your baby reaches a certain weight or gains the ability to roll over or sit up.

Co-sleepers

A co-sleeper is great for your family if co-sleeping is what you would like to do. This product enables you to have your baby very close by, even in your bed with you, for ease of feeding in the night. A co-sleeper allows you to expand your bed, if the size of your bed was precluding you from considering co-sleeping.

Most co-sleepers come in portable and wooden varieties. The wooden ones can be converted into benches or desks as your child grows. The sleeping area in a co-sleeper is larger than a cradle or bassinet, but slightly smaller than a crib. The co-sleeper tends to cost less than your standard crib.

Cribs

Cribs tend to be the largest-size sleeping area of all the baby sleeping items available. They come in a large variety of shapes, colors, materials, and styles. Some cribs are able to convert into toddler beds or daybeds as your child grows.

Because of the size of a crib, most cribs are housed in a nursery or room other than your room. You may decide to keep your baby's crib in your room and move it later or begin your baby's night life in another room. Cribs can also be used for naps or for playtime while you're working on something else in the room.

If you have a nursery in your house, your crib will likely be the center-piece of the room. The crib can be your expression of creativity in the room, or you can choose a simple crib that will allow you to change the look and feel of your baby's nursery as often as you like. It also makes it easier to pass the crib down to other babies in the family.

Portable cribs are also an option and provide a great middle ground. They are smaller than normal cribs, so some families use them as a daytime solution, for naps and such. You may also decide to use a portable crib con-tinuously if you are strapped for space. Some new portable cribs actually have bassinet attachments to help you get more use out of them.

Strollers

Strollers are the ultimate way to get your baby out and about. This item makes taking your baby out with you easy on you both. From getting exer-cise to simply strolling through the mall, a stroller can help you get out of the house and enjoy other activities. The key is choosing the right stroller for your lifestyle, or purchasing multiple strollers for different needs.

Umbrella Strollers

Umbrella strollers are great for fast and furious shopping trips and quick strolls. They are very portable and also easy to store in the car, for those unexpected walks in the park on your way home from the grocery store.

While umbrella strollers are ultralightweight and easy to use, they can also be less sturdy. This is usually only a problem for toddlers or older children. Though they do come in sturdier versions, these tend to be a bit more expen-sive. Umbrella strollers can also be difficult to use with very young babies.

Before your baby can hold his head up well, you will need a stroller in which your baby can lie down. Most umbrella strollers do not offer this option.

Double Strollers

Double strollers are a wonderful invention! They work great not only for moms with multiples, but also if you have an older child who wants to tag along. You may also consider a double stroller as an investment if you want more children in the future. Having the extra storage space is never a bad thing!

There are a few different types of double strollers:

- **Side-by-side stroller:** This stroller works well if you have two young kids who like to talk or play. It also works out well for one child because you can put purchases or coats in the extra seat.
- **Tandem stroller:** This stroller has one seat in the front and one in the back. Many are made so that one or two car seats will snap right into the stroller. This can make the transition from car to stroller very easy, particularly with a sleeping baby. And if you have a toddler as well as an infant, your older child can sit up front and look out while your baby snoozes in the back.
- **Other variations:** The other main variation on a double stroller allows one child to sit or stand on a small platform built behind a normal-looking stroller seat. These are lightweight strollers. They are designed for one small child and older child.

Carriages

The old-fashioned carriage is coming back into style. These buggies are usually for babies who want to lie down and not sit up. For this reason, carriages are perfect for newborns and little ones who can't yet sit up. Most carriages have a wide enough berth in the compartment to hold two small babies, if you have multiples.

Storage space is a must in a stroller or carriage. After all, you need a place to store your diaper bag and/or purchases when you're out. Be sure whatever stroller you have enables you to carry your stuff without dragging anything on the ground or tipping over the stroller.

The down side to carriages is their lack of flexibility. Most carriages don't fold and go very easily. They also do not expand to accommodate a sitting older baby. This can make them more of an expensive toy for you than a practical solution for travel and getting out and about.

Swings and Things

Swings and other baby carriers can be great ways to help contain your baby for short periods of time. These carriers also offer a way to help soothe your baby, usually via movement. The main difference between the options is in the way the motion is created—by the baby or a battery.

Swings

Swings come in many shapes and fashions. In fact, you can find them in such a variety of styles and colors that there is surely one to match your nursery. These infant seats are much like light car seats, suspended from a metal frame. A battery pack tends to power the motion for the swing.

Wait! Before you buy a swing or any other bouncy contraption, be sure your baby likes it! If you have the chance to try one out at a friend's house, do so. Different kinds of motion affect babies differently. Don't waste the money if it's going to be something that annoys and upsets your baby.

Swings can be used to help soothe a baby to sleep, or as an easy way to entertain a tyke while you get a small task done. It can be a blessing to have something to entertain the baby for a few minutes while you cook dinner or pay bills or even read a few pages of a book. Just be sure not to leave your baby unattended in a swing.

Bouncers

Babies like to bounce, and the motion is great for calming a crying or fussy baby. For this reason, there are several different bouncing gadgets on the market for babies. From bouncer seats to jumping harnesses, your baby can have tons of fun with one of these products.

Bouncer Seats

Bouncer seats are usually cloth seats fitted to metal frames. Most of these seats include a safety strap that goes between your baby's legs and secures at the waist. Because these seats recline, they can be used even for small babies.

Bouncer seats are great because they are low to the ground (safe) and lots of fun. In fact, they're often so comfortable that your baby could fall asleep in it when he's tired of bouncing. A neat trick is to keep your baby in the seat in the bathroom while you shower. This way, the baby is close and you can peek around the curtain to check on him.

Bouncer seats are great for use with little ones. They can entertain and comfort at the same time. As your baby gets older and learns cause and effect, he'll begin to learn that when he moves, the chair bounces. Most models also have a toy bar across the front for even more hours of fun. Other models have battery packs to allow for vibration—some children like this, and others don't.

Stationary Jumpers

Stationary jumpers are much like the old walkers of the past. The good news is that they are not as dangerous as walkers. (The AAP has warned against the use of walkers.) This circular-based toy has a seat in the middle, and the seat rotates 360 degrees, giving your baby access to a variety of fun toys.

ALERT!

Be cautious with any type of carrier or bouncer. It should always be placed on the floor, as opposed to a table, bed, or other surface that is off the ground. This prevents the motion from carrying the bouncer onto the floor and tossing your baby.

In the stationary jumper, your baby can stand and learn to use his leg muscles; however, some say that it isn't good to allow babies to bear weight on their legs before a certain age. Be sure to check with your pediatrician—or at least consult your maternal instinct—before buying a stationary jumper.

Johnny Jump Ups

These doorway jumpers are different from the stationary jumpers. They hang from a doorway and allow your baby to jump up and down. This can be a great workout for an older baby, but again, there is the issue of weight bearing. For this reason, this product is not appropriate for smaller babies. You should also be sure that your doorways can handle the jumper, as it requires a built-up doorframe for support.

Slings and Carriers

Babies love to be held, and adults love to hold babies. But parents have busy lives and can't sit around holding their babies all day, no matter how much they'd like to. For this reason, parents need a way to hold their babies while getting other things done, from vacuuming the floor to talking on the phone. Luckily, a sling or carrier can help you hold your baby and keep your hands free for other tasks.

Slings

Slings are pieces of fabric that hold your baby on your body, distributing the weight from shoulder to hip. They can be used from the newborn period until your child weighs about thirty-five pounds. There are several different types of holds that can be used with the slings, depending on your preference and the baby's age.

QUESTION?

Can you nurse using a sling?
Yes, nursing in a sling is a wonderful, discreet option. Once you get the hang of it, you can also learn to nurse discreetly while moving around. This can be a blessing if you find yourself running errands and need to feed a hungry baby in public.

Some slings have padding; others do not. Some slings are simply long pieces of material that must be wrapped around your baby in a particular fashion, while others are fitted to a certain shape but offer flexibility in sizing.

Front Packs

Fronts packs are just what they sound like: backpacks for the front of your body. There are many varieties available, all with different systems of snaps and buttons to help you position your baby. Your baby can face either inward or outward.

ESSENTIAL

Slings and other carriers are not just for moms! Many dads love using these items to hold their babies and bond with them. One family might even have two slings or carriers—one for Mom and one for Dad—if their sizes differ or just for convenience.

The main complaint about these types of carriers is that they can be difficult to learn to use. However, once you learn to use them, they are a snap.

Some women don't like them because using a front-pack carrier makes them feel pregnant again. Ask a friend if you can try on her carrier or sling before selecting one for your personal use.

Storing Stuff

Though your newborn baby is quite tiny, she has a ton of stuff! After the first couple of months, you may lose control over the products, toys, and clothing. Dressers, boxes, and closets may begin to overflow. Luckily, there are ways to get things organized. It just takes some time and diligence to sort it all out.

Space Issues

If space is an issue, or even if you simply want to tuck things away, look for portable or collapsible items for your baby. This might mean strollers that fold down to next to nothing, or a smaller, collapsible crib for your baby. It could also mean getting pieces of equipment that will last for a while or will serve more than one purpose, like a convertible car seat.

One way to keep organized is to select a place for each large item. You could keep the bouncer seat in your living room for when you need free hands to read mail. You can store the swing in the kitchen for times when you're cooking or cleaning. These things are fairly portable, but by assigning each item a room, you'll be able to cut down on random clutter.

As for the little objects that you have for baby, try baskets and bins. Use a container of some sort in each room. It should hold any small toys or books that you have for baby. As your baby gets older, use these containers to teach cleaning up. Simply show your baby that everything goes in the container when he's done playing. Eventually, your baby will get the hint and begin to clean up on his own.

Toys

Very small toys can be kept in a large bucket or basket. This can be placed in the room where they will be used the most. Larger toys can have their own spots on shelves or tables, depending on how much surface area you have.

Labeling a toy basket with your baby's name or a picture of an animal will show him that this is a place for his toys and encourage him to clean up after playing. You can simply show him how to place items back in his basket (or the elephant basket). Small children get very excited about ownership or personalization of items.

You may also want to limit the number of toys your baby has out and available. Put age-inappropriate or seasonal toys away until it's time to use them. Remember to also remove toys that your child outgrows. You can either store them for future children or pass them on to friends or charities. Keeping too many unused toys in the house is a surefire way to find yourself buried in clutter.

Clothes

Everyone loves cute little baby clothes, and people will be lining up to give them to your baby. But before long, you'll have nowhere to put them all, and your laundry duty will spin out of control. Too many baby clothes means clutter, and you don't have time to deal with clutter as a new mother.

A chest of drawers can work well for storing baby clothes, but don't waste your time folding the clothes. They are too small to really do much good folded. Also, you might consider labeling drawers for specific types of items. Some examples might be: onesies, pants, shirts, dress-up clothes, etc. You can also hang up a few clothes, though this is not necessary for the majority of your baby's wardrobe.

Babies grow quickly! Hesitate before you buy a ton of clothes that fit her right now, or before you give away clothes that are currently too big. Remember, your baby may grow at a different rate than other babies and might need to wear sizes that are above or below her age level.

A lightweight laundry bin is another good thing to have. Some really organized moms also have laundry sorters to separate light- and dark-colored clothing. Either way, it is immensely easier to keep clothes in order if you can store dirty clothes in one location. Just be sure that location is handy enough to actually get the clothes there. Keeping your laundry bin by the changing station or in the bathroom is usually a good choice.

Finding Deals

Caring for a baby can be wildly expensive. Tiny clothes can cost as much as you would pay for an adult article of clothing, sometimes even more. Other items like car seats are useful only for a short period of time. So how can you get what you need and some of what you want without breaking the bank?

Hand-Me-Downs

Hand-me-downs have a negative connotation for many people. After all, who wants to wear all their big brother's clothes after he's done with them? But the right set of hand-me-downs can be wonderful. Consider using hand-me-downs for the everyday outfits that get the most wear and tear. This would include items like undershirts, play clothes, bibs, and socks.

Hand-me-downs don't have to be just clothes. You can reuse bigger items as well. If you save money by not having to purchase a high chair or baby bath, that's great! You can always use the money you saved on that purchase elsewhere.

Using hand-me-downs is a great way to save money. Some hand-me-down clothes haven't even been worn much. This is also true of big-ticket items like car seats, high chairs, swings, and cribs. Many of these items were designed to be used multiple times by multiple children.

Bargain Shopping

Be a shrewd shopper. Look for coupons and deals every time you shop. Sometimes when you sign up for a baby registry at certain stores, they will give you a coupon for a decent amount of savings on a larger purchase. So even if you don't want to use a baby registry, sign up and enjoy a pretend shopping trip. When you're done, you'll come away with a nice reward.

ALERT!

Be a smart shopper. If you're buying an item with which safety is a huge issue, like a car seat or crib, go online to check for any company recalls. Make sure safety standards that were applied when that item was made are the highest standards available today. It's also a good idea to fill out the warranty cards that come with products you buy, as companies often use the information you give to send out recall notices.

You can also consider shopping at secondhand stores and discount stores. Many times you can get the same baby items for a lot less money at these places. Some stores also allow you to use a layaway plan to pay for more expensive items over time.

Last but not least, yard sales are great places to do bargain shopping. You can find clothes, toys, and even some larger items at these sales. You just have to be sure you're given the correct information about the item before you buy it. Be sure to ask for the user's manual that goes with the item, where applicable.

When you buy clothes at yard sales, be sure to wash all garments prior to using them for your baby. Use warm water and even bleach (on white items) to help remove any stains or soil. Cleaning toys and equipment is also a good idea; do so with hot, soapy water. The only items you might want to avoid buying at yard sales are toys and other items like bottles that go in a baby's mouth.

eBay

eBay is the hottest place to shop for baby bargains. Many of the rules of bargain shopping also apply on eBay. The key here is to really understand what eBay is and how it works. While it is a bargain hunter's paradise, you can get burned. Learn about the feedback system and use it. If you're new to eBay, make several small purchases before bidding on something large. There are also books that are prepared every year to help you find the best prices and safety features for your money. *Baby Bargains* by Denise and Alan Fields is a great read and well worth the cost.

Getting Out and About

Now that you have all these products available to help you carry your baby, you're ready to go! Fold up the stroller and put it in the trunk. Load your diaper bag and throw in the sling. Once your baby is safely in the car seat, snap the seat into the base and head out to the mall, a park, or just take a drive on a nice afternoon.

Even armed with all these products, you may still be leery of leaving the house with your little baby. It can be a daunting task to take your small baby and all this stuff to another destination. Before heading out into the world, be sure to give each item a thorough test drive at home. One reason to do this is that certain items may not be capable of all that they claim.

With all this handy stuff to help you hold your baby, be sure to remember that babies need to be held in arms as well. The body contact that they get from you and others is vital to their survival and emotional development. You don't have to hold your little one until your arms are sore, but do try to fit in some cuddle time each day.

For example, if the manufacturer of your stroller says it's collapsible with one hand, put it to the test. Learn how to snap the car seat into and out of the base. Mastering these skills now will prevent you from standing in a parking lot in the rain or snow, trying desperately to make things work. The more often you get out and use these items, the better you'll feel about trusting them with your baby. It will take you a few extra minutes to load up the car and get around a busy mall with a baby carriage and diaper bag, but the more you do it, the easier it will become.

The biggest key to keeping your life simple and under control is carefully considering each purchase before you make it. Assess your situation, including what you can afford, what you have room for, and what you truly need. Always search for deals before paying full price, and practice using items at home before taking them out into the world. These few precautions and time-saving tricks will ensure a happy life for your baby.

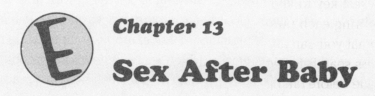

Chapter 13

Sex After Baby

Probably one of the last things on your mind after you have your baby will be sex. You'll have a ton of things requiring your attention, particularly the needs of your newborn baby. You won't be getting much sleep, and your body will still be returning to normal. You'll feel far from sexy. But don't worry—the feelings of love and affection will return. You and your husband do remember what life was like before the baby came, and postpartum sex will become a reality.

Getting Clearance

Most sources you consult will give you a generic six-week rule before you can have sex after birth. Yet, while six weeks may be just the right amount of time for one person, it may be too long or too short for you. Your doctor or midwife may give you guidelines for returning to sex after birth, and in most cases, you should follow them. However, if circumstances change, feel free to call and discuss this with your practitioner. For example, your midwife might advise you to avoid sex for six weeks, which is about how long it could take for bleeding to stop. But if you stop bleeding at four weeks and feel ready, call and get clearance from your midwife before proceeding with sex.

Physically

When assessing your physical preparedness to resume sex, you must consider several factors. First, you need to consider how you gave birth. Giving birth vaginally may provide you with certain reasons to be cautious about resuming sex. A cesarean birth would provide you with a different reason to be cautious.

Bleeding

As discussed earlier, it is important to know that any bleeding or other discharge from your vagina indicates that your uterus is not done healing. If you have any discharge, you should not engage in sexual intercourse. If you're unsure if you've been bleeding for a normal length of time, do not hesitate to call your doctor or midwife.

Once you have quit bleeding or your discharge has stopped, you can usually be cleared to have sexual intercourse. If you see a return to bleeding, you must stop. This may be a return of your normal menstrual cycle if it has been longer than six weeks, or it may be a sign that you were not truly healed.

Perineum

Obviously, giving birth can cause trauma to your perineum. If you did not have an episiotomy or require a repair, your perineum will heal more quickly and you will have less likelihood of infection. Your perineum should feel normal within a week or two after birth.

If you had an episiotomy or required stitches in the perineum after birth, you may take longer to heal. This can also make you very nervous when you begin to think about having sexual intercourse again. The good news is that even after an episiotomy or repair, your perineum will probably be healed within six weeks of giving birth. Just don't be surprised if you still feel sore for a while, even after you are completely healed.

Incision

If you gave birth via cesarean surgery, you might feel like you've lucked out of the problems associated with the perineum. That is true. However, you will need to pay attention to your incision. Sexual intercourse can place an extra strain on your incision, even though it's not located around your vagina.

You will want to ensure that your incision is free from redness and that it is not tender prior to even thinking about sex. If your incision is red, tender, or seems to leak or seep fluid, call your doctor. These may be signs of infection.

Emotionally

After giving birth, most women feel completely drained of energy. After giving of yourself all day to a tiny human being who requires so much care, the last thought on your mind in the evening is cuddling up with your husband. The good news is that this doesn't last forever. It is a temporary feeling.

In fact, talking to your husband about your predicament can actually help solve the problem. Maybe he can offer to bathe the baby after dinner and play with him a bit so you can enjoy a luxurious shower alone. Maybe even a nice walk alone or trip to the store would be helpful in refreshing your spirit. You may find that once you get a bit of time to yourself, you will feel like a completely different person. A few minutes each evening can be enough for you to recharge and find that you really do have some extra energy to spend with your husband, whether or not that means sex.

Talking about your feelings—and his—is a very important part of preparing for your new sexual relationship. If you each understand how the other is feeling, then it becomes easier to deal with these personal issues. This will also help ensure that when you do resume intercourse, you both feel comfortable with the situation.

The First Time

You and your husband have decided that you are both physically and emotionally ready to have sexual intercourse again. In some ways, it's like being a virgin all over again. You're both nervous. You've got to find the right time and the right place. Your husband is probably worried about hurting you, and you might be worried about getting pregnant again.

FACT

You can ovulate prior to having your first postpartum period. This means that you can get pregnant before having a period and thereby receiving a warning that you are fertile. This means every act of passion can lead to a pregnancy. Be sure to discuss this fact with your husband before resuming sex.

Timing

Finding the right time to have sex can be difficult. Do you wait until you're both exhausted at the end of the day simply because the baby will be asleep? Or do you wait for a weekend when Grandma can come take the baby for a long walk? There are no easy answers to this dilemma. You and your husband need to figure out what works best for you. Again, keeping an open line of communication is key to a positive experience.

ALERT!

Don't force yourself into the stereotype of having sex in your bed. Instead, act like someone who has to sneak around to have sex. Try different rooms in the house and also consider different furniture. The more exciting your romantic encounters become, the more likely they are to be enjoyable for both of you.

If the baby is in the house when you have sex, it is quite possible that in the middle of it all, your baby will wake up crying and screaming. In this case, you'll need to decide whether to quickly finish or to satisfy the baby and quickly return to bed. This choice is a tough one, and you may have several unsuccessful sexual encounters before it finally goes according to plan.

Positions

Prior to the birth of your baby, you may have had some favorite positions. There is no reason to throw these out the window after having a baby. In fact, there are no off-limits positions in the postpartum period. The only exception is lack of comfort.

If you are worried about pain from actual penetration, you may decide to choose a woman-on-top position or a side-lying position. Both of these positions allow for a more shallow penetration. If you decide to be on top, you will have more control over how deep penetration goes and how quickly penetration happens.

If you had a cesarean, you may wish to use a woman-on-top position to prevent pressure from being placed on your incision. This may be more comfortable for you and your partner for a while, but in time you'll be able to use other positions just as comfortably.

Sometimes your breasts may leak as you have an orgasm. This is perfectly normal. You can choose to wear a bra with pads for the first couple of encounters or you can elect to keep a blanket or towel nearby in case you need it. An alternative would be to assume a rear-entry position, perhaps on your hands and knees. If your husband is behind you, he cannot see the milk leaking and you can simply let it fall onto a towel.

If any position you try is painful, reassess the situation. Do you need to add a bit of personal lubricant? Lubricating the vagina can make penetration easier and less painful. Of course, the best personal lubricant is natural. This type of lubricant is released during orgasm. This being the case, you might try ensuring that you have an orgasm before attempting penetration.

Whatever you do, make sure to keep your sense of humor during the first few encounters after birth. From leaking breasts and crying babies to a large helping of personal lubricant, postpartum sex is definitely a bit different from your usual experience. The good news is that it does eventually work itself out.

Making It Work

From finding the time to finding the inspiration, getting your sex life back on track can be a challenge. If you and your husband feel differently about resuming sex, be sure to communicate openly about it and come to an agreement. If the problem is simply that you can't find the time for sex with a new baby in the house, call on some friends and family to babysit.

Whining Versus Wining

Sometimes your husband might decide that he can whine about not having sex as often as he would like it. This can be very difficult on your relationship. In fact, it may even make you less inclined to have sex with him. Here's an old trick: Remind him about wining and dining rather than whining. Ask him to put a bit of romance into your lives. Whether it's flowers, poetry, or a clean bathtub, he should do it.

Once you communicate openly about your differing points of view on the subject, you'll probably experience a lot more wining than whining. The foundation of many problems between a husband and wife is a lack of communication. The two of you experience your baby's birth and early life very differently, so it makes sense that you would not be on the same page.

Finding Time to Be Together

Adding a new little one to your life can seem to take over every available moment. The truth is, where there is a will, there is a way. As your baby gets older she will begin to sleep for longer stretches of time. Figure out when you can anticipate these stretches and plan accordingly. You can also consider asking for reinforcements. If your parents or siblings are dying for a chance to take your child out for a walk, or to the mall, give it to them.

However, there is also something to be said for spontaneity. While the above methods will get you through in a pinch, you have to remember that your life will not always involve planning when and where to have sex. This is a temporary solution. Sometimes the mood will strike and the timing will be off. Be wild. Take chances. Occasionally it will all work out perfectly. Occasionally you'll both wind up a bit frustrated or laughing about how everything turned out. No matter what, there is never any harm in trying!

Rekindling Romance in Five Minutes or Less

The key to keeping the flames burning is keeping romance alive. Now that you have your attention more divided because you're a mommy, you're going to have to adapt. Don't panic, mommies are good at adapting. You're going to be no different.

Try to remember to spend five minutes a day being romantic with your husband. This can be something as simple as a full-bodied kiss good-bye in the morning as opposed to the half-focused peck on the cheek. You'd be surprised what a bit of body contact will do. Also, consider slipping a love note into his lunch or brief case. If you can't find any paper or you're too embarrassed to send a note in crayon, consider sending a love note via e-mail. He will love this, even if he doesn't fully admit it.

Worried you'll run out of time to send a note? Find a few minutes to visit a free e-card site and prepare notes to send on future days. Hallmark is one company with such a site. Visit *www.hallmark.com* and explore their various e-card options.

When you're having dinner, try playing footsie. Bring some candles to the table one night, even if you're serving leftover take-out food. Or serve dinner after the baby is in bed and play nice music. Dancing in your pajamas doesn't have to be unromantic; this may rekindle some spark between you. Once your husband sees the effort you are making, it will be much easier for him to put the right foot forward. Don't be surprised if he starts planning surprises of his own. Nothing is as wonderful as finding notes of your own during the day!

What to Do When You Have a Headache

Surely, you're familiar with the headache excuse. The fact is that sometimes you just don't want to have sex. This happened before your baby was born and it will happen afterward. Your new role as a mom isn't necessarily at fault for your lack of sexual desire. Sometimes you and your husband are just on different wavelengths in this department.

Talking to your husband about the fact that you don't always have matching libidos and that it may not be because of the baby is imperative. He may believe that the baby is taking his place in your life. He won't know this isn't the case unless you tell him.

It may take a while for you and your husband to get back on track. In the meantime, consider alternatives to sex. Sometimes snuggling is a nice happy medium. You may find that this meets his need for physical companionship and meets your need for affection without actual intercourse.

FACT

Sometimes your desire not to have sex can be overcome by initiating romance. For example, there might be times when you think you are too tired, but a little kissing quickly gets you in the mood. This is fine; just be sure to let your husband know that you hold the right to bail at any time.

However, cuddling may not always do the trick. If he is really in the mood for sex and you are not, there are still alternatives. You can consider sending him off to take a cold shower. Or you could offer to shower with him and use it as a chance to take care of his needs through masturbation, with or without you. Remember to be considerate and respectful of his needs, just as you'd like him to be toward yours.

Frequency of Encounters

One thing most people seem to disagree on is how often a couple should have sex. Some people might feel that once every two weeks is sufficient, while others might argue that every other day is more like it. The truth is that there isn't one right amount of sexual contact to have. What works for you and your husband is the perfect amount. It really is the old argument of quality versus quantity.

If you and your husband are okay with the amount of sex you're having, why listen to what others feel is right? This goes even for national studies. If you're having less sex but enjoying it more, who cares? Do only what's best for you and your husband.

Sometimes you may find that your sex life is improved after having a baby. This could be because giving birth has changed your body and made it more pleasurable to have sex or easier for you to achieve an orgasm. It could also be because you know your body better now that you've had a baby. Either way, enjoy it!

ALERT!

One mistake many women make is comparing how often they have sex with how often their friends do. If you do have a close enough friendship to share this information, remember that every couple is different. What works for your friend may very well not work for you. Additionally, this kind of competition can quickly kill a friendship.

Birth Control

Preventing another pregnancy may or may not be on your mind. However, it is absolutely possible to get pregnant again soon after having a baby. Therefore, if you're not ready for another baby, be sure to talk to your practitioner about birth control well before you resume having sex.

Barrier Methods

Barrier methods of birth control are very common. They are easy to obtain and relatively inexpensive. Most methods require at least some thought prior to having sex, though spontaneity is not completely out the window.

Condoms

Condoms protect you from pregnancy by preventing the sperm from reaching the egg. They are about 88 percent effective in preventing pregnancy. If you decide to use a condom with spermicide, you can further decrease chances of pregnancy.

Condoms can be kept around your house and used with water-based personal lubricants. You will need to have them handy for when you want to have sex. This is also a great way to make sex a bit less messy, if speedy cleanup is something to think about.

Diaphragms

This barrier method actually goes inside the vagina and covers the cervix. This prevents sperm from entering the cervix and reaching the egg. With the aid of spermicide, it is considered to be 98 percent effective in preventing pregnancy.

ALERT!

If you used a diaphragm prior to getting pregnant, you will require a new prescription after your baby is born. This is because giving birth may change the size of diaphragm you require, and an ill-fitting diaphragm can lead to an unwanted pregnancy.

Your midwife or doctor must fit a diaphragm, as it is a prescription item. A fitting involves a vaginal exam. You can reuse a diaphragm for about a year before you need to obtain a new one. A cervical cap works much like a diaphragm.

Hormonal Methods

The hormonal methods of birth control are all prescriptive items. There are many new ones out today, each with a different hormonal combination. Only your doctor or midwife can help you find the right combination for you.

Oral Contraceptives (The Pill)

The pill is considered to be about 97 percent effective in preventing pregnancy when taken correctly. There are multiple formulas available for use today. This method of birth control allows for spontaneous sex, but requires that you remember to take a pill at the same time every day. Every missed or late pill can increase your chances of getting pregnant.

There are other considerations to take into account when thinking about the pill. One would be that while you are nursing, you might wish to consider using progesterone-only (mini) pills. Some forms of oral contraceptives can decrease your milk supply. Be sure to let your doctor or midwife know that you are nursing.

Intrauterine Device (IUD)

The intrauterine device is a piece of shaped metal wire. Your midwife or doctor places the IUD into your uterus during a vaginal exam. The IUD prevents pregnancy by discouraging implantation into the uterine lining. Some IUDs actually release hormones as well.

Patches, Rings, and Things

Other delivery systems for hormones are via the patch or a ring. These are both prescriptive medications provided by your practitioner. However, they do not require any action before you have sex. They are always in place.

The patch is simply worn on your hip or shoulder. It delivers a continuous amount of medication through your skin. The patch is changed once a week. It is barely noticeable on the skin and is not worn in an obvious area.

A ring is actually inside the vagina. It also delivers hormones to prevent ovulation. Both of these methods of birth control are easier to use than traditional oral contraceptives.

You may also opt for injectable hormones. They can be given monthly or every three months, depending on your prescription. This requires a visit to your practitioner.

Permanent Birth Control

Permanent birth control is usually chosen after you feel you have completed your family. Some states or physicians will have certain restrictions about whether you are a candidate for permanent birth control. This usually revolves around your beliefs about family and your spouse's beliefs, how many children you have, and your age.

Vasectomy

Vasectomy is permanent surgical sterilization for a male. This procedure involves altering the vas deferens on each side of your husband's scrotum and interrupting the flow of sperm to the penis. This is usually done very quickly and easily in a urologist's office. It is considered 99 percent effective in preventing pregnancy.

ALERT!

Your husband will need to return to the urologist after several ejaculations following the vasectomy procedure. A sample of his ejaculate will be tested to ensure that there is no live sperm in it. This is considered very important, to determine the success of the procedure and how safe it is to have unprotected sex.

Many men can have this done on Friday and return to work easily on Monday. Ice packs and tight pants (to prevent bouncing) can be very helpful for dealing with discomfort. Talk to your urologist for more information.

Tubal Ligation

This is female surgical sterilization. It is considered to be more than 99 percent effective in preventing pregnancy. Female sterilization is more complicated surgery than male sterilization.

FACT

If you are planning a cesarean section, you can also request that a tubal ligation be performed during your cesarean surgery. It does not affect your recovery time or the length of your surgery. This is a great option if you want the child delivered through cesarean section to be your last.

This surgery involves interrupting the pathway of the egg to the uterus. It can be done after a vaginal birth, while you are still in the hospital, though it will increase your recovery time. You may be a candidate for what is called Band-Aid surgery, or laproscopic surgery, which consists of small incisions in three or four locations on your abdomen. If you are not a candidate for this type of surgery, it will be required that you have a more open procedure, much like the surgical incision for a cesarean section. You can also choose to have this done after the postpartum period.

Since permanent birth control is considered just that, permanent, you should be very sure you are done having children before opting to have this procedure. Many couples wait until their youngest child is at least a year old before making that decision. Others are completely fine with having permanent birth control done during the birth or shortly afterward. Most forms cannot be undone with much success, despite attempts at reversal surgeries for both men and women.

Breastfeeding as Birth Control

Breastfeeding can be used as a method of birth control. This method takes a lot of research on your part before it can be effective. By using the signs of your body and fertility awareness, you can accurately predict when you will begin ovulation. The book *Breastfeeding and Natural Child Spacing* by Sheila Kippley outlines the specifics of this method of birth control.

Breastfeeding tends to delay the body's natural return to fertility. This can be a welcomed relief from the potential burden of birth-control worries. However, it is important that you learn more about breastfeeding as birth control, called the Lactational Amenorrhea Method (LAM).

The basics of using breastfeeding as birth control are not hard to follow, but there are quite a few rules. Your baby cannot have supplemental feedings by bottle, no matter what the bottle contains. He also cannot use a pacifier. Additionally, your baby must have free access to the breast, particularly at night. By letting your baby regulate when he nurses, your body responds by suppressing ovulation. Be sure to read up on this method for other very important rules that must be followed to prevent pregnancy.

Chapter 14

Returning to Work Outside the Home

Returning to work as a new mother can be both a blessing and a curse. There are many reasons why you might be going back to work, from finances to the simple fact that you want to work. Even if work is where you want to be, it can be a difficult transition for even an experienced mother. There are ways to make that transition easier on you and your family.

Easing Back into Work

As the date for you to return to work draws closer, you may have a lot of questions about returning. Will your job be the same? How will you be treated? Will your projects be intact? There are also questions about your family. Did you take enough maternity leave? Will your baby be okay during the day without you?

How Long to Stay Home

How long you are able to stay home before returning to work will depend on many things, including how long you have for maternity leave and how long you want to stay home. This is often a very hard decision to make. It's also important to note that how you feel during pregnancy may be different from how you feel once your baby is born.

The average length of time to stay home is between six and eight weeks. There are also families who take much more or much less time off after the birth of their baby, though many families are able to negotiate a period of twelve weeks, per the Family Medical Leave Act (FMLA), discussed in Chapter 1.

Your Plan of Return

During pregnancy, it is a must to talk to your supervisor or Human Resources Department at work about your maternity-leave plans. They may not require anything written in stone. Sometimes they simply ask for an estimate of the time you anticipate taking off, knowing that once your baby is born, things may change. Once your baby has arrived, have a plan in place to let people at work in on the good news. This also allows them to plan to cover your duties during your maternity leave. You don't necessarily need to do this personally, unless you want to do so.

Avoid the temptation to be available to answer work calls when you're home with your baby on leave. Once people at work know you'll answer the phone or e-mail, it may be difficult to get a moment's peace. Keep in contact with work while on maternity leave, but make sure it's on your terms.

Also, have a way to stay in touch during your maternity leave so that you can update work as needed. This should not, however, be a time to catch up on work. You might consider e-mailing your boss every week or couple of weeks, however, to say, "Hey, I'm still alive, and here's the plan."

When you have a week or two until your return, talk to your work about setting a date to come back. Starting back to work toward the end of the week can help ease your transition back to work. Consider working a half day on Thursday and a full day on Friday. This gives you an easy week with enough time to work out issues at home. It also gives you a very nice break on the weekend.

Corporate Mommy

Returning to work may feel awkward or great. More than likely, it will feel like a combination of many emotions to you. You may welcome the return to a busy schedule or adult conversations that don't revolve around diapers. You may also be worried about missing your baby. These are all normal as you ease back into the corporate world.

Getting Back into a Routine

Before you left work to go on maternity leave, you probably had a nice routine worked out. You had a flow to your workday. This is probably not how it felt at home with your baby, particularly in the beginning. The hard part of being back at work is finding that flow or routine again. Your first days back will likely be hectic. You will probably not get a lot of work done, so be prepared. Most likely you will spend the first few days sorting through e-mails, catching up with your coworkers, and reorganizing your desk.

Be sure to bring plenty of pictures of your baby to show off to your coworkers. Also be prepared to tell your birth story to plenty of people. This can be a welcome distraction as you ease back into work, or it may get in the way during busy moments. Be sure to have answers handy for either situation.

If you had a temporary helper while you were away, try to arrange to have her stay at least for a couple more days. This gives you time to ensure a smooth transition back to your work duties. The temp can help fill you in on projects that have been worked on while you were gone.

If there wasn't a temp to help out while you were gone, find out who helped with your assigned duties. If no one touched your work while you were gone, you may have a larger pile on your desk. Sit down and methodically go through each item. Once you have done that, set about prioritizing the jobs you must do. You may ask for direction from your supervisor if you aren't sure about what needs to be done and in what order. Expect that this task will take a while. No one expects you to be on top of everything immediately.

Breast Pumps and Pumping at Work

Using a breast pump at work shouldn't be scary or worrisome. There are many ways to pump discreetly and easily while at work. If you have your own office, you can simply shut your door. If you have a lock, use it if you think someone might enter. Some mothers hang a sign on the door saying simply "Do Not Disturb"; others hang signs that proudly declare "Pumping in Progress." Your sign can be as bold or as mild as you need it to be to ensure your privacy.

If you work in a hospital, you may be given access to pumps in the newborn nursery. Simply check with the director of the nursery to see if this is possible. If so, borrowing a pump will save you money and the hassle of having to bring yours to work with you.

If you do not have your own office, you will need to find a space that works for you. Some businesses actually provide rooms for pumping moms. Check with your employer to see if you can help set one up in your workplace. Since breastfeeding mothers have lower absenteeism rates than nonbreastfeeding mothers, many businesses are more than willing to work something out.

If there's no pumping room available, perhaps there's a vacant office or meeting room you can use for short periods of time. Check for any available space. Also, be sure to get clearance from your supervisor to do this;

you don't want an expectant group of coworkers banging down the door for a meeting while you're holed up inside pumping. Another alternative would be to pump at the day care or other place your child is during the day. Sometimes you may even be able to get a true feeding in, if your work location is close to your baby's.

If none of the aforementioned options work out, talk to other nursing and new moms in your office. Ask them where they pumped at work and how they managed to fit pumping into their schedules. With a little guidance from others who know, you can surely find solutions to your pumping problems.

Alternative Schedules

When going back to work, you may wish to find an alternative schedule. This is simply a schedule that is more flexible for your new needs. This may be a part-time work situation, a combination of working at home and working in your office, or even job sharing. These are all great solutions for flexibility in your job.

Splitting Time Between Home and Office

Doing some of your work from home is a great way to buy yourself some more time there. Not every profession lends itself to working from home, but many do. If you have certain duties that you could manage from home, consider talking to your supervisor about splitting time between your home and office.

ALERT!

If you work from home, talk to your tax consultant about possible tax deductions you can take for your home office and other related expenses. Not only does this allow you the convenience of working from home, but it also helps you save money on supplies you might need.

With new technologies, it is very easy to stay connected to your office. Nearly every home has not only a phone but also a computer with some form of Internet connection. If you are able to connect to the Internet and read e-mail from home, it may be quite possible for you to effectively work from home some of the time.

Having a home office is not necessarily easy. It does take some work to figure everything out. Sometimes you may find that work calls you, even though you'd rather be with your family. Having twenty-four-hour access to work can have that effect. Setting "office hours" even when you're home can help alleviate this distraction.

Job Sharing

Sharing your job with someone else might also be another option for flexibility at work. Perhaps you each work two full days and split the last day each week. Some jobs have you alternate three- and two-day weeks. Another schedule that might work for you would be five half days.

Be creative. Find a way to work out your schedule. Be sure that you are capable of getting all the work done. Talk to your supervisor about your idea. She may have someone else in the office who is already willing to do part-time/job-sharing work, or she may be willing to find someone to share your job with you. Either way, don't be afraid to ask for alternatives to a regular schedule to ease you into new motherhood.

Balancing Home and Work

The hard part about working is that you're not done when you come home. Unfortunately, your job as a mother is not nine to five—it continues around the clock. There's no way you can handle all your responsibilities without help. Your primary partner in child care is your husband, so the two of you should divide up the work that needs to be done.

Sharing the Workload

One of the hardest parts of having a baby, whether you work outside of the home or not, is the division of labor within your home. No matter if one or both parents work, there are still chores to be done at home. Meals have to be made, laundry must be washed, home repairs must be taken care of, and bills must be paid. Who will do what?

There isn't one right way to divide up the chores. You may decide to go by whatever chores you both prefer to do. If it's even enough and you and your husband are fine with the arrangement, go for it.

Find any way that works for the both of you and divide the chores. Think of everything that needs to be done to run your household. Make a list and check it twice. You may wish to trade some chores back and forth. This works particularly well for the chores that no one wants. Once you have done this, your house will run much more smoothly. You and your husband can quit fighting about dishes and get back to real life.

Your Personal Life

When you work, you may feel that you're taking time away from your family. This can lead you to believe that since you are away from your family, you're taking time for yourself. This logic just doesn't hold up. The truth is that when you are at work, your time is not your own. You work for someone else. Even if you are the boss, you have business to take care of.

One of the most important skills you can learn is how to say no. No doesn't mean never; it simply means not right now. You have a lot on your plate. There will be time in the future for you to take on projects, volunteer, and do other things. This first year should be about your family.

Be sure to make time for yourself, even if it means constructing a balancing act. The first year after having a baby is not the time to be overcommitted, so don't devote your time to unnecessary ventures. You will quickly lose your mind if you don't find time to relax and simply enjoy life with your baby. So do whatever it takes to make this work.

Missing Your Baby

In addition to getting back into the swing of things at work, you'll also have the challenge of being away from your new baby. You have just spent every minute of your life with your new baby, and now the focus is changing. It is perfectly normal to miss your baby when you first go back to work.

Easing Your Pain of Separation

Whether you want to be at work or you have to be at work, you are there. The separation from your baby can be worse if you'd rather not be at work, but either way, you may still miss your baby. There are several things you can do to help ease the pain of separation.

For one, bring a picture or two of your baby to work. Place these where you might normally see them, like your desk or your locker. You might even consider wearing a locket with your baby's picture tucked safely inside. The frequent sight of your baby's face will help you transition into days of separation.

A must for getting used to being away from your baby is having absolute confidence in your child care. A little nervousness is natural, but if you are sincerely worried about your baby's well-being while you're at work, you're not going to get much work done.

Be sure that you know how to get a hold of whomever is watching your baby during your work hours. Feel free to call just to check in, even though your little one is too small to talk to you. Chances are, she'll always be fine, but the ability to check can do a lot to reassure you.

Also consider visiting your child or having your husband visit your child during the day. This can help ease your fears. You may even be able to have lunch with your child. If you hire someone to care for your baby at your home, try to go home for your lunch break and spend some time with your baby in a comfortable setting.

The truth is that many moms have trouble dealing with initial separation from their babies. It usually gets easier with time, but if you feel that you are not getting any more comfortable with the situation, perhaps you need to get help. If you have continually intrusive thoughts about your baby during the day, to the point of not being able to work or concentrate, consider talking to your doctor or midwife. Some medical help may be in order.

Dealing with Your Baby's Anxiety

Most babies are blissfully unaware that their parents have gone to work during the day. They are aware of their new surroundings and the new people around them, but it is usually not distressing to them. What may be distressing to your baby is a change in the lifestyle they were used to having.

FACT

Some babies will have a preference for a particular parent. If this is true, try saying good-bye to that parent from home and having the other parent take the baby to child care. If your husband is the favorite at one point, don't be hurt. Children are fickle at this age and change their minds often.

Did you pick a child-care facility that will listen to what your baby's schedule has been? Do they have enough people or few enough babies to give your baby the attention he needs? As long as your very young baby has his needs met, he should not become stressed over being someplace other than with you. However, as your baby gets older, separation anxiety can become a very real issue. This can happen as early as about six months. It can also happen later, or your baby may skip it all together.

Wishing You Were Home

Perhaps you've always been the working type but now that you've had a baby, you've changed your mind. Maybe you've always wanted to stay home, but you didn't feel like your circumstances would allow it. Either way, you may want to be home right now.

Making Your Way Home

Sometimes the solution comes from simply making the decision to stay home. You may not have even realized that you wanted to be home until after you had your baby and went back to work. This is rather common among new mothers. Once you've made the decision about where you'd rather be, it's time to take stock. Do you have a workable solution? Is there a way to arrange your finances so that staying home would be possible?

ALERT!

Don't burn any bridges on your way out. Do your best to retain good relationships with your employer and coworkers. If you ever go back to work or decide to do freelance work from home, these contacts will surely come in handy. Simply make it clear that though your job is important to you, your baby is your priority at this time.

Once you know that you'd like to stay home with the baby, discuss this with your husband. Perhaps the two of you can come up with a workable solution. Then take action as soon as you can. Figure out how much notice of your resignation you need to give your supervisor. You may also need to give your child-care provider some notice that you'll no longer be needing his services. The first weeks of your new arrangement may be challenging, but with your maternal instinct to guide you, things will eventually work out.

Dealing with Disappointment

Sadly, no matter how hard you look, there may not be a way for you to stay home. This can be very disappointing, especially if you've gotten your hopes up. The disappointment of a plan gone awry can also make your work life seem unbearable. But since it is your situation, you'll need to find ways to make it easier on yourself.

One way to provide some light at the end of the tunnel is to plan for the future. Just because your financial or home situation isn't compatible with your staying home right now, that doesn't mean it won't ever be. Just keep your eyes open for future opportunities to try your plan again.

In the meantime, work hard to find an alternative schedule for home and work. While you may not be able to leave work totally, a flextime or part-time position might be better for you. Be creative in searching for ways to spend more time with your baby.

Making the Most of It

When both you and your husband work, chores are not the only thing that may need to be divided. Sometimes you may find that you are both fighting over time with your baby. This can be an awkward situation. You are both the baby's parents and your little one needs both of you.

Dads Matter

Part of the problem with working full-time is that by the end of the day, there may be relatively few hours left when your baby is awake. By the time you've sat down and had dinner, it will probably be time for your baby to go to bed. As a mother, you have the advantage of nonnegotiable nursing time with your baby. Dads, on the other hand, have a trickier situation.

You may be tempted to leave your husband chores disguised as bonding time with the baby. Yet, bathing and diapering are not ideal times to connect with your baby. Your husband needs time to read to, cuddle with, and play with your baby just as much as you do. Try to work out a plan that gives you both the bonding time you need with your baby.

Snuggle Time

Getting in snuggles before bedtime is a chore for some. But try to pass the duties around. If you're cooking dinner, let your husband play with or sing to the baby before bedtime. If your husband needs to go to a meeting or plays sports one evening a week, it'll be your turn to take over bedtime preparation with the baby.

Your baby will enjoy whatever time you can give him. Try to grab as many minutes as you can. For instance, if you usually carry your baby in a car seat, consider adding some more physical closeness by using a sling or other carrier to keep baby closer. Another way to increase time with your baby is to share sleep. By co-sleeping, your baby gets lots of time to be with mom and dad. This is an arrangement that works for many new families. Little tricks like these can greatly increase your bonding time with your baby.

FACT

While you're both running around your home and offices, you and your husband may neglect one another. Simply because you've become parents doesn't mean you don't need couple time. Do whatever it takes to maintain your relationship with your spouse. If this relationship takes a beating, everyone will suffer, including your baby.

Having Your Cake and Eating It Too

Is it possible to work and still have an awesome home life? Can you be a working mother and still have a child who knows who you are? The answer is absolutely yes; you just have to work at it. And remember, things will never be perfect. The key to success is isolating trouble spots and working to improve them, while simultaneously appreciating the good things you already have.

It often becomes way too easy to focus on what you don't have. You don't have time to go to places you used to go to. Perhaps you don't have the energy to devote to a hobby you previously enjoyed. Maybe you wish you had more time to be with your family. Focusing on all these negative aspects will get you nowhere.

In the midst of their new responsibilities, new parents have the tendency to make mountains out of molehills. But despite lack of sleep, lack of time, and lack of patience, you still have quite a lot. Take the time to stop and look around you every so often. Look at your baby and remember everything you have to be thankful for.

Being a mother is hard work. Being a working mother is doubly hard. Finding the time to meet your needs, the needs of your family, and those of your employer can be overwhelming. But even in the darkest of tunnels, there's usually light at the end. Don't give up until you find a situation that works for you and your family.

Chapter 15

Staying Home with Your Baby

Many modern mothers are choosing to stay home and not work when their children are young. In doing so, they fight stereotypes galore. The good news is that they also reap numerous benefits from their new adventures as stay-at-home parents. Despite the stereotypes, there are many rewards that come with this position. Not only do you get to watch your baby grow into an energetic child, but you also get to retain control of your little one's care during these first crucial years of development.

The Decision to Stay Home

The decision to stay home is not an easy one to make for many mothers. You may be worried about losing your career or your mind. Perhaps your worries are of a financial sort. No matter what your worries are, you are not alone.

Your Choice

The decision to stay home is an easy one when it is your choice. You may have decided long before you ever became pregnant that home was where you wanted to be when you had your own children. This does not make you old-fashioned, conservative, or any of the other labels that might be thrust upon you. You're simply a woman who knows what she wants.

The problem may come when you realize that your dream job isn't what you expected. Being a fabulous mother of three is an easy concept but a difficult task. Be cautious about forming expectations for being a stay-at-home mom. Talk to other mothers and take in both the good and bad observations. Ask them how their lives differ from what they expected. You'll hear some women complain about lack of sleep and others excitedly babble about their little one's latest accomplishment.

Preparations

With prior planning, you may come into the home-parenting situation more prepared to deal with the ups and downs. If you've had long-term plans, you're probably more financially prepared for the prospect of staying home. You may also be more emotionally ready for the task at hand.

Preparations may mean not only setting money aside but also setting yourselves up in a financial situation that is better able to adapt to a one-income family. This may mean a bigger down payment on your home so that your monthly mortgage payments are lower. It may mean cost-cutting efforts throughout the years to reduce your monthly bills.

While being financially and emotionally prepared for staying at home is not critical to the success of your time at home, it can make your life much easier. Of course, even if you have some trouble at first, this is not an indicator of a failed attempt at stay-at-home parenting. This arrangement takes time to get used to, whether or not it was your choice to begin with.

Not Your Choice

If you are required to stay home with your baby and it's not really your choice, you will certainly have a tougher time getting used to your new role. Sometimes this happens due to illness, location changes, job markets, or finances. Any of these situations can quickly find one or the other parent at home with the children, and many times this is the mom.

Your first instinct may be to grit your teeth and tough it out. This is a fine coping mechanism; however, it won't help for long. You need to either commit to being a stay-at-home parent or find an alternative solution.

Stay-at-Home Dads

Perhaps what works best for your family is for one parent to stay home. While many people assume this will always be the mother, your husband may be the better choice for a stay-at-home parent, depending on your situation. In choosing one parent over the other, there are many factors to take into consideration. Some of these include:

- Who has more earning potential?
- Who has more job-growth opportunity?
- Who has the better/less costly insurance?
- Who is better suited to staying home?

If you have a very lucrative career in a quickly growing field, you may be very hesitant to leave your job. As long as you and your husband agree that his staying at home is the best option, this will work out just fine. And don't worry; even though your husband doesn't have your maternal instincts, he does have paternal ones. Any initial problems he has will soon disappear with practice.

Finances

The money issue is often the deciding factor for most families when it comes to deciding if a parent should stay at home. Even if you desperately want to stay home, it may not be clear how your family can survive without your income. Do some investigating. There may be a workable solution hidden beneath your doubt.

Only One Income

You may wonder if it's possible for your family to make due on only one income. Though your family would lose your income if you stayed at home, the truth is that you would also be free of a few extra expenses. Sit down and think of all the things you'd no longer have to pay for if you didn't work. Some of these might include:

- **Transportation:** Whether your drive, carpool, or use public transportation, there are some fees involved. Gasoline, car maintenance, auto insurance, bus fares, or train tickets might be on your current list of expenses.
- **Wardrobe:** There are very few jobs that allow you to wear your everyday clothes. You may need to wear a uniform or dress up, but either way, you spend money.
- **Day care:** Babysitters, nannies, or day-care services might eat up a huge chunk of your paycheck. As a stay-at-home parent, you would eliminate these expenses.
- **Other hidden costs:** Perhaps you eat out, get clothes dry cleaned, travel, or purchase supplies more frequently while working. While some of these expenses are tax deductible, you still spend a lot on random things.

FACT

There are simple tricks to help you calculate the costs of working versus staying at home. For instance, a special calculator available online can be very helpful. Visit *http://homeparents.about.com/library/weekly/ blworkcalc.htm.*

Shifting Your Thinking and Spending

You might find that no matter how much you wanted to stay home, it's a difficult adjustment for you and your husband. However, there are some things that you can do to make the shift more economically feasible. By lightening your load, you can make it more possible to enjoy your new job as a stay-at-home mom.

First, consider how you can reduce your spending. Can you consolidate your debt into one payment? Sometimes you can even get a better percentage rate when you do this. Can you refinance your home? Rates fluctuate, so sometimes you can get a better deal than when you first applied. This is a great way to put more money into your pocket every month.

There are a few companies with Web sites that will actually help you shop for a new mortgage. You simply enter your information once and sit back and wait. One such company is LendingTree. Visit *http://lendingtree.com*.

Start planning menus to help you save on grocery bills. Some locations actually have online grocery shopping. While you may spend $5 on the service, you eliminate all impulse buying and you don't have to go inside the store. But even if that doesn't work out, planning ahead can keep you from spending more than you wanted and keep you from heading to a restaurant on a whim.

Defining Your Role

Your role as a stay-at-home mom is a different one than probably any other job you've had in your life. You don't really fit in with the working crowd. You're new to the mommy crowd. It is quite awkward at first. Once life settles down, you'll be fine. You just need to jump in with both feet first and hit the ground running.

Wearing Different Hats

Going from having a defined title at your job to being a stay-at-home mom is a difficult transition. Suddenly you might be a housekeeper, care giver, cook, chauffer, and banker. This is why defining your role is so important. Supermom is not a title you want to even begin to try on, let alone earn. It is important that both you and your spouse are on the same page when it comes to sharing responsibilities.

One of the biggest subjects to discuss is what can reasonably be accomplished during the day. It is simply too much to believe that you can keep your baby well entertained and safe while maintaining a spotless household, paying the bills, grocery shopping, and cooking dinner every night. And don't forget the laundry!

FACT

Let's face it: housekeeping is a chore that often falls on the wife. In defiance of this trend, you can declare that whoever stays home should reasonably assume the bulk of these chores. However, the working parent may be able to pick up some slack in the evenings.

Talking about your expectations is the only way to address the situation. If you don't discuss these issues, your life will quickly spin out of control. Your husband will expect one thing and get another. You'll be wondering why he's not helping, and he won't even know you expect help.

Play to likes and talents when divvying up chores. If he's a great chef, let him cook a couple of nights a week, while you supply the groceries for the meal and clean up. Or if you absolutely hate garbage and he absolutely hates laundry, trade! There are reasonable solutions that can be worked out when you put your heads together.

Life as Full-Time Mommy

While it may seem that all there is to being a stay-at-home mom are chores, this is far from the case. The tiredness you feel from all these responsibilities will instantly fade away when you look at your baby. After all, he is the reason you do all this work. In the end, you'll find it's absolutely worth it.

Always keep why you are doing this at the center of your mind-set. When you remember the reasons behind your decision to stay at home, it can make the execution of the plan easier for you. Let chores slide in favor of your baby. This little bundle of joy is the essence of your life, and no amount of work can overshadow that.

You may be itching to clean out a closet, but your baby is particularly needy that day. Maybe your baby is being so much fun that you can't tear yourself away to do laundry or clean a bathroom. Don't sweat it. The chores can wait. Make sure you find the balance that works for you and your family.

Staying Sane

In your new life as a stay-at-home mom, you may sometimes look around and realize that the only people you've talked to that day are under the age of one. Soon cartoons will become your favorite shows and you'll find yourself humming silly kids' songs in the shower. When you notice your motherhood taking over your life, it's time to take a break.

Getting Out

The easiest way to stay sane is to occasionally get out of the house. This can mean going out to the mall to walk around or going to a park or library to read in peace. What do these activities have in common? The company of other people, of course. You can't just talk to your baby all day. You need to have adult conversations as well. So get out there and talk to people.

What if you're shy and don't feel comfortable talking to strangers?
The good news is that babies and children are automatic conversation starters. You may never have to say a word, just look receptive. Before long someone will be telling you how cute your baby is. Simply continue the conversation and make a new friend.

You can also try some organized activities for moms and babies. This can be music classes or baby gym classes. Perhaps you can find a mother's walking group or a playgroup for babies. There are many activities that you can find to do with other moms and babies. Whatever you do, don't hesitate to get out of your house. Getting out will help you keep your sanity and expose you to potential new friends.

Staying In

There may be reasons you can't get out of the house, but this doesn't mean that you are destined to go nuts in your home. Sometimes it's a transportation issue. You might not have a car during the day. Or maybe your baby isn't feeling well. Sometimes distance can keep you more isolated than you'd like. No matter what the reason, don't panic. You can find ways to stay stimulated.

Call a friend whom you haven't talked to in a while and gaze out the window as you chat. Consider watching a bit of television or a movie when you're home. Catch up on the news or read a book you've kept waiting on the shelf. Do what it takes to stay sane, and remove yourself from your immediate situation (without neglecting your duties) from time to time.

Intellectual Stimulation

Keeping yourself intellectually stimulated is tough when you're a stay-at-home parent. The silly, musical sounds of kids' shows will always be in the background, your baby's picture books will outnumber your New York Times best sellers, and finding the time to pick up the newspaper will be a big challenge.

Saving Your Brain Cells

You probably remember being pregnant and feeling like you were losing brain cells faster by the minute. The early daze of postpartum feels much the same. However, your hormones do eventually settle, causing this feeling to occur less frequently. Once you feel you've regained some control, consider doing things to stimulate your brain while you're at home.

Reading is always a good way to relax and entertain yourself. If you are able to simply pick up a book and go, good for you. If you need a bit more motivation, try a book club, either online or at a local library or bookstore. Puzzles and brain teasers can also be a lot of fun to do. These keep your brain nimble and quick. They are also easy to do in terms of time, location, and money. You might like word finds or the crossword puzzles in your daily paper as well. There are also puzzle books, magazines, and Web sites where you can find more puzzles than you ever imagined. Be careful, these can be addicting!

The Scholarly Route

While you may not consider yourself a scholar, attending a class a couple of times a week might be just what you need to stay intellectually stimulated. This can be any sort of class that tickles your fancy, from a literature workshop to a studio art class.

FACT

Distance learning poses a great opportunity for adults who can't get away to regular classes, either because of timing or location. There are lots of places to choose from, but this site will help you answer common questions and find classes: *http://distancelearn.about.com*.

You may consider continuing or furthering your current educational status. Maybe you'd like to take a course in child development to help you in parenting. There is also something to be said for taking anything you'd be interested in, even if it doesn't seem that practical. For fun, try something like a baking or sign-language course.

This doesn't have to be an academic challenge, just something to keep you interested. You might enjoy a fitness class of a different variety. Many community centers offer classes on belly dancing, water aerobics, and other fitness specialties you may not have thought of prior to reading their brochures. Regardless of what you choose, decide on a goal to drive you. The point is to get out of the house and be with other adults for a while. Enjoy yourself!

It's Not All about Cooking and Cleaning

Do not be put off by the thought of staying home just because you don't like doing dishes, laundry, and other housework. The main focus when you stay home should be on caring for your family. Housework is a potential extra, but you'd be doing some even if you worked outside the home. Caring for your baby can be a lot of fun and very rewarding.

Add Structure to Your Day

Structure can be something to help you figure out how your days will go. You may love a routine, and you are welcome to use the same theories when you have kids, but obviously, flexibility is a must. Find out what you like to do with your baby and plan for these activities.

When you get up in the morning, have a plan for what you'll do. Obviously, breakfast is one of the first items on your agenda. Will you immediately shower and get dressed, or will you play a bit with your baby first? Finding a rhythm that works for you and for your baby can help you approach each day with purpose. Some babies do thrive on routines, though not stringent ones, particularly when it comes to feeding.

After playtime, it's a great idea to teach your child to pick up, even if at first he only watches you do it. Try to show your little one that picking up toys after playing is not only necessary, but it can also be fun. Sing a song about cleaning up toys as you put them back in their places. Your baby will love this.

Fill your calendar with fun and laughter, and don't be afraid to go out and have adventures. Just remember to alternate periods of play with periods of rest. You can overschedule even a small baby. And, of course, you need your rest as well.

What to Do All Day

When faced with the prospect of spending each and every day at home with your baby, you might become overwhelmed. What will you do all day, anyway? This is totally up to you, so be creative. Do you like to exercise? Does your baby enjoy the stroller? Try taking a walk with your baby. The more your walk, the more exercise you get. Turn each walk into a lengthy discussion of what you see. Every time you point to the neighbor's dog, your baby is storing the information. One day you'll be rewarded with your baby's shouting out, "Dog!"

Remember that your baby learns through playing. This means that all the playing that you can do with your baby is a great opportunity for him to learn. Singing learning songs, like your ABCs, counting out the number of objects you lay on a blanket or the number of kisses you give your baby— these are all learning situations for him. They also tend to be fun for you.

Working from Home

You might decide that you want the challenge or the money that working from home can provide you. Working from home can give you the best of both worlds, but it can also have some bad points. There is a fine line of balance that has to be met to make a work-at-home arrangement not only pleasurable but profitable as well.

Finding a Job

While staying home with your baby, you may decide to look for work that you can do at home. Whether it be freelance work, in-home sales work, or another job, you first have to find an opportunity that suits you. Keep your eyes and ears open for any job that fits your situation.

Before you sign on the dotted line, be sure to check out your potential new employer with the Better Business Bureau. They can tell you if the company has ever had any complaints lodged against it. Always do this before accepting a job offer. Visit *www.bbb.org*.

Where to Find a Job

You can find job listings in most newspapers on a daily basis. The same can be said for local and national magazines. Their classified sections can be filled with work-at-home offers. You can find jobs doing anything from stuffing envelopes to making jewelry. Be very careful about jobs that ask you for money up front. Check out the business in detail. Ask to speak to employees. And remember, things that seem too good to be true often are.

However, there are plenty of legitimate businesses that need help on a part-time basis. Many of these jobs can be done in your home. If you can't find a job you're looking for, take inventory of your skills. Is there a business you could run from home? A product or a service you could sell? Do you have a way to market your service or product?

Home-Party Businesses

The home-party business is booming. From toys to stamps to candles and more—there are tons of things you can sell from your home. These businesses work through social gatherings where products can be sold to friends, family members, and other guests.

The companies that originally sell the products usually offer training and support. Many offer incentives as well—surely you've seen the pink Mary Kay cars out on the streets. These opportunities can be a great start for you.

You've probably heard of multilevel marketing or pyramid schemes. Be sure your new business doesn't fall into this category. Look for the Direct Seller's Association logo or affiliation with any sell-from-home business you join. Visit *http://dsa.org*.

The key to a successful home-party business is finding something that you really love. Your passion will help you be the salesperson that you need to be. This way, you won't feel like you're begging people to buy your products.

Fitting a Job into Your Life

The problem with working from home is time. Most jobs from home will require you to find the time to do them. Skip the tendency to put it off until bedtime. This will only make you cranky and push your body out of whack.

If you are going to work from home, most experts agree that you need to set office hours for yourself. This can be very difficult to do when you're dealing with a newborn baby. It does get easier as your baby gets older. Naps and routines do become more predictable, making it easier to say, I'm going to have office hours during nap times. Office hours might be when you make calls, do paperwork, or even complete your actual job.

Having the support of your husband is crucial to making an at-home job work. Be sure to talk to him about all the possibilities before you accept a new assignment. Having his support will make finding the time and the effort easier, not to mention curtail fights over your job.

Holding Your Head High

There are some who feel that staying home and raising children is not hard work. Or they feel that it is work not worthy of smart women. The truth is, staying home is some of the hardest work you'll ever do. No one has the right to diminish your commitment and devotion to your family.

Rude Comments

Believe it or not, there are people out there who will make rude comments to you about your choice to stay home. They might say things like, "You're too smart to stay home," "What a waste of a good mind," or "You'll be so bored." These small-minded people aren't able to see that raising children is a very important task that is best left to those who are smart and competent. Parents are not only caregivers but playmates, teachers, homemakers, and role models. Some argue parenting is the most important job in the world.

What do you say to a friend who constantly remarks how awful it must be to stay home all day?

Your friend may have no idea what you do at home, so offer to enlighten her. Or she may simply be projecting how she would feel if she were at home all day. Either way, be sure to point out that your choice works for you and that being a stay-at-home parent has its challenges, just like any job.

You can be prepared with a snappy comeback for when you hear these remarks, or you can take the high road and ignore the comments from people who don't understand. No matter how you choose to respond to the negativity of others, always maintain your confidence in your choice.

A Noble Job

Children really are the future, no matter how clichéd that sounds. When children are given good, healthy starts in life, they grow up to teach the same qualities to their families. This helps them to be good leaders in the future. Your investment in your child is not only a great experience for you, but it is also a contribution to the future of society. Parenting is a noble job; don't let anyone convince you otherwise.

The time you spend in the playroom with your baby may very well be preparing your child for the boardroom. Think of all the great things you learn as a child. You learn about sharing, being friendly, bargaining, and other negotiations. These are the skills that will guide your little one through school, friendships, jobs, relationships, and, one day, his very own family.

Staying at home works very well for many families. It can be fun, exciting, and cost-effective. Remember that your children are only young once; being with them as they grow is an investment in their future. Chances are you'd only regret missing these important years of your child's life, but you'll never regret being there for every exciting milestone.

Chapter 16

Day Care and Babysitters

The thought of leaving your baby is probably a very difficult one. However, while half of mothers will return to work, the other half will eventually need to hire someone to help them with child care, even if only for a brief time. By utilizing a wide variety of choices and options, you can arrange child care that works well for you and your family.

Choosing Child Care

There are more decisions to make today than ever before when it comes to child care. With all of the options available to you, you may feel like you're swimming in choices. This doesn't necessarily make your decision any easier. In fact, it may seem to complicate things for you. However, there are ways to help yourself in this regard.

Know Your Options

Before you make a decision, you need to fully explore all of your options. Look at what is available around you. Do not limit yourself to only what you see on the surface. Dig deeper into the culture of child care in your area. Are there professional organizations? Home day cares? Leave no stone unturned while searching for the best option for your family.

Ask people you know what types of child-care options they know of in your area. Talk to the people who you work with and those who your husband works with. Talk to the childbirth educators in your area, as they often work with new families and may be aware of other options.

You may think of looking for child care near your home. That is never a bad option, but it can limit you. Do not forget to look at choices for child care near your workplace or your husband's workplace. You may also find a perfectly good location at the halfway mark, so do not limit yourself too much geographically.

Questions to Ask

One of the best ways to gather information is to ask questions. First, you need to question yourself. What types of care do you know about? Which do you think matches your child? How would explain your theories on child raising to a child-care provider? What hours do you need? Are you flexible?

FACT

For a great review of options available all over the world, from questions to ask a child-care provider to quizzes to help you determine a child-care match for you, look on the Web. Visit *http://childcare.about.com.*

Once you've gotten the basics down of what you need for your baby and family, it is time to start figuring out which type of care is right for you. Do you prefer that your baby be in your home? Someone else's home? A day care? Do you want your child alone or with other children? What policies does the facility have for sick children and sick care providers? What are the hours of the facility? Or how many hours can a single provider work per week?

Ask about pay rates. How often is payment expected? How does the provider wish to be paid? Will they provide a tax ID number so that you can claim the money spent on child care on your taxes? Do they have part-time rates? Are there other fees expected, like a registration fee or a materials fee?

What about feeding your baby? Will you bring breastmilk? What about other solids? Are they provided or are you expected to provide them? What do they do about allergies?

Is the facility certified? Are the staff trained? Is the staff trained in emergency management or infant/child CPR? There are many questions to ask. Some will be more important to you than others. Be sure to have all of your questions answered prior to signing a contract.

Day Care

The licensed facility that houses numerous children, usually broken down into groups by age, is probably one of the most well-known types of child care. There are some chains that are nationally known and others that are local. Your state or local authorities should license all of these facilities. Be sure to ask to see copies of their current licenses if they are not posted.

The Benefits of Day Care

Day care offers many benefits, though some will vary depending on the facility you choose. One of the biggest benefits is that someone will always be there, even if a certain worker is ill or needs vacation time. This can be a very big issue for you, depending on the flexibility you have at your job.

You may also enjoy the routine that has proven effective through use for a long period of time. If this is a national chain, you know that there was probably a lot of thought put into the curriculum, even for the infant ages. This curriculum probably follows a pattern throughout the year.

Another nice thing about a day-care setting is the other children. Even in the youngest age group, your baby is likely to have others around of the same age. Many of these children will stay together as they grow, providing long-term relationships for your baby.

The Drawbacks of Day Care

Yes, there is a downside to day care as well. One drawback many parents talk about is the inflexibility of the hours and off days. If your job doesn't have rigid quitting times and there are days you need to stay late, this can cause a problem if your day care closes before you leave work. You may also have a job where you work certain holidays but the day care is closed.

QUESTION?

How old does a baby have to be for day care?
Generally speaking, the youngest most day cares will allow is an infant who is six weeks old. So if you need to return to work sooner than six weeks after birth, you may need an alternative, at least for a while.

If your child is sick, you cannot bring her to day care. In fact, most facilities have a twenty-four-hour rule. This means that if your child was sent home sick in the morning on Tuesday, your child can't come back to day care for twenty-four hours after the last symptoms disappeared, which may mean more than one missed day of work.

One of the biggest drawbacks to day-care facilities is the mass-market feel. Your child may get less individualized care and attention than she may get in other child-care settings. It can also be that your child is exposed to behaviors that you aren't very pleased with. That can vary from poor grammar to biting and hitting.

Family as Child Care

Using family as a form of child care is not a new or unpopular concept. The family member can be your husband, a grandma, an aunt, a cousin—nearly anyone you call family. You may feel more comfortable with this as a new mother, because you know the people who are caring for your baby.

All in the Family

The opportunity to use your family as child care may present itself while you are pregnant. Your loving mother or mother-in-law might begin to drop delightful hints about how wonderful it would be to watch the baby while you go to work. For many families, this works out very well.

You typically pay your family members less (if at all) to help out while you work. They are also usually more flexible in terms of hours. Your baby will be either in your home or in another home that is familiar to him.

FACT

One benefit to having family members care for your baby is that they can drive your baby around. You will feel comfortable enough to have your baby ride in the car with them, which means you might be able to have your baby driven to well-checkups, photo appointments, and play dates, without your ever having to leave work.

This option usually results in fewer sick days, due to your baby's lack of exposure to other children. However, if the family member you have chosen is sick one day, you are left high and dry. Obviously, planned away dates can be worked around, but it's often these unexpected days off that can be troublesome.

Good Families Gone Bad

There are also problems with using your family for child care. One of the largest problems can be if your philosophies in child rearing don't match. It's much harder to have control over a family member than over other providers. If the baby's grandmother disagrees with you about when to start solids, how to dress your baby, or other parenting decisions, you may find your wishes being violated while you're not at home.

The real problem with family members as child-care providers occurs when they do not work out. Part of this is because it is personal. Termination of such a child-care situation can be awkward and hurtful for one or both parties.

Try to spare hurt feelings up front. In the beginning, sit down and have everyone involved agree that if it's not working out for either party, you'll agree to amicably part ways with no hard feelings. This is not a foolproof precaution, but it's worth a shot.

If the family member terminates the agreement, you might find yourself stuck having to find replacement child care right away. You might not be mentally, monetarily, or otherwise prepared to handle the sudden search for child care. The good news is that this is usually harder on you than it is on your child.

If you're on the other side of the fence and you find yourself having to end the child-care arrangement, you'll have a bit more control of the situation. You can find replacement child care before you let the family member know it's not working out. Whatever your reason for terminating such an agreement, be kind about it; you don't want to ruin relations with a well-loved relative over this.

Au Pairs

An au pair is usually a trained nanny from a different country. This is someone who you hire to live in your home and help you with child care for a set number of hours a week in exchange for a room of her own and a basic salary. Au pairs are great for many types of situations, including families with odd work hours, multiple children, or other special needs.

Choosing an Au Pair

Au pairs usually come from au pair agencies located around the world. The amount of training and experience of each au pair may vary wildly, as will the language your au pair speaks, depending both on the agency and the au pair.

FACT

Most au pairs are allowed to stay with a family for only a year or two. This can be heartbreaking to a young child if she grows attached to her au pair. Sadly, the rules are fairly inflexible. Keep this in mind when choosing an au pair as your form of child care.

Most au pairs are supposed to speak English, though this doesn't always work out as well as some families hope. On the other hand, some families choose an au pair mainly for her ability to speak a different language to their baby. Be sure to screen not only your agency, but also the au pair, for your desired level of English-speaking ability.

Au Pair as Family

Having someone live with you can be a blessing. You never have to worry about your au pair being on time for work. Your au pair can play with your baby in familiar surroundings. And your au pair is with your baby and family a lot, so you know what kind of person he is.

While having your au pair around can be very handy for last-minute trips, it can also be a bad situation. Remember, most au pairs are allowed to work for only about forty-five hours per week. It is easy to overwork your au pair by accident, and this will put you in violation of contract.

Having a stranger in your house can be hard to adjust to. Not only will you lose some privacy, but you will also have to put up with this person's personal lifestyle and habits. You may not approve of her choice of music or friends. In effect, you are inviting a complete stranger into your home to live with your family and care for your baby. Be absolutely sure about this person before entering into a contract.

ALERT!

Be aware that some au pairs do not work out. Some find that living abroad is more stressful than they imagined and want to go home before your contract is up. This is a situation you want to avoid, if possible. Good screening can usually prevent this from happening to you.

Nannies

The concept of a nanny may seem outdated to you, but this is actually still a popular option. You may opt for a live-in nanny or a nanny who comes in daily to help you out. Nannies do not usually come from other countries, but they may. Again, careful screening and interviewing will serve you well when choosing a nanny.

The Benefits of Nanny Care

One of the biggest benefits of a nanny is that your child receives one-on-one care from the same person every day. This can be a huge advantage for some families. This is particularly true if you have special requests or your child has special needs.

A nanny may also provide you with extra services. Obviously, you need to preplan these with your nanny, but you might ask for such services as laundry, light (or not so light) housecleaning, dishes, errands, and others. What you pay your nanny should be commensurate with her duties.

Nanny Training

There are actually nanny schools popping up in several areas around the country. These schools teach things like the basics of child development, infant and child CPR and first aid, infant care, and other important skills.

Other nannies have simply gotten on-the-job training. They may have years of experience or be just starting out, having only babysat previously. Some are college students looking to have a steady income while finishing school in the evenings, while others intend to make child care their career. Only you and your husband can decide whom you feel comfortable with.

FACT

Many nanny-training schools offer placement services. While this sounds good, it can also be quite costly. Some services charge over $1,000 to help you find a nanny. The good part is that they handle all the criminal and background investigations that may be difficult for you.

Babysitters

Even if you do not need regular child care, babysitters are common for nearly every parent. A babysitter might watch your child while you and your husband go out for dinner and a movie. Or this person might help out a bit while you catch up on things at home. No matter why you might need supplemental child care, babysitters can be very handy.

The Neighborhood Teen

Often a local teen girl in the neighborhood is adequate for most families when it comes to babysitting needs. Another neighbor with children usually recommends her. Or maybe she's a budding entrepreneur who leaves a flier in your mailbox.

FACT

Ask what the current going rate is in your community. If your parents charged babysitters $1 per hour when you were young, you're likely to be quite shocked by the fees these young people charge. The wage you choose should match her experience and what she is responsible for during her stay.

The local babysitter's training is likely on-the-job experience in conjunction with the caretaking of younger siblings. Yet, some communities do offer Red Cross babysitting training. This training teaches teens about the basics of child care, safety, and even some marketing skills.

Babysitting Services

The nice thing about a babysitting service is that they do all the screening for you. They also hunt down someone for whatever dates and times you may need. They may or may not take requests for certain providers.

> Unlike the girl who lives in the neighborhood, these sitters drive themselves to your house and drive themselves home! This is always a blessing after an evening out. Additionally, you might find individuals with more experience through a babysitting service.

You will usually pay a bit more for the service than you might pay your neighborhood teens. There are also usually a minimum number of hours that they will work, so if you don't stay out that long, you still have to pay for it. Sitters from a service are usually older and have more experience, but the drawback is that you might not have a chance to meet them until they show up at your door, ready to work.

Monetary Issues with Child Care

There is no doubt about it: child care costs money. You will be paying for a valuable service, and this service can come at quite a high price. Trying to figure out how much to budget for child care can be a difficult task. This is particularly true if you don't have a real clue about current child-care costs. Begin researching different child-care costs for day care, au pairs, nannies, or babysitters as soon as you become pregnant. Consider the following information about the costs of each option:

- **Day care:** Day-care costs will depend on whether it is a chain or a large day care versus a family-run day care. You may also receive cost breaks as your child grows. Some chains even run coupons or offer price breaks for referrals to other parents.

- **Family care:** Family care can be free or low cost. Just remember that you might get exactly what you pay for. Even if a family member begs to babysit for free, you might consider insisting on a pay rate to keep the arrangement professional.
- **Au pairs:** The weekly cost of an au pair is not as much as other child care, but there are hidden costs. There is the agency fee and the fee for health insurance for the au pair, not to mention basic room and board.
- **Nannies:** Nannies may cost the same or a bit less than day care. The good news is that the price may be the same for one child as for two or three. There is also less likelihood that the nanny will charge based on the age of the child.

There are cost incentives to almost every type of child care. The main questions to keep in mind include what you are asking of the child-care provider, how many children she will be expected to watch, the ages of the children, and how many hours per week you expect to need her services.

One of the benefits of having to pay for child care is that there are certain tax incentives available. What type of tax incentive and how much of an incentive it really is will depend on many factors. Part of this is based on the cost of child care, your annual combined income, and other factors.

ALERT!

Tax law changes very frequently. Be sure to contact your tax advisor or the Internal Revenue Service (IRS) about the actual amount of deductions and what type of child care can be deducted. *Visit www.irs.gov.*

The Flexible Spending Account (FSA) is a great way to save money on child care. You choose the amount you wish to set aside for child care by taking a pretax portion out of each paycheck. You then apply to receive these funds back over the course of the year.

However, once you have placed the money aside, it is difficult to change your elections for deductions during the year. You usually have to wait for open enrollment to make changes. You will also be unable to get a regular tax break on monies that have been reimbursed through your FSA.

Making Child Care Work

Finding the ideal situation takes time and research. It also takes a leap of faith. This is particularly true if you had to choose your child care prior to the birth of your baby. Sometimes conflicts don't arise until after you've been with a provider for a while, and other times it is apparent immediately. Still, there are solutions for most problems.

Conflict with Care Providers

There will be times when you and the person caring for your baby don't see eye to eye. This may be a small issue, a large one, or even several small issues. No matter how big or small, it deserves your attention. If you are constantly worried about what is going on with your baby during the day, you will be distracted and anxious at work.

Try a quick chat with the person you are having the conflict with as soon as possible. Explain the situation and how you feel about it. Tell the person what you need done to rectify the situation. You don't need to be rude or loud or point fingers, but do be succinct and clear. Remember, you are your baby's advocate. If this solution does not work, you may need to go above the person's head, to their boss. Use the same tactics as before. If the issue still cannot be resolved, it may be time to find new child care.

Not the Right Match

If you are simply not meshing with the person or people taking care of your child, that is also a problem. Low-level stress can eat away at you. You might even wonder if the person is taking the bad situation out on your child while you are at work.

There is also nothing wrong with admitting that your choice isn't right for you or for your baby. There may be personality conflicts. It may be that the location or times of the day care provider don't work as well as you had thought. Whatever the reason, be sure to speak up.

You probably signed some form of contract with your day-care provider. Be sure to read it thoroughly, particularly in terms of breaking the contract. This will include how much notice you are to give the provider as well as other technical details. Be sure to hang on to your copy of this agreement.

Gross Violations

You may also find yourself in the unlikely situation of suffering gross violations of state regulations. If the problem is with regulation set forth by the state or local authorities, you will want to contact them directly. You should also remove your child from any dangerous situation.

There may also be gross violations of your personal desires, like feeding your child something you've specifically said not to feed him. Perhaps they let your child go home with someone else, like a grandparent, without checking for ID. Maybe even a personal nanny or an au pair drove your child somewhere when you specified against it. These may all be grounds for termination or serious probation. Only you can decide how serious these situations are for your family.

Overall, finding the right type of day care for your baby can be time consuming. There are many choices that may be available to you, though not every choice will work for your situation. Take all factors into consideration before choosing a child-care solution for your baby. It should be one that you feel comfortable with from the beginning.

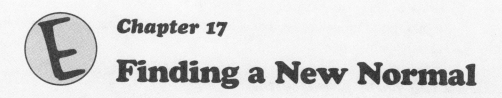

Chapter 17

Finding a New Normal

Having a baby changes your life. No one doubts this statement. Once your baby arrives, you'll probably be longing for your life to go back to normal. But the truth is, your life never goes back to the way it was before giving birth. You must instead find a new normal. This means that you will find acceptable changes to eating and sleeping habits, different quantities of free time, and even a whole new outlook on life. But relax; this task isn't nearly as scary as it sounds.

Becoming the Mother You Want to Be

You probably have a good idea of how you want to mother your child. This usually comes from a combination of your life experiences and role models. Or perhaps you have singled out what you judge to be poor parenting decisions and hope to escape committing them yourself. No matter what kind of motherhood guidelines you have set for yourself, things will always change as your baby grows.

Drawing from Experience

When you were growing up, you likely kept a running list of all the things your parents did that you didn't want to do to your children. Yet, as you grew older, you probably realized that your parents didn't do as bad a job as you once estimated. After all, they raised you, didn't they?

While it's certainly a good idea to learn from your own less-than-perfect childhood experiences, remember that your vision at the time may have been skewed. Kids often overreact when they are young, and no one likes being told what to do. You'll soon realize that this is part of your job as a parent. Telling your child what she should and shouldn't do is your way of keeping her safe while she's young. Just be sure to keep in mind that nobody's perfect. You, too, will make mistakes as a parent. But just as you once did, your child will likely come to a realization one day that even parents are only human.

Parenting as a Partnership

The hard part of parenting may not be deciding how you want to parent; it may be hashing out a parenting philosophy that works for both you and your husband. When the two of you agree, the chances are good that things will go smoothly. This means that you won't have to argue and debate every time it comes to making a decision about your baby's needs or even discipline. Having the same thoughts helps present a united front in parenting, something that becomes very important as your child grows up.

Remember that this is a partnership. Talk to each other and figure out if you have similar goals. Perhaps it's just how you intend to get there that is different. If you both believe that your child should learn to respect his elders, how do you intend to get there? One of you might believe that constant reinforcement by encouraging your child to say respectful things is best, while the other may believe that role modeling respect is the key.

Finding Time to Be a Wife

Yes, there is a life after baby. You can successfully be a mother and a wife, though some fine tuning may be necessary. Priorities shift, free time shrinks, spontaneity issues arise, and generally, life is different with a baby. It will take some effort on both your and your husband's part to make your relationship work with a new baby in the house.

Feeling Sexy

It can be really tough to feel sexy as a new mother. This may have nothing to do with your sex life; it is more connected to how you feel about your body. Giving birth changes how you feel about your body. You may feel very powerful and lovely after giving birth, or you might feel tired, run down, and out of shape. These are all normal variations.

Don't forget to treat your body well! Consider a manicure, pedicure, or massage to give yourself a boost and help you feel attractive. Often these simple things can be very helpful in getting your healthy body image back. You haven't lost it forever; it's just hidden.

How you feel about your body may be very different from how your husband feels about your body. If you feel negative about your body, don't keep repeating it out loud for others to hear. They may think you look great. The constant repetition will convince them they are wrong. Just remember sexy is more a state of mind than a physical state of being.

Date Nights

Date nights are simply times you carve out of your hectic life to be alone with your husband. This is a foreign concept to most postpartum families.

However, it is a necessity to help you continue to strengthen your relationship with your husband.

Dates do not have to happen at night, or even on the weekend. A date for you and your husband can simply consist of a few uninterrupted hours together. You can sit and talk over a quiet dinner out or curl up on your couch to watch television. This is not the time to do laundry or even answer the phone.

FACT

Company parties or picnics do not count as date nights, nor does any other occasion where you are surrounded by people who desire your attention. This time is meant for you and your husband alone. Do whatever it takes to get this time to yourselves, whether it be hiring a babysitter or asking a family member to come pick up the baby for a while.

You may choose a time when your baby is sleeping to reconnect with your husband. This option does not require that you hire help for the baby, but if the baby wakes up, this will certainly distract you from your date. Do whatever you can to limit distractions during these intimate times.

A Sense of Self

You might have worried that becoming a mother would completely change your identity, and in a way, it did. You can't become a mother without making huge changes in your life. However, the person you used to be is not gone forever—she has just evolved.

This evolution takes time. Your transition to motherhood doesn't end when your baby is born. While the pregnancy does confer the rite of motherhood upon you, the growth over that first year is what changes you. There are ways to influence these changes so that you don't lose yourself.

Time for Yourself

One of the most important things you need to remember to do is to find time for yourself. This can be difficult as a new mother. You may feel torn between home, work, and family. By the time you try to add the demands of being a daughter, a wife, a friend into the mix, you may feel that there is nothing left for you.

Taking a break for five or ten minutes a day to do something you want is not always easy. You may need to schedule this time to ensure that you get it. You might even try setting the alarm for a few minutes before your baby is due to awake.

To ensure that this doesn't happen to you, set aside time for self. This can be merely ten minutes every day. Those first few days of motherhood you may decide to use this time to shower. As your baby grows and becomes less dependent, you can move away more easily. This enables you to get away and take time for yourself.

Sometimes you might believe that this is a selfish attitude. Don't feel guilty—just think of the long-term benefits to you. You are much more able to think clearly and enjoy your family when you've been alone awhile. It's about self-preservation, not just a preference.

New Hobbies

One way to get out a bit more often is to take up a hobby. You might have a hobby you've done for a long time and wish to continue. Perhaps you'll pick up a long-lost hobby. Or as you evolve as a mom, you might find that a completely new hobby interests you. Any of these options is fine.

There are many hobbies that you might find interesting. Scrapbooking is a natural extension of becoming a new mother. It's the perfect time to begin to chronicle the journey of your life and your family's life. If you like singing, look for a local nonprofessional or semiprofessional singing group that performs a couple of times of year. A reading group that meets monthly might be another great idea for you as a new mother.

What if you don't have time to get out to do something?
Try the Web! For example, if you like to scrapbook, you can learn every-thing you need to know, from techniques to materials. Check out sites like *http://scrapbooking.about.com* and *www.twopeasinabucket.com*.

Whatever you decide to do, remember to have fun. If you're a type-A mom, avoid going out and immediately taking over the organization or join-ing the board of directors. Remember, this is a hobby. Your hobby is for fun. If it's not pleasurable, don't do it.

Changing Friendships

One of the hardest aspects of becoming a mother is the way your friend-ships change. Some of your old friendships will change at this time. They may not even survive. Your new friendships are great, but they are probably baby related. You may miss the combination of old friends and everything that comes with them. Still, you have entered a new phase in your life. Not everything from past years can follow you where you're going.

Old Friends

Old friends are great. You have a history with them. You know their secrets and they know yours. The problem? Sometimes having a baby makes the friendships change, and not always for the better. If your old friends already have children, this is easier, particularly if their kids are the same age as yours. This means it's just something else you've all gone through together. That journey just strengthens the bond of friendship.

Pay attention to the news that an old friend is having a baby; it might just be time to renew the friendship. You might be able to impart valu-able advice to her, and she to you. A fresh perspective on the topic could be beneficial to you both.

If your friends don't have kids, the problem is simply that they don't understand the changes in your life. While they mentally understand that you can't drop everything and run out to a late-night movie, emotionally this is hard for them to take. This can be hard on you as well.

Try talking to your friends if you notice tension. This doesn't mean the friendship is over; it's simply changing. All relationships require work. This is true even of the best of friendships from years past. Do the work to keep friendships strong and up-to-date.

Finding Time for Friends

It may seem like you are trying to divide your time between lots of places and people. Friends will be one of the slices of life that will need to be addressed. It can be a lot of fun to go out with your friends, and you may find going out with them to be a great source of relief.

Turnabout is fair play. Don't forget to let your husband have a night out with the guys occasionally too. It can go a long way toward friendly relations in the home if he can get out and be with his friends for a while. If you appreciate this small luxury, doesn't it make sense that he would too?

Going out with your friends can be a sanity saver. Your friends can be people that you can talk to about your life and its many changes. They can also be people whose company helps you forget your cares for a while and relax. It tends not to matter where you go or what you do. The simple act of getting out affirms the good feelings associated with being with friends. Sometimes a nice dinner or a movie at a friend's house can change your whole outlook.

Try to find new ways to be with your friends. Invite them to go on a walk with you at the park. Consider going to a less-crowded matinee during the day, where your baby can come along for the ride. Finding creative new ways to be together will help you nurture your friendships as well as incorporate being a mother into your existing life.

The Importance of Alone Time

You may find it hard to believe that your baby is not connected to your hip permanently. It is perfectly acceptable to get out of your house without taking anyone with you. Realizing this is one of the hardest hurdles you may face, unless of course the hardest hurdle you face is actually leaving the house. There will be days when you may consider begging your husband to watch the baby while you go to the grocery store alone. Alone has a whole new meaning now that you're a mom. When you start believing that the grocery store is a hot hangout, it's time to get out alone more often.

It can be difficult to leave your baby in the care of someone else, even if it is just your husband. Regardless, you need to get away. Your baby needs to learn that sometimes Grandma or Daddy or Aunt Rosie will be in charge. And certainly your husband needs to learn to take care of your child without your help.

ALERT!

If you can't get out and be alone, take a mental holiday. When your baby is asleep or safely occupied, put on some music that reminds you of a pleasant time and relax in a chair. Close your eyes and imagine the beach, or consider taking a warm bath alone. Sometimes alone time can happen in a room full of people.

It is understood that no one takes care of your baby quite like you do. But sometimes the learning curve of leaving your husband and his child alone, despite harmless mistakes, is a good thing. Remember, you should not feel guilty about needing to be away for a while. To care for your family, you need to be in tip-top emotional shape. A moody, neglected mom can't help anybody.

Pampering Yourself

The idea of pampering yourself usually brings to mind a massage or a pedicure. While these are definitely enjoyable, they are not the sole ways of looking after your mental, physical, and emotional well-being. Pampering yourself contributes to all sides of you and is a necessary part of being a mom.

The Mental Side

One of the many disheartening feelings of pregnancy is one of forgetfulness. You perhaps lost your keys more often than not. Maybe you forgot your mother-in-law's birthday or some other important event. You basically had days where all you wanted to do was scream, "Give me my brain back!"

FACT

While pregnant women will usually tell you that the last thing they feel is smart, research shows the opposite. Despite feelings of forgetfulness, pregnancy actually increases the intelligence of women. Even though you feel frazzled, you aren't losing brain cells by the thousand.

Somehow, you probably tricked yourself into believing that as soon as the placenta was out, the hormones would leave and your brain would resume its normal functioning. The bad news is that it doesn't often work that way. However, there are things you can do to help yourself. The key to staying mentally fit and alert is to use your brain. You've probably heard the phrase "Use it or lose it." This holds true for your brainpower. The postpartum period is a great time to stretch your mental muscle.

You may find that a local college or organization has a monthly lecture series that you can attend. Consider switching your radio station in the car to some of the higher-brow talk shows. Basically try to engage your brain with thought-provoking activities. If you love to read, do it often. Consider joining a book club. If you don't have time to read, try playing Books on Tape while you are at home with your baby or driving in your car.

If you are working, check for a local "lunch and learn." These are often seminars held during lunch hours, where you bring your lunch and eat during the lecture. They are often less formal, but still informative. The timing of these also eliminates the issue of guilt for leaving at night when you're gone all day.

Anything that you do to stimulate your brain will help you stay mentally alert. Staying in the habit of taking a class or exercising your ideas is a great way to build the love of lifelong learning. A side benefit is that as your baby grows up, he will also inherit your love of learning.

The Physical Side

While the physical benefits of exercise for the body are well known, many new moms still don't tend to give fitness a fair shake. Energizing the body can help you stay physically and mentally alert. It can also help you stay in touch with your new postpartum shape, contributing to your positive self-image.

FACT

There are physical benefits to massage aside from relaxation. It can actually help boost your immune system, increase your flexibility, increase your sense of well-being, increase blood flow, and promote relaxation. All of these are good things for your mind and body.

When you feel good about your body, you tend to have better self-esteem. You also are less susceptible to illness and infection. Having kids makes you a bit more prone to catching everything that comes around, simply because you're exposed to more. This is particularly true if your child is in a day-care or school situation. So your physical health has physical, mental, and emotional benefits.

The Emotional Side

The relationships around you are so important these first years of being a new mother. Having others to turn to for support and conversation can make a world of difference. It helps prevent you from feeling isolated and gives you a sounding board as well as support for your decisions.

ALERT!

Don't be afraid to let go of a relationship that is constantly sour. This only poisons your mind and heart. As a new mother, you need to avoid unnecessary stress at all costs. A friendship that makes you upset is not a friendship at all, and not worth your time or energy.

If you find that there are certain people who are constantly negative toward your attitudes and opinions about parenting, you may need to address this issue with them. If this is your parent or a friend, explain your beliefs and ask her to explain hers. Don't worry about convincing her, just let her know you're not going in blind; you do have theories and you'll deal with the outcomes. Everyone has to parent his or her own way, including you.

Keeping this emotional barrier is a way to grow strong and healthy while you stretch your wings and learn to fly as your own parent. Emotionally you will be stronger for everything you've learned being a mother yourself. Just remember to feather your nest with the tools and people that you need to survive the journey of new motherhood. As you go and grow in your confidence in parenting, you'll figure out what works for you, meaning you'll rely less on others. Try new things out and see how they work and how they feel. Remember, as your baby changes and grows, you'll need different sets of skills to help him.

Moving Forward as a Mom

As your baby gets older, you'll start to look back at his life so far. Try to remember the first few moments you held your tiny, precious newborn.

How did you feel? What did you see when you looked ahead? It is often amazing to you to realize how far you have come in twelve short months.

Recording Your Progress

One of the first gifts you probably got at a baby shower or for a newborn gift was a baby book. These can be fun places to record memorable firsts and funny stories during the first year or two of your baby's life. These books usually have a place for you to write a sentence or two and include some pictures and other memorabilia, including hospital tags, cord clamps, locks of hair, and the like.

You can also use a "baby's first year" calendar to record much of the same information. This is usually a much more compact format, and you may find it less intimidating than an entire book. This is also handy for mothers of multiples.

If you have older children, a baby book or calendar is a great tool to help them stay involved and busy at the same time. Allow them to have their own version. Not only will it keep their hands busy, but also it will be a great gift as you look back!

You can move beyond the baby book concept in your records. Try a journal or a scrapbook or a combination. This will help you capture more of the flavor of everyday life and not simply keep a chronological record of illnesses, steps, shots, and baths. This can be done with images of the first year, journals, letters, and quotes. The idea is to be creative.

As you write things down, you'll see that you have come a long way in mothering. Being able to reflect back through your journals will show you the amazing growth you've made. This is one way to gain confidence in your mothering.

Gaining Confidence in Your Mothering

The confidence you gain as you experience new things with your baby is amazing. Many times you don't even realize what you've gained over the course of a year. You've learned not only to give birth to a new human being, but to care for her and raise her from a tiny, helpless creature to a toddler who desires some independence.

FACT

There are days in your journey of motherhood, and these go well beyond the first year, where you will consider your day a success if everyone is alive at the end of it. Don't let this shake your confidence; it's a period of learning and growth for everyone.

In the beginning you may have been unsure of your decisions as a parent. You, perhaps for the first time, realized that you and your husband alone were completely responsible for another human being. You made careful choices according to your and your family's needs, and you learned from your mistakes. You have become the perfect mother for your baby, mistakes and all.

Though the period of the first year is one of adjustment as a new mother, don't be frightened. Find yourself. Do what you need to do to take care of yourself and your family. Find joy in life. Rejoice with your friends. Be alone and like yourself. Flex your spirit, your mind, and your body. Celebrate motherhood!

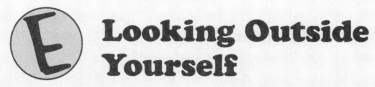

Chapter 18

Looking Outside Yourself

E ventually there comes a time when you need to get out of the house. Your world will begin to revolve less around just your new baby and more around your new life as a whole. This change comes at different times for everyone. If you feel like getting out and being social at six weeks postpartum, go for it! If it's later, don't worry. There are lots of ways to get out and enjoy other grown-ups. They can be old friends or new friends. It really doesn't matter, as long as you enjoy their company.

Finding New Friends

A good friend is worth her weight in gold. This is really true when you are in such a state of flux as the first year of your baby's life. The changes that you go through physically and emotionally require the ear of a good friend. Though your relationships with old friends have changed over the years, you may still have some of them in your life. If so, you're lucky. However, you also need to find new friends to share your new life with.

One of the great things about having a baby is the opportunity to make new friends. A baby is always a great conversation starter. Not to mention that you might even make friends in all the prenatal, childbirth, and other classes you take. You have an instant bond! These friendships that are built around your children are wonderful in many respects. They give you a wide variety of children the same age to look at and enjoy. It also gives your baby instant playmates as he gets older and begins to play near other children.

As your and your friends' children grow, you may notice that they want to play together less and less. This doesn't mean an end to your friendship. Just remember, kids have opinions too. You and your friend will just have to figure out a normal state for your friendship without the kids.

The hard part is that your children may be the only things you have in common. This is not always a bad thing. It is just something that might make your friendship a bit harder to manage, like changes to older friendships. Consider it variety—the spice of life! You never know when these new friends will be very old friends.

Baby Rivalry among Mothers

It is only natural to think that your baby is the cutest, smartest, and best at everything. In fact, you may absolutely know this. That said, it is also normal to look at other babies and wonder if your baby is on target, ahead, or behind the natural curve of things. This may lead you to compare your baby with others in your neighborhood.

Why Making Comparisons Is Normal

It is perfectly normal to look at the baby next to you in the pediatrician's office and wonder if your baby is doing the same things. Or you may see another infant in baby gym class rolling over while your precious bundle still just lies there and smiles.

Making comparisons from baby to baby is natural and normal. It's simply a part of human nature. You want to know that your baby is where he should be for his age. You want to reassure yourself that there isn't a problem with his growth or development, and comparisons are the easiest way to reassure yourself.

Why Comparisons Are Dangerous

While it is perfectly normal to compare, remember that it can be dangerous. Pay attention to your obsessing over the skills of your baby. If your concerns are that great, be sure to have a chat with your pediatrician. She should be able to give you a handy chart showing some ranges for normal activities of a baby the age of your little one.

The key to remember is that there is always a range of normal. Just because your neighbor's baby rolled over at two weeks of age doesn't mean your baby is destined for subpar schoolwork for not rolling over until six weeks. There are many considerations to take into account, including the gestational age at birth (remember, preemies take a while to catch up), body weight, freedom to move around and play, parental involvement, and many others.

The constant comparisons will serve only to drive you crazy. Remember, less is more, and every child is an individual. Real concerns should be taken to your pediatrician; push the silly stuff aside.

Mothers Groups

Mothers groups can be such a blessing! You've got women to talk to and babies to play with—who could ask for more? These groups are designed to help boost your confidence as a new mom and educate you on issues that you may not have thought about since becoming a mother.

Many groups will have monthly or biweekly meetings. Usually, part of the group time is spent in an educational endeavor, in a loosely based, kid-friendly way. Topics might be postpartum depression, knowing when to call your pediatrician, weight loss, choosing child care, or other hot new-mom topics.

ALERT!

Don't hesitate to breastfeed at these meetings or to change a diaper. The loose format is there so that the members and speakers know that the needs of the babies come first. These won't be anything like the meetings you have or had at work. Instead, they'll be noisy and fun!

The rest of the meeting is usually social in nature. The kids can lie on the floor and play, or toddlers can play together. The moms can talk and socialize, usually over light snacks. This can be a great way to get out and meet other moms, while learning about taking care of yourself and your baby.

Where to Look

Some obvious places to look for a new-mothers group would be from your local birth network. You might also try the hospitals or birth centers in your area. There may also be community-based programs, so check the paper.

Ask other mothers if they know of any in your area. Some groups are formed from other groups; for instance, your local La Leche League may have a new mother's discussion/playgroup outside of their regular meetings. Check with local preschools to see if they run formal or informal groups for new moms and babies.

How to Start One

If you don't have any luck finding a group in your area, consider starting one of your own. Start by gathering new moms. The perfect place to start is at your childbirth class reunion. Simply tell everyone there that you're interested in starting a new-moms group.

If you want to start a mothers group in your area, ask for help! You don't need to do this alone. Ask other moms to help you. Don't be afraid to ask for help from baby-related entities, like doctors, hospitals, or toy stores. They might offer to provide speakers, space, or even snacks for your meetings and events.

From there, consider creating a brief flier and asking local birth centers and hospitals to distribute them. Be watchful, though, that you don't get too big. If that happens, ask the hospital to provide space and a coordinator. This may be the perfect outreach to new moms that they are looking for.

Rotate who brings snacks, or have everyone bring something. Consider finding a speaker to come to every meeting. Poll your new members to see what topics they would be interested in hearing about.

Dealing with Other Mothers

Being a mother can be great fun. But every now and then you run across a mom who makes your head spin. The lady doesn't know when to quit. Often, these women are insecure in their own situations and that's why they give you such grief. These moms who drive you nuts might fall into a few basic categories.

The Know-It-All Mom

This mom needs no introduction. She knows everything. At first it may seem like a great relationship. You ask a question and she has an answer. You probably even look up to her. But eventually you realize that in her answers it's her way or the highway. If you don't follow her advice to the letter, you may have to answer questions from her about why not. Or perhaps you didn't even ask her opinion and just went out on your own. How dare you! Now you'll get an earful.

Know-It-All Mom has an answer for everything. She can quote to you from every manual and every pediatric association on what to do when. The problem is that there is no room for flexibility. Babies need flexibility.

Follow your gut instincts. Be your own person and do what is right for your baby, even if it goes against Know-It-All Mom's advice. You and your baby will be just fine.

While you can't completely ignore Know-It-All Mom, just smile and nod as she doles out advice. Stay strong in your convictions. Take what advice you can use and toss the rest.

The Superwoman Mom

Superwoman Mom is a hard act to follow. She may work, have a spotless house, and have a spotless car all while caring for her immaculate baby. (She and baby probably wear matching clothes too.) Even though this woman is not out to get you, you may feel that way. She probably doesn't say anything to you about being Superwoman Mom. She doesn't have to say a word. You feel inadequate simply by being near her.

You don't invite her over because you have cookie crumbs on the floor and dirty laundry stacked higher than the book shelves. You wince when you notice the baby stains on your clothes and the specs of dirt on your baby so microscopic you need to look to see them. But you know she notices.

The truth is Superwoman Mom doesn't notice. She's too wrapped up in making her life spic-and-span to notice anyone else. She's also not out to get you or out to make you feel guilty. She's just a bit of a perfectionist and absolutely harmless, once you get over how you feel when you see her.

Mother of the Perfect Baby

The Mother of the Perfect Baby is probably the hardest person to get along with. No matter what your baby does or doesn't do, it simply isn't a match for her perfect tyke. Her baby is bigger, smarter, faster, and can speak six languages before he is three months old. You'll find this mother lurks nearly everywhere. She reels you in with chitchat about your baby. She will compliment you on your baby and then pull you in when you innocently return the compliment for her baby.

These mothers are hard to ignore. They demand attention. Sometimes the best method for dealing with them is a direct method. Simply tell them you and your child are going to go play elsewhere with the normal babies. Don't get bent out of shape over the ordeal.

Creating Playgroups

Playgroups are different than new mothers groups. These groups focus more on babies than on mothers, though social time for moms is often built in. The idea is to gather together with similar-aged children for playtime. Playgroups can give children a great foundation for lifelong friendships.

If you want to start your own group, there are a few things you need to do. Looking for members for a playgroup is usually very easy. You will probably want to limit the number of members to six to eight moms. This allows you to usually be able to meet at homes rather than find a place to meet outside or at another location.

FACT

Some playgroups can also act as babysitting co-ops. If this is something you are considering for your group, be sure to have it all in writing so no one gets ripped off of time. This is the perfect solution to help for errand running or date night with your husband.

Locating other moms or dads with kids for playgroups is the easy part. Just look to where you know you'll find kids of similar ages. Childbirth classmates are always a good place to start. Look in your neighborhood, at the grocery, at your place of worship, or anywhere you see kids. Don't hesitate to invite people you know, but consider expanding your group to include some new people as well. The diversity can make for a great mix, not to mention some new friends. While the more the merrier is true, be sure you don't overbook your group. If so, it just becomes very crowded.

Consider locations when choosing moms. Do they all live within a reasonable driving distance from each other? Can they all drive?

If you all live close enough, trading houses isn't a problem. It can be more of a problem if you must drive far distances to make it to playgroup. If your group prefers a central location that is donated or you can rent, then that works too.

Once you have your members, figure out who will be in charge of what. Someone should take over meeting scheduling and rotating houses.

Someone else should be in charge of snacks. These jobs can rotate and should be kept very simple.

ALERT!

> If you decide to take turns providing snacks for the whole group, you may want to poll for allergies prior to doing so. While no one may have allergies, it at least helps alert you to potential problems. Giving peanut butter to a child with a peanut allergy is a recipe for disaster.

Someone should keep a calendar and a phone directory. Someone else can make notes as to who will provide snacks. Do you want the hostess to provide them? Do you want each family to bring its own snacks? There is no right answer.

A playgroup is a great way to get out. The work involved for running your own group is not as great as it seems, and it is well worth the effort. By recruiting a couple of other moms to share the workload, it can become something to really look forward to, particularly as the babies begin to play together.

Playgroups Gone Bad

Unfortunately, not every playgroup will be a great experience. You may find that the distance you must drive makes it less likely that you'll attend. Or perhaps Know-It-All Mom is there and she annoys you. These groups are probably more trouble than they are worth to you.

When to Leave

If you encounter a problem within a playgroup, ask yourself if it can be dealt with. Can you talk to the person who is annoying you? Or avoid that person?

If the group is far away, can you offer to host the group at your house occasionally? Perhaps you could suggest an alternative meeting place? Look for creative solutions.

If, however, there doesn't seem to be any good solution or the people you've talked to haven't been able to help, it may be time to leave. If you find yourself dreading playgroups or making excuses not to go, don't panic. Simply make the break from the group.

Making the Break

Leaving shouldn't be a mean or nasty process. Simply explain to the organizer that you need to move on for personal reasons. Point out that there is now an opening for another new mom to join.

Sometimes leaving a playgroup really isn't about anyone but you and your family. If you simply can't find the time or energy for playgroup, don't sweat it. Your baby will have other opportunities to play, and you will make your own opportunities to have time with other adults.

You don't need to make a big deal of it. You might choose to say something to the group at your last visit or simply just disappear. You should consider calling those with whom you were friends to let them know that you've left the group. Offer to continue the friendship outside of the group.

Internet Friendships

The Internet has done a lot for parenting and pregnancy. As we have moved away from our families and friends and started families of our own, that lack of personal touch has been difficult. Not only can the Internet and it's associated technologies help us stay in touch with our families, but it can help us meet friends we'd never have met any other way.

Support at Convenient Times

One of the biggest benefits of the Internet for friends is that it can be done at our convenience. You can post a message to an e-mail group or bulletin board and return later to collect your messages. This means that if you have time to read online at 2 A.M. after baby has fed, so be it!

Real-time chats are available through many different programs or services. Some of these are free while others require a service fee. These require a bit more specific timing but are optional in many online communities.

Commonality

In addition to being very convenient, these groups are often built around a common theme. This may be a due date group, where everyone is due the same month and continues after the birth. It may be a geographic region. Some groups often gather over other commonalities such as parenthood after infertility, babies after forty, younger moms, military moms, etc.

ALERT!

While these groups are great for advice, remember, they are not your pediatrician or other health-care provider. Be careful what advice you follow and adhere to from these lists. Use your common sense.

This can help create a bond between women who may never have met otherwise. It brings you together and is a safe place to ask questions. It's often a great place to ask the embarrassing questions about baby poop or bloody discharge as your periods return.

RL Meetings

Sometimes these groups even wind up meeting in real life (RL). These meetings can be very strange and exciting. Your family and friends may think you're a bit nuts, but think of it like a blind date. Always plan your out, in case you feel uncomfortable, and be aware of what's going on.

The new social you after baby is an important side to nurture. It can be difficult to find a way to integrate your motherhood with your personhood. Take the time to try to reach out to others, both near and far. Find those with similarities and differences. Be bold and confident but mostly have fun!

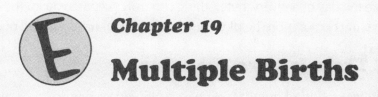

Chapter 19

Multiple Births

The rates of multiples births are skyrocketing. More and more families are dealing with babies that come in pairs or more. Most people picture their first baby being just that—one baby. However, the incidence of twins, triplets, and even more multiples is higher than you think. If your babies came together, you might feel overwhelmed and alone. Fortunately, you're not on your own. There are lots of support systems in place to help you through the shock of multiples and get on with your new life.

Dealing with Shock

Wow. Babies are definitely awesome. However, they usually come one at a time. When you happen to get an immediate second helping, you may feel completely caught off guard. Of course, you will know that you're having multiples before the day of delivery, but nothing can truly prepare you for the experience of having two or more helpless newborns in your arms instead of one.

Finding Out There Is More Than One

Hopefully you found out that you had multiples far before the birth day. Chances are you figured it out early on, or at least by twenty or so weeks. Once you found out, your reaction, and the reaction of your husband, could be wildly varied.

FACT

Multiple births are on the rise. Much of this increase in incidence is due to the advances in reproductive technologies. Though not everyone out there is pregnant with multiples because of fertility drugs or IVF, this is a common reason for multiples.

You may have been excited and happy. Perhaps you were worried or frightened. Overwhelmed is another way that many new mothers of multiples (MOMs) feel. Your husband probably experienced similar feelings. Once the initial shock wears off, there is a sense of calm. Though sometimes it's easy to mistake glazed over for calm. Be sure to seek out support from others who have been there. Ask lots of questions about how this will change things for your pregnancy, birth, and postpartum period.

The Birth

Giving birth to more than one baby is not as difficult as it may seem. While I hate that a childbirth educator might say, "Oh, you just have to push two out rather than one," that is basically the truth.

For a vaginal birth, you will have only one labor. Your cervix will dilate, much the same way any singleton mother's cervix would dilate. Though some experts say this will happen faster because of the weight of more than one baby, others say it will actually be a bit slower because of the potentially different positions of your babies. Either way, it opens once.

Once your cervix is dilated and you feel the urge to push, you will push out each baby individually. The average time between the birth of the first baby and that of the second baby is generally about seventeen minutes, though it can be less than a minute or it can be several hours. If you can, take this time to enjoy a small break to play with your firstborn.

Be sure to try to encourage your baby to breastfeed, even while you're waiting on the rest of the babies. This will help stimulate your uterus to work and give birth, as well as prevent excessive bleeding. It also gives your baby a great head start at feeding.

Between the birth of the first baby and the subsequent baby, your birth team will continue to monitor your other baby(ies). They will do this by listening to the heart rate and assessing the position, either by ultrasound or manually feeling your abdomen. This is standard procedure, no matter where you give birth.

For a cesarean, your surgery will happen as any other cesarean. You will have each baby separately lifted out of your abdomen, one at a time. This usually doesn't take any longer than a cesarean surgery for a single baby. There is rarely more than a minute or two between the births of each baby.

Prematurity

Most twins are born slightly sooner than the average singleton. Some of these multiples will be born early enough that they require special care from the neonatal intensive care unit (NICU). If your babies are born prior to thirty-six weeks' gestation, know that you'll have a special team of care providers who are used to taking care of babies born early.

ALERT!

The more babies you have in your uterus, the more likely they are to come early. It also means that they are likely to be smaller than your average multiple. Talk to your doctor or midwife about how best to prevent early labor and to increase the birth weight of your babies.

Interventions

Because you carry a higher risk for complications, you will tend to have more interventions such as fetal monitoring and IV drips and to be asked to remain in bed. You may also be moved from your labor and birth suite to the surgical suite for the actual birth of your babies, even if they are born vaginally. Be sure to ask your doctor or midwife what other interventions may be likely because you are carrying more than one baby.

Body Double

While multiples may multiply the joys, they multiply other things, too, including postpartum woes. Your body is even more tired than that of a mother of a singleton, because you just grew and gave birth to more than one baby. You may also find that you feel weaker, due to more stress and a higher blood loss with multiples.

Postpartum is difficult, any way you slice it. The sheer stress of giving birth to more than one baby also takes its toll. Add the stress of a multiple pregnancy, which may include bed rest, preterm labor, prior hospitalizations, et cetera, and it's more than twice as difficult. All of the symptoms that one would normally experience in the postpartum period are multiplied.

FACT

Having multiple babies increases the cesarean rate. Twins have a 50 percent cesarean birth rate, while triplets have about a 90 percent cesarean birth rate. Giving birth by cesarean increases the recovery time physically, making it harder to care for the multiple infants.

Getting past the immediate recovery from giving birth to multiples, you will have different recovery issues for the long term. Your abdomen is going to be more stretched than you can imagine. You will have a greater likelihood of separating your abdominal muscles. Your stretch marks will be greater in number and length.

Two for Tea: Feeding Two or More Babies

Feeding multiple babies is a challenging task, but it is one that can easily be taken on with a bit of knowledge and support. The key is preparation. Learn all you can about feeding multiples way before you are actually faced with those two or more hungry, expectant faces.

Breastfeeding

The good news is that your body knows how many babies you are having. In response, it will create enough milk to feed all of your babies. In fact, your body will usually provide more milk than one baby needs, even when you only have one. This is to ensure that the baby is never left hungry.

Make your life easier—figure out how to tell your babies apart during middle-of-the-night feedings. It can be very easy to feed the same baby twice, which means you have to wake up more often! You can use bracelets or other ideas to help tell your babies apart so you don't even have to turn on a light.

Take a breastfeeding class during your pregnancy. Find other mothers of multiples who have successfully breastfed. Talk to a lactation consultant during your hospital stay. Ask her for support in feeding your babies. They will be able to offer great positioning advice as well as other tips on feeding multiple babies.

Be sure to nurse as soon as possible. The AAP recommends that you nurse within the first hour of life when possible. If your babies are ill or for some reason cannot or do not wish to nurse, be sure to ask for help with a breast pump. Nursing and pumping in the first forty-eight hours is key to helping you establish a great milk supply for your babies.

Once you get past the hurdle of figuring out how to breastfeed and accommodating each baby's personality, it gets immensely easier. Remember, breastfeeding may be uncomfortable at first, but any discomfort should subside after the first few days, and any pain should never be extreme or long lasting. If you do experience ongoing, intense pain, get help immediately. Often, pain is caused by a very small, very fixable problem.

Your babies will let you know when they need to eat and for how long. Throw away the clocks and resist the urge to feed using any timing device other than your baby. This is the key to having them grow and nurse successfully.

After the first few days of life, you should see two to three bowel movements a day and five to six wet diapers. Your baby should have periods of sleep and periods of alertness. You should not use the way your breasts feel as a gauge for how much milk you have.

As your babies get bigger, they will go longer between feedings. You can experiment with feeding positions to find a way to feed them comfortably at the same time. There is no rule about feeding multiples at the same time; some MOMs say that feeding their babies together is great, and others prefer individual feedings. Do what works for you and your babies.

Your babies will need no supplements of water while breastfeeding. They will also not need solid food until about six months of age. The perfect first solid food will depend on the recommendation of your pediatrician, who has access to your family's health and allergy history.

As you add solid foods, the number of times a day you nurse will begin to decrease. Breastmilk still has enormous benefits for your babies. The AAP recommends that you nurse at least until the age of one.

Bottle-Feeding

Some multiples will need supplementation by alternative means. This can be by finger feeding, cup feeding, syringe feeding, or even bottle feeding. However, nursing moms (especially those with multiples) should try to avoid bottle feeding until their milk supply is well established. If any of your babies is having trouble latching on, consider avoiding bottles and using alternative methods of feeding your baby. This will help prevent additional problems with a breastfeeding latch.

Anyone can help you with these alternate feedings. Your husband, a family member or friend, even an older child can feed the baby. Be sure to use these alternate feedings as a potential break, even if you wind up using a breast pump during the feeding.

You may wish to alternate feedings of your multiples, particularly when the number of babies outnumbers the number of breasts available. For example, with triplets, you may wish to give Baby A the right breast, Baby B the left breast, and have Baby C simply rotate onto both breasts at the end of a feeding. At the next feeding, Baby B gets the right, Baby C gets the left, and Baby A nurses at both at the end of the feeding. Continue this rotation every feeding.

Multiple bottles or cups can be a pain to keep clean. Be sure to enlist help in the washing, drying, and sterilizing of these items. Microwavable sterilizers can be very handy, and they decrease the need for huge numbers of feeding accessories. They are also good for sterilizing toys, breast pump parts, and other baby items.

To warm up a cold bottle of breast milk or anything else, simply put the container in a large cup and let hot water pour over it from the sink. Never microwave the contents of a bottle, no matter what is inside, as this can cause hot spots.

If you use artificial baby milk, it is possible to mix or make up what you need only once a day. Many families do this in pitchers, stored in the refrigerator. Be sure to check labels for how to mix ABM, particularly when making it in larger quantities. You can actually harm your baby by making it incorrectly.

Getting Support

Everyone needs support after having a baby. While many women like to think they can go it alone, it is simply not true. The idea that you can be Supermom with one baby, let alone more than one, is absolutely ridiculous. Everyone needs support, and the more babies you have, the more support you need.

Family and Friends

While your family and friends are the most obvious sources of support, it is important to ensure that they really supply the help that you need.

Have a list of chores or things that you need done. Do you need someone to run to the grocery? Can they bring you dinner? Do you have an older child who needs some special play time? Perhaps you simply want a shower. Be sure to be specific when you are asking for what you need.

Try to limit the amount of visiting your family and friends do, particularly when you need help. You may even consider setting specific visiting times; anyone coming over at any other time had better be prepared to help.

Postpartum Doulas

The easy way around asking for help from friends and family is hiring people specifically to help. This brings us to the blessing of a postpartum doula. A postpartum doula is a trained woman who specializes in helping families in the early months after the birth of a baby or babies.

She is trained to help you keep your house in order, do light housework, and teach you baby care. A postpartum doula not only knows what you need, but she is able to anticipate it before you can ask for something. In the new world of multiples chaos, there is nothing like having someone else to help out as well as take care of some of your needs.

FACT

Postpartum doula certification is available through DONA International. This organization also certifies birth doulas. Using a birth doula can help reduce the likelihood of unnecessary interventions during birth, which can make your recovery easier. Visit *http://dona.org*.

There is a certification process for postpartum doulas. I would warn you that it is fairly new, so not many doulas have had the opportunity to take part in this certification process. Ask your postpartum doula candidate about her educational history and her experience, and always talk to her references. Many postpartum doulas will have references from other parents of multiples.

Multiples Clubs

Talking to someone else who has been there can be so important. A multiples club is usually comprised of parents or other caregivers with multiples. Some groups separate themselves according to the number of multiples each member has: twins, triplets, et cetera. Other groups are all-inclusive. You may also find that clubs segregate by parents, that is, clubs for either all moms or all dads. Finding a club in your area, no matter how it is divided, is very important.

The largest organization for multiples is the National Organization of Mothers of Twins Clubs (NOMOTC). This group offers support for all multiples, not just twins. They also maintain a Web site with helpful hints and a locator for a club near you. Visit *www.nomotc.org*.

The support that you can get from the local multiples club is irreplaceable. From telling you how to manage more than one baby at a time to finding local discounts for multiples, you'll find lots of ways to benefit from your club. It is always great to be able to ask questions of other parents who have been there before. Sometimes it is nice to simply go to a meeting and be away from home for a short time.

In addition to social benefits, many clubs have special programs. Some programs include meals for new families, bed rest support for problem pregnancies, clothes closets, a library of multiples-related books, a group clothing sale, and many more projects and activities. If you have trouble finding a local club that is already organized, considering asking the hospital that delivers the most multiples in your area to consider starting a club or at least putting you in contact with others who have had multiples.

Leaving the House

Leaving the house is a must for your sanity. It also doesn't hurt to put groceries on the table. However, it can feel overwhelming to bundle up more than one tiny tyke and try to head out the door.

Planning Ahead

There is something to be said for planning ahead when you have multiples. You never know when a call will come and you'll need to go rushing out the door. Or the more likely scenario is that you need to take one of your children to the pediatrician or lactation consultant immediately.

Always have the car seats ready to go. When possible, they should always be installed in the car. When your babies are younger, bases make it easy to snap carrier car seats in and out. Consider investing in this type of system. Older babies' car seats should stay strapped in when at all possible.

Have an emergency diaper kit in the car. Put several diapers, some wipes (sealed in a plastic baggy), and one emergency outfit in a plastic grocery bag and leave it in the trunk of your car. This is not to replace anything you'd normally take on a trip. It is only for emergencies. Your normal diaper bag should be well stocked and by the door as well.

You may also want to plan on how you will carry your babies. Do they sit well in a stroller? Can you carry them in a sling or other baby carrier? Whatever works for you. Plan to bring these items.

If you can plan when you're going out, try to avoid times of day that are particularly cranky. For most families, this is nap time and feeding time. Consider planning a nap followed by a feeding right before your outing. This should give you a couple of hours to get out. Your babies will be as calm and comfortable as possible, allowing you a bit more sanity as you try to manage the gear of multiple babies.

Handling Multiple Babies at Once

It can be frustrating to have a small creature totally dependent on you. This is particularly true when you can't speak his language or always read his signals perfectly. The more babies you add to the mix, the more potential for frustration.

Staying Sane

The hardest part of having any baby is staying sane. While your previous sanity may be questionable, your mind definitely feels less fresh after having a baby or two. Part of this is due to hormonal changes that every new mother goes through. The rest will depend on your situation. And once again, multiple babies multiply the feeling of insanity.

Support

Support will help you feel sane. It will help you feel like you have a handle not only on the babies, but on your home. It doesn't matter where this support comes from as long as you get it.

Adult Time

It may seem like you spend time with only the under-one crowd. Some days you answer phone calls from people you normally would not talk to, simply to talk to adults. The top ten songs you know are mostly written by a hot chick named Mother Goose.

Do not panic! Your days like this are numbered. Just be sure to find other moms, or any adult for that matter, who you can talk to on a regular basis.

Mommy Groups

Consider visiting a new moms group. This might be specifically for moms with multiples or it could be a general group, open to all. You can usually find them in the community by contacting a local birth network or hospital. Sometimes playgroups are organized by neighborhoods as well.

Girls' Nights Out

Consider having a night a month to go out with just your friends. This could be a quick dinner at a favorite restaurant or coffee in the afternoon—no kids allowed. Hire a babysitter or get dad or another family member to watch the babies while you get out and be an adult for a while. Remember, time away from your babies can help make you a more sane mommy.

Date Night Out

An even wilder concept would be a date night out with your honey. Try to get away, just the two of you, at least once a month. Even if you can't go away overnight, there is nothing like a luxurious meal that you don't have to cook or clean up after.

Even if you can't get out of the house, spend time together. Try to ensure that you have time alone with your husband. Consider serving dinner late one night after the babies have fallen asleep. Or even order Chinese food or pizza for a less stressful meal. The trick is to have time to talk about anything but the kids. This is harder than it seems.

Dealing with Preemies

Many multiples will be born prematurely. In fact, the more babies you are carrying, the more likely you are to have the babies early, and the earlier they tend to be born. Prevention of preterm labor is a must.

Talk to your doctor or midwife about prevention of preterm labor. While these measures don't always work, they certainly don't hurt. You also need to discuss how to tell if you are having preterm labor. Early detection allows the best chance at stopping preterm labor. Even with all of these measures, many babies will be born early.

The NICU

The neonatal intensive care unit (NICU) can be a very frightening place. Tiny babies in bassinets with wires and monitors all over the place. This is likely not how you imagined your first days as a mother.

Talking to other parents who have had babies in the NICU can be very helpful. Know that this does not mean that your world has ended or that your baby will always be tiny and fragile. Finding that support for the sorrow and worry that accompany a trip to the NICU is a must for the long journey.

You will be assigned a social worker or nurse care coordinator. This person will be your go-to person when you have questions or need help. However, you should never hesitate to talk to any nurse or physician on shift. Remember, the same rules of informed consent apply in the NICU.

You will learn a whole new language as those who care for your babies explain detailed procedures to you. Don't hesitate to ask for more information. Also, remember that the babies belong to you and not to the hospital. If you have ideas about their care, particularly holding and feeding your babies, speak up!

Coming Home

When the time comes to graduate from the NICU, you might experience joy and fear. After days or months in the NICU, you've grown accustomed to having support at the drop of a hat. Remember that your babies will not be sent home until the doctor is sure that urgent medical care is not needed. In fact, most babies spend several days or weeks in a step-down unit to ensure just that.

Ask about infant CPR classes or other safety classes to help you feel more confident about parenting premature infants. Many hospitals make such classes mandatory before your babies can come home. Be sure to have a list of numbers to call if you have questions or need medication or information about caring for your babies.

Moving Forward

After dealing with the issues of prematurity, you may wonder if you will ever feel normal about your children. You may feel the need to be overprotective about your once frail children. Remember, as your babies grow up and grow stronger, these feelings will fade. You'll see them run and scream like other kids and forget that they were once tiny babies in a small incubator.

Tips to Make Life Easier with Multiples

Let's face it: you're not perfect and you can't do everything. You can't carry more than one or two babies at a time. This is particularly true when they get heavier. So even the mother who swears she'll never use a container for her babies will have to come to the realization that there is a time and a place for everything.

Strollers

Strollers are an amazing invention. That's particularly true for the fancy new strollers that hold more than one child. You can get strollers that hold three, four, five, or six babies nowadays.

FACT

Multiples draw a lot of attention. If you prefer to avoid some of that attention, consider carrying one baby in a carrier and putting one in a stroller—it lessens that multiples effect. More than two? Each parent can take a baby and one or more can be pushed in a double stroller. Twins, when very little, can both lie down in one stroller.

Choose a stroller that will be the most beneficial to you. Think of the number of children you have, including any older children. Will you have more children in the future? Does the stroller in question transport well? Does it fold up or even fit in your trunk?

The perfect stroller can be a blessing when you're out and about. Whether it is used to take a walk around the block or for shopping at the mall. The right stroller will be a great help to the mother of multiples.

Carriers and Toys

From carrier seats to swings and other containing toys, there are many choices available. These devices allow you to ensure your babies are safe while you do necessary things like go to the bathroom or feed yourself. The important thing is to remember safety first.

QUESTION?

Do you need multiples of everything when you have multiples?
No, you can easily get along with only one or a few of certain things. Items like swings, bouncers, and other containers can usually be purchased in fewer quantity than, say, car seats. Babies can use different items if you need to use something simultaneously. So one baby goes in the swing while another sits in the bouncer while you're feeding a third.

Are the devices you're using age appropriate for your children? Are they new or recent models? Do your babies like them? You need to re-evaluate these questions every so often. These items can be very expensive, even with the lower-end models. Consider borrowing some of these items or purchasing them at yard sales or discount stores. You might consider contacting your local multiples club to see if they have a lending closet or have a way to put you in contact with someone who might be getting rid of all their baby stuff.

Carriers, high chairs, bouncy chairs, and more can be great sanity savers for any mother, particularly when dealing with more than one baby. Do remember to pick your children up occasionally, as these devices can become addictive to both you and your children. Remember, tummy time is an important part of development.

Breastfeeding Pillows

Breastfeeding pillows help you breastfeed in a number of ways. They free up your hands to help you position your babies correctly or read a book while you nurse. They support your back by allowing you to sit properly in your chair or other location. And they provide a comfortable place for baby to rest while eating.

This hands-free lifesaver is a must for all breastfeeding mothers. There are special pillows made just for mothers who have multiples. Get recommendations from your friends and other parents in your multiples club. Consider asking your lactation consultant what her clients have worked well with.

Having multiple babies at once can be a wild ride. It can be frightening and overwhelming, but it can also be twice or thrice as wonderful. Once you get past the first year, life changes. Yes, it is easier to get around in many senses of the word, but it also presents its own challenges, like multiple babies running in multiple directions! Get ready!

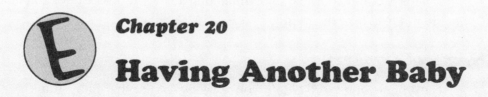

Chapter 20

Having Another Baby

Y ou've successfully survived the birth of your baby and the subsequent year. While it's been a year of changes, it has also been a year of growth. At some point during this time, you may begin to wonder if you'd like another child. This is a pretty common thought, even if it is not acted on. However, this is a big decision. There are certain questions you need to ask yourself and your husband before you even think about having another baby.

What Are You Thinking?

You've probably just been getting too much sleep if you're thinking about another baby! Or maybe the sight of your once tiny newborn blowing out his first birthday candles has you craving a tiny baby again. Whatever your reason for wanting another child, think long and hard before deciding that you are ready to take the plunge.

Practical Concerns

When trying to decide if you're ready for another baby, think not only of the high points of the first year, but the low points too. How did your first birth go? Are you ready to give birth again? Are you ready to lose sleep again? Do you have the physical and mental stamina to take care of two children, even if you will be working outside of the home?

What about monetary concerns? Do you have enough income to afford another baby? While you certainly can reuse many of the big-ticket items from your previous child, diapers are expensive!

There are also issues of medical care. Do you have insurance? What types of deductibles are in your policy? What will your out-of-pocket expenses be for this birth?

Once your new baby is here, how will you afford day care? Will it be less expensive for you to get a nanny? Perhaps the next child will be the one that breaks the budget and sees you considering staying home. There are many things to think about before having another baby. This is not to say that having another baby is a bad idea. It is just an idea that requires a lot of decisions.

Societal Pressures

Perhaps you feel like society is pressuring you to have more children. Maybe you've seen all the stories on late-night television about only children gone bad. Whatever your reason for wanting another child, you have to remember that it is yours and yours alone.

You need to not give in to societal pressures. Say no to your mother-in-law who really wants another grandbaby. Tell your child that Mommy and Daddy will be the ones to decide if they need another baby in the family. This can be hard to do.

The pressure we get from almost everyone is amazing. Once you have a baby, everyone automatically expects the next one to follow a couple of years later. And when that baby doesn't come, surely something must be physically wrong, because you obviously want another baby, right?

The Ideal Age Difference

Everyone will tell you that he knows what the perfect distance is between children. The truth is that there are benefits and disadvantages to nearly all age spreads. You need to figure out which of these benefits and disadvantages are most important to you, and which will have the most impact on your life.

Physical Healing from Previous Pregnancies

The truth is that pregnancy can take a toll on your body. How heavy that toll is depends on multiple factors. If you had a relatively easy pregnancy, stayed healthy, and had a fairly straightforward and normal birth, you will have a much faster recovery than someone who was ill, in poor shape, or had a surgical birth.

If you gave birth by cesarean, it is imperative that you wait the requested eighteen months before becoming pregnant. Getting pregnant prior to this time gives your incision less healing time and may be associated with a greater risk of uterine rupture at the incision site.

Talk to your doctor or midwife to see if they have a recommendation about how long to wait between pregnancies. They may have medical reasons for you to wait longer or shorter periods of time. Your practitioner can base this on your personal medical history rather than reading a chart someplace. Being physically ready for a future pregnancy is very important, not only to your health, but to the health of the baby as well.

How Many Kids Should You Have?

The decisions surrounding how many children you should have are personal ones. They may be made by you and your husband long before you are married, or they may come as you start to build your family. Your personal, medical, and financial well-being may all be determining factors in how many children you decide to have in your family. There is not one right answer for every family.

Only Child

You and your husband may decide that one child is enough for you. There are many families choosing to have only one child. Some benefits of having an only child are that more time, attention, and monetary resources are given to a single child since they are not divided among siblings.

FACT

The average household in the United States has about 1.86 children in it, according to the U.S. Census in 2000. However, this number is decreasing. This is not to say that there aren't still families with seven, eight, or nine children out there, because there certainly are.

Having an only child can be wonderful. You and your husband don't have to divide your time between other children and can focus on the one child. You can both go to the science fair or the school play and not tag team each other. Whatever your reasons for wanting an only child, remember that the decision is yours. Be careful to avoid pressure from family and friends who think they know what is best for you.

Perhaps the decision to have only one child was not your decision. It may have been made for you due to medical or other personal circumstances. This can be difficult to come to terms with, but families come in all shapes and sizes.

Full House

Having a house full of kids can be a wild ride. The proponents of large families say that the sibling experience is not one to be missed. The interaction and love that goes on in large families is amazing. It's also quite the operational venture for the parents as well.

Larger families learn to cope with sharing parents with each other. They also quickly learn to work together. Large families learn to share resources and take care of each other. If you came from a family that was larger, you may want either to have a larger family or to avoid one, depending on your particular experience within your family background.

You must be careful to watch what others say to you when you express your desires for a large family. Don't be discouraged by the thoughts of others. You'll often hear, "Not for me!" or "Are you crazy?" Just ignore these comments and make decisions that feel right to you and your husband.

But how many is too many? This is a very good question. The answer varies widely. The only ones who can decide how many children to have would be you and your husband. Ultimately, you shouldn't have more children than you can financially, emotionally, or physically manage.

While you may have an idea in your mind of the ideal family size, be flexible. I would advise you to have a settling-in period after the birth of each child, and then readdress the issue of more children. This prevents you from finding yourself overloaded based on a random number you may have pulled out of your head long before your wedding night.

Cost Considerations

How much could a teeny, tiny baby cost? The answer is lots and lots of money! Many times you don't think of all the costs of having a baby when considering starting or expanding your family.

What Will Another Baby Cost?

When you are considering having another baby and the discussion of cost comes up, be sure to address all of the needs of your new baby. Regarding just the pregnancy, you will need to consider the expense of prenatal medical care and figure in the cost of any additional maternity clothing. The good news is that you can save some money by recycling your old maternity clothes.

FACT

The closer together your children are, the fewer baby items you can reuse. This means having to buy an additional big-ticket item or two, such as a car seat and/or a crib. This may influence your decision on when to expand your family.

After pregnancy, the big costs of your new baby begin to add up. Child care may be the biggest cost of having another baby. You can save money by reusing some of the big-ticket items your older child has already out-grown. You may also be able to reuse some of the clothes, depending on the gender, size, and season of the births of your babies.

Planning for the Costs of Two

Having two children, even at different ages, can be a huge burden on the pocketbook. The good news is that with some planning, there are ways to make having two children affordable for most families. (And it doesn't even involve selling the first child!)

Child Care Costs for Two

Child care may be the biggest expense when you have more than one child. Planning ahead and thinking about the placement of your children can help you. For many families with two children, it will be more cost-effective for one parent to stay home with the children.

FACT

If you already use a child-care facility that you love, you may want to ask if they offer discounts for multiple children. Many child-care facilities do offer such discounts, which can be a big help to mothers of two or more children.

If staying home is not an option for either of you, there are other possibilities. One great option is in-home care. This means finding a nanny or babysitter who can come to your home to watch your children. This can be a savings of time as well as money for you. Many families find that they spend less money by using an in-home care provider for their children.

Fertility Issues

With a successful conception and pregnancy behind you, the thought of fertility issues may not have entered your mind. Your body obviously figured out what it was doing before. You got pregnant. You gave birth to your baby. That should be the end of it, no?

Will I Suffer Again?

If you had problems conceiving your first baby, you probably wonder if you will experience similar difficulties. The answer is maybe. It all depends on the diagnosis you have for infertility. Some conditions seem to go away miraculously once a pregnancy is achieved, while other conditions may have to be dealt with for every conception.

Sometimes patients find that the second time around isn't as bad as the first, because they do not feel as desperate to have a child. This is not true for everyone. Be sure to tune in to how you are feeling and use the mental-health services associated with your fertility clinic.

If you do require medical intervention to get pregnant, your reproductive endocrinologist or other specialist will be more than happy to help you achieve a second pregnancy. The more aggressive the therapy that you required the first time, the more likely you are to require therapy this time, though not always. Obviously, this can have a negative impact on finances and on your mental and emotional health.

Secondary Infertility

The rates of secondary infertility are hard to define because many women do not seek help for secondary infertility. After a year of failing to conceive in spite of well-timed intercourse and no birth control, you should seek help from your doctor or midwife. Depending on your age, they may begin testing right away or advise other, less invasive measures first.

ALERT!

If you are over thirty-five, your doctor or midwife may advise you to seek help for fertility issues after six months of trying to get pregnant with no luck. This is because of the natural decline in fertility as you age.

Suffering from infertility after previously having a child can leave you feeling stuck between two worlds. You don't really belong with the primary infertility sufferers because you have a child, and yet you are not really a part of the fertile world. This can be very painful emotionally. Finding a practitioner who will really listen and get to the bottom of your fertility situation is your best bet.

Planning for Pregnancy

The best things you can do if you are contemplating a second baby are to be healthy and to plan your pregnancy. Planning your pregnancy means that you are taking a proactive approach to becoming pregnant, not just becoming pregnant accidentally. While many unplanned pregnancies do turn out well, planning gives you the extra boost to keep you and your baby healthy.

Preconceptional Health

Planning your health is a great way to prepare for your new baby. It also gives you something to focus on in the pretrying phase. There are many ways to get healthy while planning your pregnancy.

A visit to your doctor or midwife will get you started on the right track. There, you can discuss lowering your risks of pregnancy complications prior to pregnancy. This is usually accomplished by being at an appropriate weight, eating well, exercising, and taking good care of yourself. You will also talk to your practitioner about the discontinuation of birth control in preparation for getting pregnant.

Diet

Being at your ideal weight when you become pregnant can lower many risks in pregnancy. It can help you reduce the risks of some really terrible complications from pregnancy-induced hypertension to gestational diabetes. These complications can endanger not only your life, but also the life of your baby.

FACT

The March of Dimes and other organizations dedicated to prepregnancy prevention of birth defects recommend that every woman of childbearing age have 400 mcg of folic acid every day. They estimate that this can reduce your risk of certain birth defects by up to 70 percent.

Your doctor or midwife can help you identify your ideal body weight and your body mass index (BMI). She will help you find additional help in planning your diet. This may include printed materials or books. It may also include a trip to the nutritionist.

The key to a healthy prepregnancy is eating a variety of fruits and vegetables in addition to protein and fiber. If you eat more whole foods and vegetables, you'll find that you not only lose any excess weight you may have had, but that you will also have more energy. This can be vital to you if you are going to be pregnant while dealing with another child, particularly if that child is a toddler.

Exercise

Exercise is vital to staying healthy. If you already have a workout regimen, then planning for pregnancy shouldn't be a huge issue. You will probably simply want to be sure that your workout is one that can be continued safely during pregnancy. To do this, simply share your routine with your doctor or midwife.

FACT

Your BMI is an important indicator of health. You can calculate it online with the Centers for Disease Control and Prevention: *www.cdc.gov/nccdphp/dnpa/bmi/bmi-adult-formula.htm.*

Perhaps you've never gotten into the swing of the exercise thing. This planning phase is the time to really get into it and start your routine. Your prepregnancy workout doesn't have to be wild or horrific. Be sure to include your family; this will help you keep up the routine.

Your workout doesn't necessarily need to be hard-core. Start simply by walking around your block once a day. This will help get you moving. Getting moving is often the hardest part. From there, simply add on to your walk when you feel able to do so. For most people, this is when the old path is no longer physically challenging.

Timing

The timing of your pregnancy may be important to you. You might be in a job where you have built-in time off, like a teacher or seasonal worker. Being able to maximize your built-in time off can enhance your use of your maternity leave. The hard part is that you can't always plan everything the way you want to plan it. You may be lucky enough to get pregnant right away or right on time, but a pregnancy could just as easily come before or after you hope.

The best way to help predict the exact time to get pregnant is to use some form of ovulation prediction. This can be done by taking basal body temperature or with store-bought individual ovulation prediction kits or other, more sophisticated kits to help you predict when you will ovulate. This certainly can't hurt your chances of becoming pregnant.

Pregnancy While Caring for Another Child

Expecting a new baby is great! You are probably excited to be expanding your family. However, caring for a first child while pregnant with a second is very challenging. You probably thought you had the pregnancy thing down, but with your added responsibilities of caring for your first baby, things can get messy.

A Different Ball Game

Pregnancy the second time around can be a whole new world. You may think you remember what it was like to be pregnant. However, having another child to care for can really throw a wrench into your plans.

Remember how, in your first pregnancy, you simply lay down to nap when you were tired? There will be none of that, unless you can convince your toddler to nap too. There are days when you will break every rule you ever set, like letting your toddler watch television for an extended period of time, just so you can catch a couple of winks on the couch.

You may find yourself comparing your pregnancies. If in your first pregnancy you felt movement at sixteen weeks, you may panic when week eighteen comes and goes without a flutter. You may also be more involved in your medical care during pregnancy, since you are now able to see the larger picture.

Physical Changes

The physical changes that one can usually expect during pregnancy aren't a huge shock the second time around. What might really shock you is how soon the changes seem to happen in comparison to your first pregnancy. You will probably find that you start to show much sooner with your second (or more) pregnancy. This is often thought to be because of the laxity of the uterine and abdominal muscles from the previous pregnancy.

Don't forget to get help if you need it. There is nothing wrong with asking for someone else to help you with tasks that simply become too much to handle during pregnancy. Soon you'll have two little ones in the house, and you'll need all the strength and energy you can muster.

The problem with the physical changes is getting around. You might think that's nothing new, but think of new duties that you have now with an older child. Do you lean over your car to buckle your child into a car seat? What about lifting groceries? Can you do that while holding your toddler's hand and minding your protruding belly? Try leaning over and giving a bath when you are nine months pregnant!

Tiredness will be one of the biggest issues you'll face. Your child doesn't understand why you aren't able to go to the park and run around every day like you used to do. Take a nap when you can. The same goes for sleeping in when you can. Don't hesitate to ask your husband to take over some of the middle-of-the-night or early-morning duties when appropriate. Remember, growing a new baby takes a lot of work.

Preparing Your Baby to Be a Sibling

One of the most exciting parts of becoming a new mother all over again is making your child an older sibling. However, encouraging your child to welcome a new baby and preparing him to have a healthy relationship with his new sibling can be both fun and frightening.

When to Tell Your Older Child

There are many answers to the question of when to tell your child that there is a new baby on the way. Most families choose to wait until at least the end of the first trimester. While pregnancy loss is a normal part of life, it is terribly hard to explain to your children. (This doesn't mean that you shouldn't tell your child earlier if you want to.)

Warning! Don't tell your child about your pregnancy until you're ready for the whole world to know about it. There is something about a secret this awesome that makes it impossible not to talk about. So if you don't want Grandma or teachers to know, don't tell your child.

The biggest part of the decision of when to tell will revolve around your child. Part of that determination will be based on the age of your child. An older child can handle a deeper understanding of pregnancy. A younger child may be able to handle only a couple of months of notice prior to the birth.

Sibling Preparation

There are many sibling preparation programs available. What you choose should be age appropriate. It should also match your values and ways of thinking when it comes to birth and parenting.

Classes

Sibling classes may be offered at your local hospital or birth center. You may also find a private educator who holds sibling classes. The majority of these classes are designed for children between the ages of three and seven. This does not mean that they would not have benefits for children of other ages.

Most classes cover a variety of topics. They may discuss what new babies look and sound like. Most classes will cover the dos and don'ts of having a new baby in the house. You may even find that the class offers a tour of the hospital or birth center. This can help make the separation from mom, even if it's only for a short time, a bit easier.

You may need to take special classes if you plan to have your child attend the birth of his or her sibling. There is no one right age for an older sibling to attend a birth; it depends more on the child. The big keys to a sibling's attending the birth are preparation for the birth, a support person solely dedicated to her, and that the child has the ability to come and go as she pleases.

Books

There are many books and videos that you can use to show your child some of the aspects of a growing family. Books are very widely available in many topics. You may decide to offer a variety of books to your child to see what appeals to him.

Pick books for your children that match your circumstances as closely as possible. If you're planning a home birth, find a children's book on home birth. If you are having a baby in a hospital, find one that takes place in that setting. This will help familiarize your child with common happenings in the setting you have chosen.

Pregnancy books are a great start to answer the inevitable series of questions that will follow your pregnancy announcement. There are some great books that describe how babies grow inside you. Kids of all ages are thrilled with these books. They also can help pass the long months ahead as you discuss what your baby is doing on a weekly basis. *A Child Is Born* by Lennart Nilsson is a parental favorite.

Books on new babies are also important. What is a day in the life of a new baby really like? Find books that talk about how your child may feel once the new baby gets here. Kevin Henkes has a wonderful book called *Julius, Baby of the World*. There are many books available on the subject of new babies.

There are also videos available. They range from the "favorite cartoon character gets a new sister" type to those featuring a variety of personified animals having babies. Kids are okay with this type of show, but they don't get overly excited. They know that there is a huge difference between cartoons and real life. Always watch the videos with your child; some may be a bit frightening for some children.

Deciding to have another baby can be a lengthy process. Are you ready mentally and emotionally? Is your body ready to have another baby? Or do you need to take some time to prepare your body? Once you do get pregnant, there's no going back. So be sure you're ready! Expanding your family is a lot of work, but it's also great fun. Do what you can to ensure every pregnancy is better than the last and that each child becomes comfortable in his role as a sibling. Enjoy your journey!

Appendix A

Helpful Hints for the First Year

0 to 3 Months

- Sleep when the baby sleeps. These catnaps may be the only chance for sleep you get for some time.
- Always use a car seat whenever you take your baby in a car.
- Your baby should sleep on his back to reduce the risks of sudden infant death syndrome (SIDS).
- Be sure not to let your baby get too warm. One light layer more than you would wear is plenty.
- Talk to your baby often to stimulate brain development.
- Always support your baby's head when holding or carrying him.
- Never leave your baby on a couch or other high surface, as he could easily roll off.
- The human face is very interesting to your baby; give him lots of face time.
- Tummy time is a very important part of play. Your baby should spend some time on her belly every day to help build her neck muscles.

4 to 6 Months

- Be wary of toys that put weight on your baby's legs, as they may cause strain on undeveloped muscles.
- Do not start solid foods yet, as they may cause food allergies.
- Start babyproofing, if you haven't already. Mobility isn't too far off.
- You can't spoil your baby with attention. Remember to respond to her needs immediately so she will feel confident and comfortable when alone.
- Consider learning some simple sign language to teach your baby how to communicate before language abilities are developed.
- Make time every day to read to your baby, even if it's simply talking through a picture book.
- Have a car seat checkup. Your baby may have outgrown the car seat you've chosen.
- Juice is not recommended for babies. It simply leads to obesity and doesn't really offer any nutritional value to your baby's diet.

7 to 9 Months

- When starting solid foods, try one food at a time for several days to note any allergic reactions, like rashes or irritability.
- Before moving your baby into a forward-facing car seat, check with your

pediatrician to ensure that your baby is heavy and long enough for this to be safe.

- Check your home for low-hanging cords and unprotected electrical outlets. Your baby will be drawn to these at this age.
- Some sunscreens are safe for use on infants. Just be careful not to get any in your baby's eyes or mouth.
- Without going overboard, keep your baby's environment clean. Babies are very tempted to put things in their mouth at this age.
- Slings and backpacks are still great for getting around with your little one.
- Enjoy music with your baby. Different genres will inspire your little one to move and wiggle.
- Around this time, diaper changes may get a bit more hectic, as your baby won't want to be changed. Give your baby a special toy to play with to distract her during changes.

10 to 12 Months

- Zoos and petting farms are great treats for budding toddlers. Take your little one for a trip and tell her the names of all the animals. Just remember the importance of hand washing after touching animals.
- Babyproofing takes on a whole new meaning as your baby becomes more mobile. Take another look around your home for safety issues.
- Slings work well for carrying an older baby or toddler. They are also easier on your back than other carriers.
- Dry cereal is a mom's best friend during travel. Always carry a container of baby-friendly cereal with you in case hunger (or boredom) crops up.
- Don't be concerned if your almost-one-year-old is not yet walking. Many toddlers don't take their first steps until well after the first year.
- Play dates are great for older babies, but don't be discouraged if your baby doesn't want to play with a friend. At this age, you typically see parallel play, where the babies play next to each other with minimal interaction.
- Another car seat safety check is in order. Is your baby ready to turn around and be forward facing? Do you know how to use your new car seat?
- Go through your medicine chest. Do you have expired medications? Do you need to buy any new emergency meds to have on hand? Talk to your pediatrician about what medications you should keep at home.

Additional Resources

Pregnancy Resources

The following are Web sites, books, and organizations that can help you through the trials and tribulations of pregnancy.

Pregnancy Web Sites

About Pregnancy Guide
http://pregnancy.about.com

This Web site offers pregnancy-related articles, a pregnancy calendar, ultrasound photos, community support, a belly gallery, and other pregnancy-related items and information.

Childbirth.org
www.childbirth.org

This pregnancy Web site is dedicated to helping you maintain a healthy pregnancy. There are many informative articles on all aspects of pregnancy, and fun programs, including a boy-or-girl quiz and a birth-plan creator.

Lamaze Institute for Normal Birth
normalbirth.lamaze.org

Here you'll find great information on having a healthy, normal birth. This includes the researched linked six cares practices that are considered to be the cornerstone of a healthy birth.

Books on Pregnancy

The Pregnancy Book by William Sears, M.D., and Martha Sears, R.N., I.B.C.L.C.

This doctor/nurse, husband/wife team gives the facts about pregnancy and birth. The book is laid out in a convenient month-by-month format to help you find the information you need, when you need it.

The Thinking Woman's Guide to a Better Birth by Henci Goer

Ms. Goer gives you all the medical information in layman's terms to help you decide the safest, healthiest way for your baby to be born.

Pregnancy-Related Organizations

American Academy of Husband Coached Childbirth (Bradley Method)

P.O. Box 5224
Sherman Oaks, CA 91413-5224
800-4-A-BIRTH
www.bradleybirth.com

The Bradley Method of childbirth includes the use of deep relaxation and breathing with the help of the husband or partner through the labor process. The classes emphasize prenatal nutrition and exercise and their influence on a healthy pregnancy.

American Academy of Pediatrics (AAP)

141 Northwest Point Boulevard
Elk Grove Village, IL 60007
847-434-4000
www.aap.org

The AAP is the leading authority on children's issues and the governing body of pediatricians across America.

American College of Nurse Midwives (ACNM)

818 Connecticut Avenue, NW, Suite 900
Washington, DC 20006

Phone: 202-728-9860
Fax: 202-728-9897
www.midwife.org

ACNM certifies nurse midwives (CNM) throughout the United States. It focuses on the care of low-risk women through pregnancy and birth as well as other time periods of life. Well-woman care is their specialty.

American College of Obstetricians and Gynecologists (ACOG)

409 12th Street, SW
P.O. Box 96920
Washington, DC 20090-6920
www.acog.org

ACOG is the premiere organization for obstetricians and gynecologists. It manages the post–medical school training and certification of this specialty. These physicians are trained in the care of the woman during all stages of life.

Coalition for Improving Maternity Services (CIMS)

P.O. Box 2346
Ponte Vedra Beach, FL 32004
888-282-CIMS
www.motherfriendly.org

CIMS has lots of great information on choosing a health-care provider and place of birth, as well as information on making decisions for yourself in pregnancy and beyond.

DONA International (Formerly Doulas of North America)

P.O. Box 626
Jasper, IN 47547
888-788-DONA
www.dona.org

DONA is the leading organization that certifies birth and postpartum doulas. A doula can assist the family before, during, or after birth. Using a doula has been shown to decrease the incidence of many complications in labor and postpartum, including cesarean section and postpartum depression.

International Cesarean Awareness Network (ICAN)

1304 Kingsdale Avenue
Redondo Beach, CA 90278
310-542-6400
www.ican-online.org

ICAN works toward the prevention of unnecessary cesareans and the emotional and physical recovery from cesareans.

International Childbirth Education Association (ICEA)

P.O. Box 20048
Minneapolis, MN 55420

952-854-8660
www.icea.org

ICEA trains childbirth educators as well as prenatal fitness instructors throughout the world. Their Web site offers a search to help you find local instructors.

Lamaze International

2025 M Street, Suite 800
Washington, DC 20036-3309
202-367-1128
www.lamaze.org

Lamaze International is the leading certifying organization for childbirth educators. Promoting normal birth is the core of their philosophy as they train educators worldwide. Their site offers a directory, articles, and other interactive features.

Maternity Center Association

281 Park Avenue South, 5th Floor
New York, NY 10010
212-777-5000
www.maternitywise.org

Lots of great consumer advice can be found here. You can download new booklets on choosing cesarean birth, what you should know about vaginal birth after cesarean (VBAC), and more. There is even a complete pregnancy medical text available to read on their Web site.

Breastfeeding Resources

The following are helpful Web sites, books, and organizations with information and tips on breastfeeding.

Web Sites

Breastfeeding Online
www.breastfeedingonline.com

This site has great information on breastfeeding, from how to start to how to deal with complications or issues that arise. You can also submit your questions and receive answers.

Growth Charts for the first year from the CDC
www.cdc.gov/growthcharts

These charts will help you track your baby's growth during the first year of his or her life.

Breastfeeding Books

The Nursing Mother's Companion by Kathleen Huggins

This breastfeeding book has a wealth of information that is broken down for ease of use. It also has a section on breastfeeding as a working mother, including pumps and pumping.

The Ultimate Breastfeeding Book of Answers by Dr. Jack Newman and Teresa Pitman

Pediatrician Dr. Newman and Teresa Pitman explain the benefits of breastfeeding, how to prevent problems with breastfeeding, and how to handle life as a breastfeeding mother.

Breastfeeding Organizations

International Lactation Consultant Association (ILCA)
1500 Sunday Drive, Suite 102
Raleigh, NC 27607
919-861-5577
www.ilca.org

ILCA certifies lactation consultants. Their Web site has information on finding a board-certified lactation consultant in your area, as well as information on how to become a board-certified lactation consultant.

La Leche League International
1400 N. Meacham Road
Schaumburg, IL 60173-4808
847-519-7730
www.lalecheleague.org

La Leche League provides information, education, and support for pregnant and breastfeeding women. There are monthly meetings held locally in many cities around the world, as well as a wealth of information via various publications. La Leche League also has some phone support available.

Postpartum Fitness

Postpartum Exercise Books

Eat Well, Lose Weight While Breastfeeding by Eileen Behan

While breastfeeding does promote weight loss, the balance between keeping your baby well fed and losing weight can be a difficult one to maintain. Here's a different approach to the age-old question of how do you lose weight after pregnancy?

Essential Exercises for the Childbearing Year by Elizabeth Noble

Ms. Noble is a physical therapist, and the movement of the body is her specialty. She focuses on pregnancy fitness and how to stay healthy and fit while living a normal life during pregnancy. The book also includes information on proper body alignment and deal-

ing with everyday questions like how to pick up older children.

The Everything® Pregnancy Fitness Book by Robin Elise Weiss

This book is a great view of exercises for each trimester and the postpartum period. The photos are clear and the text succinct.

Web Sites

Fit Pregnancy
www.fitpregnancy.com

Fit Pregnancy is based on a magazine of the same name. Here you will find pregnancy fitness- and wellness-related articles.

Walking Guide at About
http://walking.about.com

Your walking guide for every avenue of life. Includes the free ten-week Walk of Life program.

Managing Multiple Children Resources

Books

Mothering Multiples by Karen Kerkoff Gromada, IBCLC

Not only is this advice indispensable, but it comes from the mother of twins! In this book you'll find lots of information on living with new twins (or more), from bringing them into the world to managing daily life. Also included are great sections on successfully feeding multiples, including premature babies.

Web Sites

About Parenting of Multiples
http://multiples.about.com

This site starts at pregnancy and takes you through all the stages of physical, mental, and emotional development of multiples. There is also a gallery of photos of multiples, polls, and lots of great articles on different aspects of raising multiples.

Organizations

National Organizations of Mothers of Twins Clubs (NOMOTC)
P.O. Box 700860
Plymouth, MI 48170-0955
877-540-2200

Representing over 475 clubs in cities all over the United States, the NOMOTC is the oldest and largest organization serving multiple-birth families today. Locate a club near you, read the latest news on multiples, and find ongoing research projects for multiples at their Web site.

Pregnancy Loss– Related Organizations

SHARE
www.NationalSHAREOffice.com

SHARE is an organization dedicated to helping you grieve the loss of your child, no matter at what point your child died. Through a monthly paper newsletter that is free for the first year, to conferences held all over, SHARE has support at heart.

Fertility Related Resources

Web Sites

About Infertility Guide
infertility.about.com

Infertility from diagnosis to high-tech assistance. This site includes a personal touch with lots of opportunities for loving support from others in your situation. A great place to look for cycle buddies.

Books

The Everything® Getting Pregnant Book by Robin Elise Weiss

A guide to every aspect of getting pregnant, from preparing your body for pregnancy to timing your pregnancy. Even includes a section on secondary infertility and fertility treatments.

Taking Charge of Your Fertility by Toni Weschler, M.P.H.

This is an excellent manual for learning about charting your natural fertility cycles. It goes into very great detail about sympothermal testing and charting your basal body temperatures.

Fertility-Related Organizations

American Society for Reproductive Medicine (ASRM) (Formerly the American Fertility Society)
1209 Montgomery Highway
Birmingham, AL 35216-2809
Phone: 205-978-5000
Fax: 205-978-5005
www.asrm.org

ASRM provides patient and physician information. It also helps govern and provide guidance for fertility programs, both in training and in ethical situations. You will find great handouts on various positions from ASRM here, also included in Spanish.

Couple to Couple League—Natural Family Planning
www.ccli.org

The Couple to Couple League provides training in various locations about how to use your body's fertility signals to help you achieve pregnancy and diagnose your cycle variability. This can be used to help achieve or avoid pregnancy with great accuracy. Their Web site includes information on finding local classes.

The International Council on Infertility Information Dissemination, Inc. (INCIID)
P.O. Box 6836
Arlington, VA 22206
Phone: 703-379-9178
Fax: 703-379-1593
www.inciid.org

Great information for support purposes and information. They offer chats by professionals for the layperson on various forms of fertility questions.

RESOLVE: The National Infertility Association
1310 Broadway
Somerville, MA 02144
888-623-0744
E-mail: *info@resolve.org*
www.resolve.org

Primarily a support organization for persons facing various fertility issues. Leadership positions in this organization are held by professionals in the field, as well as parents.

Society for Assisted Reproductive Technology (SART)
1209 Montgomery Highway
Birmingham, AL 35216
Phone: 205-978-5000 (x109)
Fax: 205-978-5015

E-mail: *jzeitz@asrm.org*
www.sart.org

SART runs the statistical information processing that is used in helping you compare fertility clinic to fertility clinic. It leads in its position and should be consulted when trying to decide what program is right for you.

Index

THE EVERYTHING SERIES!

BUSINESS & PERSONAL FINANCE

Everything® Budgeting Book
Everything® Business Planning Book
Everything® Coaching and Mentoring Book
Everything® Fundraising Book
Everything® Get Out of Debt Book
Everything® Grant Writing Book
Everything® Home-Based Business Book
Everything® Homebuying Book, 2nd Ed.
Everything® Homeselling Book, 2nd Ed.
Everything® Investing Book, 2nd Ed.
Everything® Landlording Book
Everything® Leadership Book
Everything® Managing People Book
Everything® Negotiating Book
Everything® Online Business Book
Everything® Personal Finance Book
Everything® Personal Finance in Your 20s
   and 30s Book
Everything® Project Management Book
Everything® Real Estate Investing Book
Everything® Robert's Rules Book, $7.95
Everything® Selling Book
Everything® Start Your Own Business Book
Everything® Wills & Estate Planning Book

COOKING

Everything® Barbecue Cookbook
Everything® Bartender's Book, $9.95
Everything® Chinese Cookbook
Everything® Cocktail Parties and Drinks
   Book
Everything® College Cookbook
Everything® Cookbook
Everything® Cooking for Two Cookbook
Everything® Diabetes Cookbook
Everything® Easy Gourmet Cookbook
Everything® Fondue Cookbook
Everything® Gluten-Free Cookbook

Everything® Grilling Cookbook
Everything® Healthy Meals in Minutes
   Cookbook
Everything® Holiday Cookbook
Everything® Indian Cookbook
Everything® Italian Cookbook
Everything® Low-Carb Cookbook
Everything® Low-Fat High-Flavor Cookbook
Everything® Low-Salt Cookbook
Everything® Meals for a Month Cookbook
Everything® Mediterranean Cookbook
Everything® Mexican Cookbook
Everything® One-Pot Cookbook
Everything® Pasta Cookbook
Everything® Quick Meals Cookbook
Everything® Slow Cooker Cookbook
Everything® Slow Cooking for a Crowd
   Cookbook
Everything® Soup Cookbook
Everything® Thai Cookbook
Everything® Vegetarian Cookbook
Everything® Wine Book, 2nd Ed.

CRAFT SERIES

Everything® Crafts—Baby Scrapbooking
Everything® Crafts—Bead Your Own Jewelry
Everything® Crafts—Create Your Own
   Greeting Cards
Everything® Crafts—Easy Projects
Everything® Crafts—Polymer Clay for
   Beginners
Everything® Crafts—Rubber Stamping
   Made Easy
Everything® Crafts—Wedding Decorations
   and Keepsakes

HEALTH

Everything® Alzheimer's Book
Everything® Diabetes Book
Everything® Health Guide to Controlling
   Anxiety

Everything® Hypnosis Book
Everything® Low Cholesterol Book
Everything® Massage Book
Everything® Menopause Book
Everything® Nutrition Book
Everything® Reflexology Book
Everything® Stress Management Book

HISTORY

Everything® American Government Book
Everything® American History Book
Everything® Civil War Book
Everything® Irish History & Heritage Book
Everything® Middle East Book

HOBBIES & GAMES

Everything® Blackjack Strategy Book
Everything® Brain Strain Book, $9.95
Everything® Bridge Book
Everything® Candlemaking Book
Everything® Card Games Book
Everything® Card Tricks Book, $9.95
Everything® Cartooning Book
Everything® Casino Gambling Book, 2nd Ed.
Everything® Chess Basics Book
Everything® Craps Strategy Book
Everything® Crossword and Puzzle Book
Everything® Crossword Challenge Book
Everything® Cryptograms Book, $9.95
Everything® Digital Photography Book
Everything® Drawing Book
Everything® Easy Crosswords Book
Everything® Family Tree Book, 2nd Ed.
Everything® Games Book, 2nd Ed.
Everything® Knitting Book
Everything® Knots Book
Everything® Photography Book
Everything® Poker Strategy Book
Everything® Pool & Billiards Book
Everything® Quilting Book
Everything® Scrapbooking Book

All Everything® books are priced at $12.95 or $14.95, unless otherwise stated. Prices subject to change without notice.

Everything® Sewing Book
Everything® Test Your IQ Book, $9.95
Everything® Travel Crosswords Book, $9.95
Everything® Woodworking Book
Everything® Word Games Challenge Book
Everything® Word Search Book

HOME IMPROVEMENT

Everything® Feng Shui Book
Everything® Feng Shui Decluttering Book,
  $9.95
Everything® Fix-It Book
Everything® Homebuilding Book
Everything® Lawn Care Book
Everything® Organize Your Home Book

EVERYTHING®
KIDS' BOOKS

All titles are $6.95
Everything® Kids' Animal Puzzle & Activity
  Book
Everything® Kids' Baseball Book, 3rd Ed.
Everything® Kids' Bible Trivia Book
Everything® Kids' Bugs Book
Everything® Kids' Christmas Puzzle
  & Activity Book
Everything® Kids' Cookbook
Everything® Kids' Crazy Puzzles Book
Everything® Kids' Dinosaurs Book
Everything® Kids' Gross Jokes Book
Everything® Kids' Gross Puzzle and
  Activity Book
Everything® Kids' Halloween Puzzle
  & Activity Book
Everything® Kids' Hidden Pictures Book
Everything® Kids' Joke Book
Everything® Kids' Knock Knock Book
Everything® Kids' Math Puzzles Book
Everything® Kids' Mazes Book
Everything® Kids' Money Book
Everything® Kids' Nature Book
Everything® Kids' Puzzle Book
Everything® Kids' Riddles & Brain Teasers Book
Everything® Kids' Science Experiments Book
Everything® Kids' Sharks Book
Everything® Kids' Soccer Book
Everything® Kids' Travel Activity Book

KIDS' STORY BOOKS

Everything® Fairy Tales Book

LANGUAGE

Everything® Conversational Japanese Book
  (with CD), $19.95
Everything® French Phrase Book, $9.95
Everything® French Verb Book, $9.95
Everything® Inglés Book
Everything® Learning French Book
Everything® Learning German Book
Everything® Learning Italian Book
Everything® Learning Latin Book
Everything® Learning Spanish Book
Everything® Sign Language Book
Everything® Spanish Grammar Book
Everything® Spanish Practice Book
  (with CD), $19.95
Everything® Spanish Phrase Book, $9.95
Everything® Spanish Verb Book, $9.95

MUSIC

Everything® Drums Book (with CD), $19.95
Everything® Guitar Book
Everything® Home Recording Book
Everything® Playing Piano and Keyboards
  Book
Everything® Reading Music Book (with CD),
  $19.95
Everything® Rock & Blues Guitar Book
  (with CD), $19.95
Everything® Songwriting Book

NEW AGE

Everything® Astrology Book, 2nd Ed.
Everything® Dreams Book, 2nd Ed.
Everything® Ghost Book
Everything® Love Signs Book, $9.95
Everything® Numerology Book
Everything® Paganism Book
Everything® Palmistry Book
Everything® Psychic Book
Everything® Reiki Book
Everything® Tarot Book
Everything® Wicca and Witchcraft Book

PARENTING

Everything® Baby Names Book
Everything® Baby Shower Book
Everything® Baby's First Food Book
Everything® Baby's First Year Book
Everything® Birthing Book
Everything® Breastfeeding Book
Everything® Father-to-Be Book
Everything® Father's First Year Book
Everything® Get Ready for Baby Book
Everything® Get Your Baby to Sleep Book,
  $9.95
Everything® Getting Pregnant Book
Everything® Homeschooling Book
Everything® Mother's First Year Book
Everything® Parent's Guide to Children
  and Divorce
Everything® Parent's Guide to Children
  with ADD/ADHD
Everything® Parent's Guide to Children
  with Asperger's Syndrome
Everything® Parent's Guide to Children
  with Autism
Everything® Parent's Guide to Children with
  Bipolar Disorder
Everything® Parent's Guide to Children
  with Dyslexia
Everything® Parent's Guide to Positive
  Discipline
Everything® Parent's Guide to Raising a
  Successful Child
Everything® Parent's Guide to Tantrums
Everything® Parent's Guide to the Overweight
  Child
Everything® Parent's Guide to the Strong-
  Willed Child
Everything® Parenting a Teenager Book
Everything® Potty Training Book, $9.95
Everything® Pregnancy Book, 2nd Ed.
Everything® Pregnancy Fitness Book
Everything® Pregnancy Nutrition Book
Everything® Pregnancy Organizer, $15.00
Everything® Toddler Book
Everything® Tween Book
Everything® Twins, Triplets, and More Book

All Everything® books are priced at $12.95 or $14.95, unless otherwise stated. Prices subject to change without notice.

PETS

Everything® Cat Book
Everything® Dachshund Book
Everything® Dog Book
Everything® Dog Health Book
Everything® Dog Training and Tricks Book
Everything® German Shepherd Book
Everything® Golden Retriever Book
Everything® Horse Book
Everything® Horseback Riding Book
Everything® Labrador Retriever Book
Everything® Poodle Book
Everything® Pug Book
Everything® Puppy Book
Everything® Rottweiler Book
Everything® Small Dogs Book
Everything® Tropical Fish Book
Everything® Yorkshire Terrier Book

REFERENCE

Everything® Car Care Book
Everything® Classical Mythology Book
Everything® Computer Book
Everything® Divorce Book
Everything® Einstein Book
Everything® Etiquette Book, 2nd Ed.
Everything® Inventions and Patents Book
Everything® Mafia Book
Everything® Philosophy Book
Everything® Psychology Book
Everything® Shakespeare Book

RELIGION

Everything® Angels Book
Everything® Bible Book
Everything® Buddhism Book
Everything® Catholicism Book
Everything® Christianity Book
Everything® Jewish History & Heritage Book
Everything® Judaism Book
Everything® Koran Book
Everything® Prayer Book
Everything® Saints Book

Everything® Torah Book
Everything® Understanding Islam Book
Everything® World's Religions Book
Everything® Zen Book

SCHOOL & CAREERS

Everything® Alternative Careers Book
Everything® College Survival Book, 2nd Ed.
Everything® Cover Letter Book, 2nd Ed.
Everything® Get-a-Job Book
Everything® Guide to Starting and Running
   a Restaurant
Everything® Job Interview Book
Everything® New Teacher Book
Everything® Online Job Search Book
Everything® Paying for College Book
Everything® Practice Interview Book
Everything® Resume Book, 2nd Ed.
Everything® Study Book

SELF-HELP

Everything® Dating Book, 2nd Ed.
Everything® Great Sex Book
Everything® Kama Sutra Book
Everything® Self-Esteem Book

SPORTS & FITNESS

Everything® Fishing Book
Everything® Golf Instruction Book
Everything® Pilates Book
Everything® Running Book
Everything® Total Fitness Book
Everything® Weight Training Book
Everything® Yoga Book

TRAVEL

Everything® Family Guide to Hawaii
Everything® Family Guide to Las Vegas,
   2nd Ed.
Everything® Family Guide to New York City,
   2nd Ed.
Everything® Family Guide to RV Travel &
   Campgrounds

Everything® Family Guide to the Walt Disney
   World Resort®, Universal Studios®,
   and Greater Orlando, 4th Ed.
Everything® Family Guide to Cruise Vacations
Everything® Family Guide to the Caribbean
Everything® Family Guide to Washington
   D.C., 2nd Ed.
Everything® Guide to New England
Everything® Travel Guide to the Disneyland
   Resort®, California Adventure®,
   Universal Studios®, and the
   Anaheim Area

WEDDINGS

Everything® Bachelorette Party Book, $9.95
Everything® Bridesmaid Book, $9.95
Everything® Elopement Book, $9.95
Everything® Father of the Bride Book, $9.95
Everything® Groom Book, $9.95
Everything® Mother of the Bride Book, $9.95
Everything® Outdoor Wedding Book
Everything® Wedding Book, 3rd Ed.
Everything® Wedding Checklist, $9.95
Everything® Wedding Etiquette Book, $9.95
Everything® Wedding Organizer, $15.00
Everything® Wedding Shower Book, $9.95
Everything® Wedding Vows Book, $9.95
Everything® Weddings on a Budget Book,
   $9.95

WRITING

Everything® Creative Writing Book
Everything® Get Published Book
Everything® Grammar and Style Book
Everything® Guide to Writing a Book Proposal
Everything® Guide to Writing a Novel
Everything® Guide to Writing Children's Books
Everything® Guide to Writing Research Papers
Everything® Screenwriting Book
Everything® Writing Poetry Book
Everything® Writing Well Book

Available wherever books are sold!
To order, call 800-258-0929, or visit us at **www.everything.com**
Everything® and everything.com® are registered trademarks of F+W Publications, Inc.